BRITISH TOPOGRAPHICAL SERIES

PEMBROKESHIRE

BRITISH TOPOGRAPHICAL SERIES

published

Beyond the Great Glen
Bodmin Moor
The Peak District

PEMBROKESHIRE

by BRIAN JOHN

DAVID & CHARLES

NEWTON ABBOT   LONDON

NORTH POMFRET (VT)   VANCOUVER

ISBN 0 7153 7171 1

Library of Congress Catalog Card Number 76–2890

© BRIAN JOHN 1976

Set in 11 on 13pt Monotype Baskerville and
printed in Great Britain by Latimer Trend &
Company Ltd Plymouth for David & Charles
(Publishers) Limited Brunel House Newton
Abbot Devon

Published in the United States of America by
David & Charles Inc North Pomfret Vermont
05053 USA

Published in Canada by Douglas David &
Charles Limited 1875 Welch Street North
Vancouver BC

CONTENTS

		page
List of Illustrations		7
Preface		9
1	Introduction: The Region and its Character	13
2	The Natural Landscape	19
3	Myths, Monuments and Mysteries	34
4	The Welsh, their Saints and their Stories	47
5	The Creation of 'Little England'	55
6	George Owen's Pembrokeshire	65
7	Changing Fortunes	80
8	Seafaring and Life by the Sea	98
9	Milford Haven and its 'New Towns'	107
10	Coal, Stone, Slate and Iron: Pembrokeshire's Industrial Revolution	117
11	Town and Country	134
12	The English, the Welsh and the Landsker	152
13	The Pembrokeshire Coast National Park	164
14	Buildings: Medieval Castles, Palaces and Churches	180
15	Buildings: Homes for Rich and Poor	199
16	The Rediscovery of Milford Haven	210
17	Conclusion: Pembrokeshire, Dyfed and the Future	224
Bibliography		228
Acknowledgements		233
Index		234

LIST OF ILLUSTRATIONS

PLATES	*page*
The single-street village of Cosheston	17
Frost-shattered rock from the Ice Age	18
The submerged forest at Marros	18
Summit fort of Moel Drygarn	35
The skeleton at St Patrick's Chapel, Whitesand Bay	35
St Govan's Chapel	36
Bethesda Chapel	36
St David's Cathedral	69
Five Arches, Tenby	69
Johnston church tower	70
Llanwnda church	70
Lime kilns at Solva	87
The 'blue lagoon' slate quarry at Abereiddi	87
The corn-mill at Carew	88
Industrial token of 1792	88
A Fishguard Fencible	121
Rosebush holiday poster	121
Pembroke's Norman fortress	122
Work on Porthgain Harbour in 1903	122
Grey seal pup	139
The Grassholm gannetry	139
Manorbier Castle	140
Orielton mansion	140
A farmhouse at Garn	173
St David's post office in 1870	174
A stepped-segment long-house in Trefin	174

LIST OF ILLUSTRATIONS

Tourist pressure at Saundersfoot   191
The new Haven Bridge   191
The Llysyfran reservoir under construction   192
The Esso refinery near Milford   192

FIGURES

The Neolithic dwelling-house at Clegyrfwya   40
The cromlech at Longhouse   41
A page from the *Description of Pembrokeshire*   66
Rebecca rioters   96
The Pembrokeshire Landsker   161
The Tudor Merchant's House in Tenby   162

MAPS

Geological map of Pembrokeshire   21
Location map of Pembrokeshire   26
English and Welsh church-types and place-names   157
The Pembrokeshire Coast National Park   166
The early medieval Landsker showing main castle types   182
Milford Haven waterway   211

PREFACE

THIS book has been written because I love Pembrokeshire. Since my school-days in Haverfordwest I have
been fascinated by the complicated history of my native
county and especially by the infinite variety of its landscapes. I
have been fascinated by Pembrokeshire's two halves and by the
invisible dividing line between them. My training as a geo-
grapher has increased this sense of fascination while it has taught
me to look more and more critically at landscape. And now that
I am able to return to Pembrokeshire relatively infrequently,
the unique qualities of the Pembrokeshire scene are impressed
upon me more deeply with every visit. Pembrokeshire is changing, and the rate of change is speeding up. This book looks at,
and attempts to analyse, the main features of the landscape and
the way of life of this little corner of Wales as it moves into the
last quarter of the century. The viewpoint is very much a geo-
graphical one, concentrating on what can be observed rather
than on what can be read or remembered. As such, this is a
book about topography.

I am very much aware that this book contains a great deal on
topics about which others know far more than I. Where ap-
propriate the text acknowledges my main source of information
and it will be obvious from the bibliography how much I have
depended upon earlier published works about the county. However, in a book of this type it is not possible to cite chapter and
verse as often as I would have liked. There are many Pembrokeshire writers who will recognise certain parts of the text as
based upon information first published or otherwise provided by
them; I am happy to acknowledge my debt to them, and
I hope I have succeeded in reporting their ideas honestly. I

9

know that they will not take it amiss that I have been unable to mention all by name, but I have learnt something from each of them. Needless to say, the opinions and the factual shortcomings in this book are my own, and I take the blame for them.

I owe a special debt of gratitude to the many people who have helped me directly in the preparation of this book. Throughout my studies of Pembrokeshire I have had the benefit of much invaluable advice from Margaret Davies and John Barrett, and I owe them both a great debt of gratitude. George Dickman and his staff at the Pembrokeshire County Library have helped me, with never-failing courtesy, to find all the written raw materials which I have needed. I am happy to acknowledge the lasting value of two source-books in particular, seen through the press by men who have served the best interests of Pembrokeshire for many years. These are the official *Guide to the Pembrokeshire Coast National Park*, edited by Dillwyn Miles, and the *Pembroke County Development Plan* prepared under the direction of the late Jack Price. These books, and many other documents published by the Planning Department of the old Pembrokeshire County Council and more recently by the National Park Office and the Industrial Development Unit of Dyfed County Council, have provided much valuable material. In addition to those mentioned above, I am happy to thank the many others involved in these publications, and in particular Frank Grout, Nick Wheeler and Dyfed Ellis-Gruffydd. I thank Mr R. Campfield, Col J. A. Sulivan, Mr J. A. Grubb, Douglas Bassett, David Watts and many others for advice on specific points. I have received much help from representatives of the Milford Haven oil companies and other commercial concerns, and from the staffs of various government departments. The manuscript of the book has kindly been typed by Suzanne Eckford, and I am grateful to the print room, drawing office and photographic laboratory staff of the Durham University Department of Geography for their great help with the illustrations. I thank Professor W. B. Fisher for allowing the use of various departmental facilities in this work. I have received generous help with illustrations from a number of sources,

and full acknowledgement is made at the end of the book
(p 233).

Several kind people have helped to make this book present-
able by reading through parts of the text, correcting errors and
suggesting improvements. In particular I thank Michael Brace,
B. G. Charles, Jack Donovan, Roscoe Howells, Brian Howells,
Richard Keen, Morgan Rees, Wilfred Harrison, David Howell,
W. G. Thomas, and Peter Smith. I hope they will not be
disappointed with the chapters of the book as they now find
them.

Finally, I thank my parents for their constant help and for
encouraging my exploration of Pembrokeshire's more remote
corners. My father, J. Ivor John, if he had had different
priorities, could have written this book far better than I. My
wife Inger, and our two small boys Stephen and Martin, have
done most of all over the past few years in making our trips to
Pembrokeshire fun; and while this book has been in the pipeline they have tolerated far too much anti-social behaviour on
my part. They, more than I, will be pleased to see the last of the
manuscript and all its attendant domestic clutter.

This is a book about places and about the people who have
made these places what they are. Some of them will be difficult
for the visitor to find, but hopefully the location map and the
other maps in the text will provide some help. In addition, the
standard guides and other published material often give grid
references to important sites, together with information concerning access. Most of the important general material is referred to in the bibliography, which is arranged chapter by
chapter at the end of the book. For those who wish to use this
book during the course of intrepid expeditions into the Pembrokeshire outback, the new Ordnance Survey 1:50,000 maps
are essential equipment. The relevant sheets are 157 (St David's
and Haverfordwest), 145 (Cardigan) and 158 (Tenby). While
hunting for fascinating localities, please remember that most of
them belong to somebody or other. Pembrokeshire has a
national park and its residents are used to visitors; nevertheless,
visitors are asked to respect at all times the private property

and the proper privacy of those who have the good fortune to live somewhere interesting.

Lanchester, Durham   Brian John
January 1975

1 INTRODUCTION: THE REGION AND ITS CHARACTER

PEMBROKESHIRE, one of the 'Atlantic ends' of Britain, is not sure whether its fortunes lie at sea or on the land. It is mostly lowland, but it has always been called part of Highland Britain. During the Dark Ages it looked westwards towards Ireland for much of its cultural inspiration; but suddenly, with the coming of the Normans, it was caught up in the great cultural dynamo controlled from south-eastern England. Since then, for almost a thousand years, it has been undecided about whether to call itself English or Welsh. But Pembrokeshire felt that in spite of its confused past it did have an identity.

Then the British Government decided that local government administration should be made less local, and in April 1974 the conglomerate county of Dyfed came into being. Pembrokeshire, kicking and screaming more furiously than any of the other Welsh counties, was exterminated. It was replaced by two local government districts called South Pembrokeshire and Preseli. South Pembrokeshire, confusingly, is comprised mostly of eastern Pembrokeshire and a sizeable part of Mynydd Presely, while Preseli includes parts of the deep south such as Neyland, Milford and the Dale peninsula. While Pembrokeshire may formally have passed out of existence, it will be a long time before local people look on themselves as inhabitants of Dyfed. And as long as people recognise and use the term 'Pembrokeshire' there seems no reason to refer to the old county by any other name. Hence the title of this book.

The landscape of Pembrokeshire is basically rural, but it does display a number of vivid contrasts. Three of these contrasts are recognised in the separate sections of the Pembrokeshire Coast National Park. In the main section of the park there is the spectacular beauty of the coastline itself, with its violent Atlantic cliffs subdued here and there by wide sandy bays and narrow inlets. Then there are the bleak rolling moorland wastes of Mynydd Presely, whose flanks were naked and windswept until in recent years puritanical foresters began to clothe them with a dull cover of conifers. Finally, there is the wooded secrecy of the Daugleddau estuary, whose tidal mudflats and steep oak woods are quite beautiful and quite unknown even to most Pembrokeshire people.

Perhaps the most striking contrasts are between the north and south of the county. In the north, moorlands and upstanding rocks often provide a wild, harsh back-cloth in a landscape of small scattered settlements. Farms are small, and fields are often bounded by bare hedges or rough stone walls. Churches, farms and chapels look Welsh, and they usually have Welsh names. In the south the landscape is gentler and occasionally well wooded, with larger villages and towns. Farms are more modern and more profitable, and the pattern of life has closer links with England than with Celtic Wales. This is the 'Little England' of the guide-books, the region of Anglo-Saxon place-names, Norman castles and tall battlemented church towers. Margaret F. Davies, who has made a special study of the historical geography of the county, has recognised a 'zone of frontiers' between these two regions, and has pointed out how closely geological, landscape, political, social and other boundaries coincide as they curve eastward and southward from St Bride's Bay to Carmarthen Bay. For something like a thousand years this vague zone of frontiers has been crystallised within the cultural landscape as the Pembrokeshire Landsker, a unique local phenomenon which has changed its character and its position several times. The Landsker still exists as a sharp language divide, and we shall refer frequently to its past and present importance.

A further series of landscape contrasts can be related to the halting progress of Pembrokeshire towards a balanced way of life in which modern trade and industry offset the traditional arts of agriculture. From the sixteenth century onwards sea-trading from small harbours on the open coast and from the creeks of Milford Haven has been of importance, as we are reminded by many traces in the landscape. Similarly, there are many traces of Pembrokeshire's coal era. The Pembrokeshire anthracite field, the remote western extension of the South Wales coalfield, enjoyed almost a century of moderate prosperity; we can still see traces of spoil heaps, pit-head buildings and machinery, railway tracks and quays in some remote localities. Milford Haven, the county's great natural waterway, was largely neglected until the towns of Milford (in this book the author follows the local practice of referring to the town as Milford and the waterway as Milford Haven), Pembroke Dock and Neyland were built in the nineteenth century. Shipbuilding at Pembroke Dock and a later important fishing industry at Milford have now practically disappeared. It was the age of the supertanker which, at long last, brought Milford Haven to the notice of British industry. Now Milford Haven is Britain's major oil port, and its shores are being transformed by industry.

The belated recognition of the qualities of the Milford Haven waterway, and the very recent arrival of Pembrokeshire's 'industrial revolution' can of course be welcomed from an economic point of view, but at present Pembrokeshire is undergoing a profound change in character which many local people regret. The outer reaches of Milford Haven lie within the national park, and inevitably there has been conflict between the interests of conservation and those of industry. In this gently undulating landscape it is difficult to hide oil refineries, and even more difficult to hide the 750ft stack of the new Pembroke power-station and the rows of pylons which leave it to march through the south Pembrokeshire countryside in close formation towards the east. Somehow Pembrokeshire has to find a compromise between the interests of industry, the interests of the local farming and urban communities, and the interests of the tourists who flock in ever-increasing numbers to the coastline during the summer months.

In the chapters which follow many of these topics are

explored in greater depth. Some of the chapters are historical, but always there is a conscious attempt to relate the events of the past to the landscape features of today. The chapters progress from an examination of the landscape's most ancient features to those which are most recent; but the approach is for the most part thematic.

Pembrokeshire still has a strong feeling of identity, and with this goes a strong feeling of unity among its people. Hopefully the pages which follow will show that Pembrokeshire has a unique historical tradition, and a unique style of life. Pembrokeshire still exists.

Plate 1 Air photo of the long single-street village of Cosheston, with the pattern of strip fields clearly seen on the village flanks

Plate 2 (above) Evidence of the work of frost during the Ice Age: frost-shattered rock on the lower slopes of Carningli; *(below)* a fallen tree-trunk resting in the ancient peat of the submerged forest at Marros

2 THE NATURAL LANDSCAPE

'As touchinge the forme and fashion thereof by the Topographicall discripcion yt is neyther perfect square longe nor rounde but shaped with diverse Corners, some sharpe, some obtuse, in some places concave in some convexe, but in most places concave and bendinge inwarde . . .'
'. . . the sea doth the like, dealeinge soe inkindely with this poore Countrey as that it doth not in anye where seeme to yeld to the lande in anye parte, but in everye corner thereof eateth upp parte of the mayne . . .'
'. . . there are fine and sweete springes runninge in small little valleys, as if worne by their course, not deepe but broade, and shallowe, not headlonge or steepe, but allmost on playne ground . . .'

(George Owen, 1603)

NOWADAYS it may be unfashionable to describe anything as beautiful, but this is the word which describes, most simply but comprehensively, the natural landscape of Pembrokeshire. Forgetting for a moment the superficial paraphernalia of man's occupation of the land—his towns, his farms, his fields, his roads—one can look a little more closely at the forms and features of the landscape which have evolved, unseen by human eyes, over many thousands of years. These landforms are the foundations upon which man has scuttled about during the past few millennia furiously erecting minute monuments to his own technical ingenuity. And make no mistake about it—they are minute. The view of Pembrokeshire from a satellite, say 100 miles above the earth's surface, is of a green and varied land without a trace of human habitation. Here the works of man are reduced to realistic proportions. The forces of nature are seen as the real creators of the Pembrokeshire landscape.

When we look a little closer, it is the variety of the Pembrokeshire scene which catches the eye. Even on the ground the most casual observer cannot fail to notice the landscape contrasts which appear on all sides: contrasts between the plunging cliffed coast of Pencaer and the gentle undulations of the Western Cleddau valley; between the heather moorlands of Carningli and the quiet woodlands of Cwm Gwaun; between the wide tidal estuary of the Daugleddau and the dry limestone plateau of the Castlemartin peninsula. Other contrasts of many types rush to mind, for Pembrokeshire is a microcosm of Great Britain. Side by side there are small-scale illustrations of the types of countryside which elsewhere merge imperceptibly one with another. In other parts of Britain, the subtle changes of scene may defy recognition by all but the most acute observer; here in Pembrokeshire they are noticed and appreciated by visitors and local people alike. The beauty of Pembrokeshire lies not just in the serenity of its deep foxgloved lanes, not just in the stark ferocity of its clifflines, nor in the tangled chlorophyll jungles which are its oak woods. Not even in the bleak wide purple vistas of Presely, or the famous wild Whitsuntide extravaganza of bluebells and pink campions on the island of Skomer, or the pastel shades of a Trefgarn autumn. For Pembrokeshire has all of these things, and infinitely more. It has the beauty of a many-sided character, a beauty of moods and seasons, of gales and calms, of seascapes and skyscapes as well as landscapes. And above all the landscapes are green landscapes, even in mid-winter; always there are green plants competing, thriving and failing in a myriad of environments. The face of the county has an instantly recognisable appeal which at the same time defies accurate description. Nevertheless, this chapter tries, even if inadequately, to describe just some of the landscape features which make up this enigmatic face of Pembrokeshire.

ROCKS AND STRUCTURE

The rocks of the county (Map 1) are to a large extent responsible for one of its most noticeable contrasts; namely that between the higher, bleaker lands of the north and the warm, wooded lowlands of the south. To generalise, the north is an area of immensely old rocks (between 2,000 million and 395 million

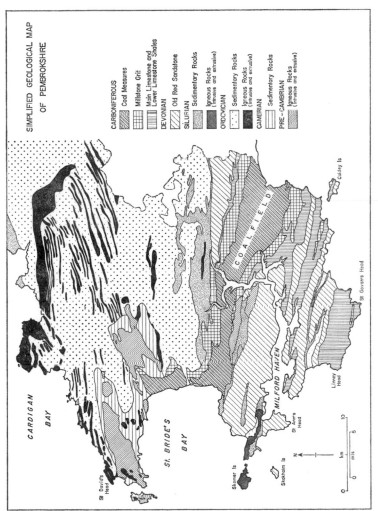

Map 1 Geological map of Pembrokeshire

years old), whereas to the south most of the rocks are much younger. Nevertheless, none of the rocks in Pembrokeshire are as young as those of south-east England; on the contrary, all of them are more than 295 million years old, classified as Palaeozoic and containing some of the oldest fossils in the British Isles. Many of the rocks of north Pembrokeshire are igneous in origin, made of basic earth materials, which have found their way in a molten state from the earth's interior to its outer crust largely by means of volcanic activity. The most prominent hill masses and carns in the north coincide with the outcrops of igneous rocks, for they have been more resistant to erosion than the layered sedimentary rocks (mainly of Cambrian and Ordovician age) around them. Examples are the massive dolerite carns of Carnllidi, Carn Treliwyd and Penbiri near St David's, which look for all the world like the stark ramparts of some gigantic distant mountain range; the long moorland ridge of Precambrian volcanic rocks which stretches westward from Mynydd Presely almost to the coast near Newgale, surmounted by the carns at Trefgarn, Plumstone and Roch; and the low smooth hills of whitish rhyolite along the coast road between Fishguard and Dinas. In the Presely uplands (always referred to by the locals, somewhat optimistically, as mountains) the carns of tumbled blocks which protrude from the generally smooth slopes are also of igneous rock. Carn Meini and Carn Alw, on the south-east slopes of the main Presely ridge, are thought to have been the sources of some of the bluestones of Stonehenge.

The oldest rocks in the north of the county are found around St David's, stretching from Ramsey Sound like a broad wedge into the centre of the peninsula, and around Roch, Hayscastle and the northern end of Trefgarn Gorge. Many of these rocks are volcanic ashes and lava-flows, but there are also more deep-seated igneous rocks such as granites and rhyolites; most are thought to be about 1,000 million years old. Somewhat unexpectedly, however, the oldest of all the rocks in Pembrokeshire are found in the south (around Benton, Johnston and Talbenny) in the midst of rocks which are generally very much younger. Near Johnston, for instance, by taking just a few paces one can pass from Precambrian rocks which are well over 1,000 million years old to Carboniferous Coal Measures which are less than 300 million years old.

Map 1 shows that the younger rocks of south Pembrokeshire are arranged quite simply in a series of more or less parallel strips, trending between w–e and nw–se. This was described as long ago as the sixteenth century by George Owen, who in addition to his other accomplishments has been called the patriarch of English geologists. He traced the main outcrops of limestone and coal in considerable detail, and noticed that some outcrops repeat themselves. The following quotation shows that he was beginning to appreciate the principles of stratigraphy also:

> . . . I found out two vaynes of lymestone to have their originale here in Pembrokeshire, and . . . theire Course holdeth estward, . . . betweene both which vaynes of lymestone the coale is founde to followe, but not soe open as the lymestone in every place with the lymestone but in many places where the stone sheweth, the coale hideth himself .& where the coale is founde, sometymes the lymestone lurketh underground, and in many places they are found neere together . . .

Hence, following in the footsteps of Pembrokeshire's Elizabethan geologist it is possible to trace several outcrops of the bright red sandstones, pebbly grits and conglomerates of the Old Red Sandstone; the hard white and grey limestones of Carboniferous age; the younger buff and brown grits, sandstones and shales of the Millstone Grit; and the Coal Measures which contain the Pembrokeshire anthracite much valued by the early industrialists for its excellent heating properties and low ash content. Each of these rocks has given rise to its own particular landscape type. A careful look reveals that the bright red soils (used especially for arable farming north of Milford Haven, on the Dale peninsula and on parts of the Castlemartin peninsula) coincide with the Old Red Sandstone outcrops. The landscape is pleasantly undulating and varied, with frequent small wooded valleys and broad swelling interfluves. In contrast, the Carboniferous Limestone lands are sometimes so short of surface water that they make up Pembrokeshire's own small desert. The limestone area within the boundaries of the old Castlemartin tank range is a platform of wide open spaces, of white bleached grass and of stunted trees. There is generally a thin red soil, but close to the coast the white limestone breaks the surface. Near Barafundle Bay and Broad Haven there are pits, hollows and areas of bare 'limestone pavement' reminiscent of more famous limestone terrains at Ingleborough and Malham Tarn. Elsewhere drifting white sand-dunes contribute to the desert image, as at Broad Haven and Tenby's South Beach. In violent contrast, the lush well-wooded landscape of the centre of the county coincides with the broad outcrop of the Coal Measures and the Millstone Grit. The soils are heavy and cold, and have a tendency to water-logging, so most of the fields are kept under grass for dairying and stock raising. Fields are small and hedges support a prolific growth of ground vegetation, shrubs and mature trees. The landscape here looks very much like the *bocage* of Brittany.

Inland there are very few clues to suggest just how complicated is the structure of Pembrokeshire, but the coast shows in fascinating detail how the rocks have been furiously tortured during geological time. In every bay, on every headland there are the signs of the massive upheavals of 1,000 million years; rocks standing on end, rocks buckled and bent and twisted, rocks melted and fused and reconstituted, rocks shattered and fragmented to the state where individual beds become quite unrecognisable. Concerning the more general patterns on the geological map of the county, there are two main trends in the arrangements of the rocks. In the north the rock outcrops trend from wsw–ene, whereas in the south the prevailing trend is wnw–ese. These trends reveal the roots of two ancient mountain chains, now worn down so drastically by the forces of erosion that hardly anything remains of them. In the north the rock outcrops show the course of an ancient Caledonian mountain chain, formed by the collision of the two ancient continents of Europe and North America some 400 million years ago. And in the south are the roots of the Armorican mountains, formed about 290 million years ago. Along a narrow zone in the centre of the county, stretching from St Bride's Bay through Haverfordwest to Tavernspite, the roots of these old mountain systems are in particularly close contact. But everywhere in the county the detailed pattern of rock exposures is related to the downwarps (synclines) and upwarps (anticlines) formed by the almost unimaginable forces released during these two main periods of mountain-building.

COASTAL CONTRASTS

The varied magnificence of the Pembrokeshire coast, which led in 1951 to the designation of the Pembrokeshire Coast National Park, is due in large measures to its geological and structural diversity. The main features of coastal configuration can be simply explained as the result of long-continued erosion of rocks and structures of varying resistance. So the broad embayment of St Bride's Bay, with its long sandy beaches and crumbling cliffs, has been formed by marine attack along the broad syncline of the Pembrokeshire coalfield, where the soft Coal Measures have been easily removed. The prominent peninsulas flanking St Bride's Bay to north and south exist in their present form because the igneous rocks of which they are partly made have proved much more resistant to wave attack. These igneous rocks can be seen on the bleak cliffs above Ramsey Sound, and on Skomer Island and around Wooltack Point in the south. Further out to sea, the wave-washed Bishops and Clerks and the gannet island of Grassholm are remote extensions of these same ridges of hard igneous rocks. The other main features of the Pembrokeshire coast can be related to geology in a similar way. The prominent peninsula of Pencaer, pushing bluntly northwards into Cardigan Bay, is made largely of intrusive and volcanic rocks of Ordovician age. The long branching waterway of Milford Haven and the Daugleddau shows how rivers and the sea have been able to exploit faults and synclines and soft rock exposures to create a winding main channel and many secret creeks and bays. Freshwater West Bay has been excavated by the sea along a line where a sharp upwarp has exposed broken and faulted rocks of many types. Saundersfoot Bay is a smaller relative of St Bride's Bay,

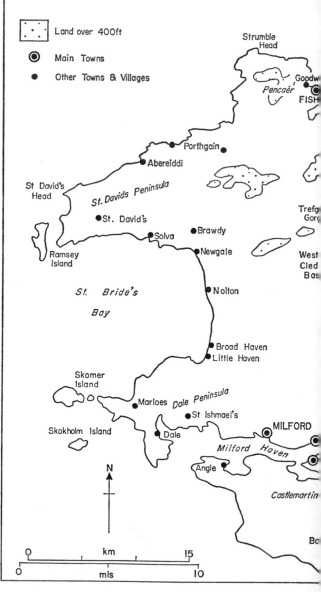

PEMBROKESHIRE
LOCATION MAP

Land over 400ft

⊙ Main Towns

● Other Towns & Villages

Strumble Head

Goodw

Pencaêr

FISH

Porthgain

Abereiddi

St David's Head

St. Davids Peninsula

St. David's

Solva

Brawdy

Newgale

Trefg Gorg

West Cled Bas

Ramsey Island

St. Bride's

Bay

Nolton

Broad Haven

Little Haven

Skomer Island

Marloes

Dale Peninsula

St Ishmael's

MILFORD

Skokholm Island

Dale

Milford Haven

N

Angle

Castlemartin

Bo

km   15

mls   10

Map 2

keshire

having formed as a result of wave attack along the centre of the coalfield syncline. At a more detailed scale, many small bays and inlets coincide with soft sedimentary rocks or faulted zones; and headlands are made of harder igneous rocks or sedimentary rocks made resistant to wave attack by their massive and homogeneous nature.

With so many geological contrasts around the coast, little wonder that each stretch has its own characteristics, its own idiosyncracies. Particular personal favourites are the coasts of the St David's peninsula, explored in minute detail a decade ago, in a bright, quiet, early summer spent largely in the company of sea-birds and soft winds off the sea. Here the cliffs are immensely varied in colour and form. The north coast between Pencaer and St David's Head, for example, is a wild, lonely coast where rocks and sea are in unceasing and uncompromising conflict. Here there are no clean wide sandy beaches like those of St Bride's Bay; except for Aber-mawr and Abereiddi the small beaches are dark and menacing, and difficult of access. Here it is not golden sand and sunlight which catch the eye, but stark shadows on grey and black cliffs. Here all that matters is measured in the vertical dimension. The cliffs rivet the attention. If the eyes stray from them they wander up to the clifftop wastes of heather, gorse and stunted bushes; or down, far below, to the caves, fissures and stacks hewn by the waves from the resisting land. The sounds are the sounds of surf crashing over a chaos of massive fallen blocks and rock ledges, echoing in unseen caves; the cries of gulls and ravens; the rise and fall of wind buffeting against sheer rock faces and rushing through fine grass. The scents carried on the wind are of salt spray and blossoming gorse. Here there is peace, and beauty to be absorbed by all the senses.

Equally, many people fall in love with the coast between Porth-clais and Solva, where the details have been etched by the waves into the subtle purples, reds, greens and greys of Cambrian sedimentary rocks dipping steeply seawards; or the high Old Red Sandstone cliffs which culminate in St Ann's Head; or the grey-white Carboniferous Limestone cliffs between Flimston and St Govan's, where the waves have created a fantastic coastline dominated by vertical walls, ledges littered by collapsed blocks, caves, arches, stacks, chasms and caverns. If one is temperamentally more attracted by the beauty which resides in peaceful things, there are the 'inland coasts' of the estuarine Daugleddau, which make up a separate section of the national park. Here, at high tide, there are no wide vistas; simply the quiet muddy river balanced between ebb and flow, the low rock cliffs and the smooth valley sides clothed by dense oak woodland. These are no ordinary oak woods. They are the fantastic remnants of the Mabinogion forests, densely inhabited by twisted stunted trees which struggle for existence amid lichens and moss and brambles and climbing ivy—except where neat, well-ordered, alien coniferous woods have rudely replaced them. At low water everything is transformed; mud replaces water, rocks draped in steaming seaweed line the shore, and waders and waterfowl appear from nowhere to see what the ebbing tide has laid bare.

PLATFORMS AND VALLEYS

The relationships between geology and landscape are a little less obvious in inland Pembrokeshire, for here the agents of landscape destruction have gained the upper hand over millions of years of geological time. Much of the Pembrokeshire landscape appears extremely flat when viewed as a panorama. Near the coast the 'erosion surfaces' are particularly spectacular, and the coastal flats cut across steeply dipping Carboniferous Limestone on the Castlemartin peninsula are justly famous among geologists and geomorphologists. Around St David's also, the level waterlogged wastes of Dowrog Common, Treleddyd-fawr and the other moorlands are similarly easy to recognise. These coastal platforms have probably been fashioned partly by wave action at times of much higher sea-level, and the St David's carns must have stood above the water surface as islands, looking much as Ramsey Island and the Bishops and Clerks look today. Generally the coastal flats have surface altitudes less than 200ft above sea-level, but there may be other surfaces at such altitudes as 400ft, 600ft, and above.

Certainly there are extensive gently undulating areas to be seen well inland in Pembrokeshire, but their edges are difficult to find, and it would be misleading to describe a landscape composed of neat steps separated by old clifflines. More simply, the Pembrokeshire land surface has been attacked by the processes of wave action, slope formation and river erosion. Over an immensely long period of time the old mountain masses have been worn down, slowly but surely, so that now the county is largely reduced to the status of a lowland. Most of the erosion responsible for the present-day landforms has occurred within the last 60 million years or so.

Apart from the past higher sea-levels relative to the land, there have also been periods of much lower sea-levels. The times of low sea-level within the last 2 million years have been linked to the events of the Ice Age (the Quaternary Period), when vast amounts of moisture were periodically extracted from the oceans and locked up in the major ice sheets of Antarctica, Greenland, North America and Scandinavia. But even earlier than this, Pembrokeshire experienced a prolonged period when sea-level was at least 100ft lower than at present. At this time the ancient valley system of Milford Haven was formed, with streams draining a large part of the county flowing generally southwards and then westwards, sometimes independently of geology and sometimes exploiting and guided by weaknesses such as long fault-lines. The coast was well to the west of its present position. Since this time the magnificent waterway has gradually evolved; several times it has been flooded by the sea during the warm interglacial periods, and several times it has been drained as the glaciers advanced and sea-level fell to 200 or even 300ft below its present level. The red cliffs of the Haven, the broad amphitheatre of Angle Bay and the more irregular Pembroke River, the quiet creeks and pills up-river from Burton, have all had a long and complex history influenced above all by the violent changes of Ice Age sea-level.

THE ICE AGE

Of perhaps greater importance to the natural landscape of

Pembrokeshire were the direct effects of the Ice Age, in particular related to the work of glacier ice, frost and water produced by the melting of ice and snow. On at least two occasions the county lay close to the southern margin of the largest British glacier, the Irish Sea glacier. During the earlier of the two glaciations which have been discovered, this glacier, nourished by the snows of the northern and western British Isles, swept southwards across Cardigan Bay, and then southeastwards across Pembrokeshire. Even here it must have been over three thousand feet thick, for the glacier had sufficient momentum to flow on up the Bristol Channel as far as Bristol and the Mendips. Pembrokeshire must have been completely submerged beneath a solid mass of glacier ice, pressing irresistibly on towards the south-east, removing mud and clay from the old sea-floor and soil, sand and loose bedrock from the face of the land. How much rock was eroded by the Irish Sea glacier is difficult to say, for this last complete glaciation of the county occurred well over 100,000 years ago; most traces of it have long since been removed by more recent erosion and deposition. In the south of the county there is little trace except for some 'erratic' boulders carried by the ice from the St David's area and further afield, and some of these have been used by enterprising locals as gravestones in the old churchyard at Flimston.

In the north, however, there is one much more spectacular trace of this glaciation—the long, wooded Gwaun valley and the little known series of deep valleys which join its western end. The Gwaun valley itself cuts right across the uplands, isolating Carningli from the main mass of Mynydd Presely. It was cut by glacial meltwater flowing in tunnels beneath thick melting ice at a time when the Irish Sea glacier was dying a slow, lingering death. The meltwater rushed westwards under enormous pressure, sometimes flowing uphill and carving a steep-sided valley which is occasionally over 150ft deep. It escaped through the western series of connecting valleys into the upper basin of the Western Cleddau and thence southwards through the deep cleft of the Trefgarn gorge. By far the most spectacular of these connecting valleys is the Nant-y-Bugail valley (unfortunately closed to the public), whose precipitous sides are in one place over 280ft high. Perhaps more beautiful, but largely undiscovered, are the valleys of Esgyrn Bottom, Criney Brook and Cwmonnen, with their steep wooded flanks and their flat floors of thick, boggy peat. In autumn when the mist is rising and there are red dying leaves on the trees and dead white grass below, these quiet valleys also have the feel of magic about them.

Once again, more recently, the ice of the Irish Sea glacier overwhelmed part of Pembrokeshire. About 17,000 years ago the glacier crossed the north coast and flowed almost as far south as Milford Haven; but this glaciation was not nearly as prolonged or powerful as its predecessors, and by the time the glacier reached Pembrokeshire its energies were almost spent. The ice changed the landscape hardly at all, but it did smooth the contours by dumping a spasmodic cover of 'till' (once called 'boulder-clay') especially in the north. On some of the moorlands near St David's and Fishguard this dark purple, sticky clay till was worked in clay-pits from medieval times until quite recently; it was described very accurately in 1599 by the ubiquitous George Owen. Here and there sands and gravels over 50ft thick were laid down by meltwater streams. Sometimes these sands and gravels have a hummocky surface, but more often they occupy the valley floors; they can be seen in gravel-pits at Trevayog, Mullock Bridge, Tre-llys, Mathry Road and elsewhere. Occasionally the gravels contain shells dredged by the ice from the floor of Cardigan Bay and then re-deposited by meltwater.

Before, during and after this last glaciation the climate of Pembrokeshire was as severe as that of an Arctic tundra, and those areas not actually covered by snow and ice were subjected to intense frost shattering. The slopes of sharp, angular blocks in the uplands, and beneath many coastal cliffs, are the result of this process (Plate 2a). In the uplands the coarser material is called 'scree', but on the coast, where it is often exposed in section, it has long been referred to by geologists as 'head'. At one or two coastal localities in north Pembrokeshire chance circumstances have led to the preservation of smoothed and ice-scratched bedrock and thick sequences of interglacial and glacial deposits; the most important of these are Abermawr and Poppit, both of which have been scheduled as Sites of Special Scientific Interest. As with many of the other natural landscape features, the landforms of the Ice Age may not be particularly noticcable to the casual observer, but they are there to be seen by those who know what they are looking for. They contribute much to the character of Pembrokeshire.

3   MYTHS, MONUMENTS AND MYSTERIES

SINCE the end of the last glaciation, the impact of man upon the natural landscapes of Pembrokeshire has gradually increased, so that today the cultural features within the landscape tend to attract much of our attention. The tempo of landscape change has increased as man's technological expertise has advanced. Technological 'generations' have become shorter and shorter. By looking at a variety of ancient cultural relics we can see that each succeeding generation has developed for itself the means, ever more efficient, of removing the landscape traces of its predecessors. But successive generations have had different territorial and economic demands, and in a region with landscapes as varied as those of Pembrokeshire this explains why many old features of the cultural landscape are so well preserved.

THE STONE AGE

The earliest known human occupation of Pembrokeshire occurred during the most recent cold stage of the Ice Age, over 20,000 years ago and at a time when sea-level was very much lower than it is now. Palaeolithic or Old Stone Age man hunted the tundra on the northern slopes of the (then dry) Bristol Channel. He occupied some of the old sea caves on the limestone cliffs of the Castlemartin peninsula and also limestone caves further inland. Caves such as the Priory Farm cave at Monkton were used, off and on, for thousands of years; and the evidence from Paviland in Gower and elsewhere shows that men using the Aurignacian culture lived here during and

34

Plate 3 *(above)* The summit fort at Moel Drygarn, at the eastern end of the Presely Mountains; *(below)* the saintly skeleton found during the excavations of St Patrick's Chapel at Whitesand Bay

Plate 4 (left) The little limestone chapel of St Govan's, wedged into a narrow cleft in the limestone cliffs at Trefalen on the south coast of the Castlemartin peninsula

(right) the fine chapel of Bethesda in Haverfordwest. It was built in 1789

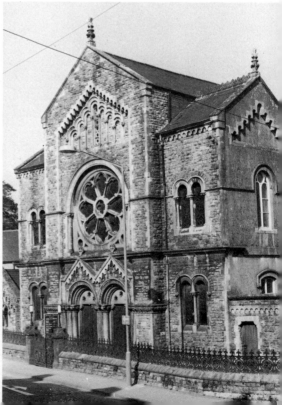

after the so-called 'Upton Warren' interstadial phase when there was a temporary improvement of climate. We do not know whether man was forced to retreat from the Castlemartin peninsula during the coldest part of the last glaciation, but archaeological finds of simple flint implements show that he was in residence again when the ice began to melt around 15,000 years ago. Caves on Caldey Island and the mainland have yielded many finds of animal bones and teeth which show that Early Stone Age man had plenty of animal company. Among the animals were woolly rhinoceros, reindeer, giant ox, cave bear, brown bear, cave lion, glutton, wolf and wild boar. One fissure in the limestone cliffs at Daylight Rock, Caldey Island, contained so many bones of Ice Age animals that they must have been dragged there by hyenas. In addition to the animals mentioned above, there were remains of mammoth, giant deer, and horse; often the bones showed the teeth-marks of the feasting hyenas.

In the following Mesolithic or Middle Stone Age, which began about 10,000 years ago, some of the traditions of the Old Stone Age were continued; in particular family groups in South Wales still depended on hunting and fishing, and many of them still lived in caves. Gradually people were moving to other parts of the county, and finds of Mesolithic tools have been made at Nab Head, Benton, and Frainslake, in addition to the well-known cave sites of Pembroke and the Tenby–Caldey area. While Mesolithic man probably roamed more widely over the Pembrokeshire landscape than his predecessors, his impact upon it must still have been negligible.

During the Mesolithic period, which lasted until about 6,000 years ago, sea-level was rising by fits and starts. At the close of the last glaciation the sea was more than 350ft lower than at present, but as the great ice-sheets of the northern hemisphere wasted away more and more meltwater was returned to the oceans. Until about 9,000 years ago the rate of sea-level rise was about 6ft per century; then after an 'interruption' of about a thousand years during which sea-level may have fallen and then risen again slowly, the rate of sea-level rise increased dramatically to about 10ft per century. This was a real natural catastrophe, and the coastal lowlands of Cardigan Bay, St Bride's Bay and Carmarthen Bay were gradually encroached upon by the sea. Peatlands, marshes and woodlands were over-whelmed by the waves, sometimes during storms of such violence that tree-trunks were snapped off like matchsticks (Plate 2b). In some of the 'submerged forests' which are occasionally exposed at times of exceptionally low tides around the Pem-brokeshire coast, the tree-trunks are seen to lie with a constant orientation, felled and then preserved in peat, mud and sand for over 7,000 years. Arthur Leach, Pembrokeshire's greatest ama-teur geologist, discovered the skeleton of a pig in the submerged forest at Lydstep. Across the poor beast's neck lay the trunk of a fallen tree. Leach and many other investigators have found flint implements among the remains of the submerged forest, together with stags' horns and many animal bones. Undoubtedly many of these drowned areas must have been the hunting-grounds of Mesolithic family groups, and probably many of their settle-ments, too, are now lost beneath the sea.

The submerged forests have frequently been described in the literature, from Giraldus Cambrensis in the twelfth century to George Owen in the seventeenth century and Arthur Leach and F. J. North in recent decades. According to Giraldus, a great storm at Newgale in the winter of 1171–2 'laid bare . . . the surface of the earth, which had been covered for many ages, and discovered the trunks of trees cut off, standing in the very sea itself. . . .' For hundreds of years the people of Whitesands, Newgale, Lydstep, Amroth and Marros have collected fire-wood from the submerged forests; but recently great damage has unfortunately been done by souvenir hunters encouraged by unwise newspaper publicity.

The rapid post-glacial rise of sea-level and the overwhelming of the coastal forests seems, even after thousands of years, to retain a place in the communal sub-conscious. Lurking darkly amid the hazy half-remembered traditions of Pembrokeshire coastal communities there are the stories of great floods; some of these stories date from the Iron Age or even from the Christian period, but some may be much older. Who knows, for instance, where lie the roots of the story of Cantref y Gwaelod? The tale has a strongly Celtic flavour, but its roots may lie amid the tree-stumps and fallen trunks and branches of the Mesolithic forests lost in Cardigan Bay. Here, according to tradition, there lay a great tract of fertile country, cultivated, densely peopled and guarded by fine fortified towns. The land, called the Lowland Hundred (Cantref' y Gwaelod), was defended from the encroachment of the sea by a strong embankment. Seithennin, the keeper of the embankment, was 'one of the three immortal drunkards of Britain'. During a splendid banquet the immortal Seithennin became so drunk that he forgot to close the sluice-gates in the embankment, and the sea surged in to inundate the whole land. Most of the population perished, and the land was never reclaimed. It is said that traces of the walls and buildings can still be seen at times of low tide, or made out beneath the surface of the water when the sea is very calm. Whether or not this is true, there are many who know that the embankments of Cantref y Gwaelod still exist: during low spring tides, the *sarnau* of Cardigan Bay are exposed as long, stony ridges running straight out to sea. Sarn Cynfelin and Sarn-y-Bwlch are both more than five miles long, while Sarn Badrig (also called St Patrick's Causeway) stretches out to sea for no less than eleven miles. Modern research shows them to be moraines constructed by the last outlet glaciers to flow westwards from the Cambrian Mountains, but who can blame our forefathers for not knowing that?

The first people who were really able to alter the face of the land we know as Pembrokeshire were the Neolithic farmers who arrived by sea some 5,000 years ago. They came by way of the Bristol Channel, probably sailing in simple skin and wattle vessels not unlike the Irish curragh or the Welsh coracle of today. They usually settled within sight of the sea, for example at Clegyrfwya near St David's. Here archaeologists have been able to make a reconstruction of a Neolithic house, showing it to have been built between two steps of rock with a wooden roof supported by eight timber posts (Fig 1). There was another Neolithic building on the same rocky hill, and there may indeed have been a real farming community here. Probably they practised cattle-raising, but their food supplies must have

Fig 1 A reconstruction of the Neolithic dwelling-house at Clegyrfwya, (also called Clegyr Boia) near St David's

been supplemented by hunting and by gathering fruits, roots and nuts. In the most favourable areas the Neolithic communities are thought to have used shifting cultivation. In the broad lush basins of the Western Cleddau and Eastern Cleddau rivers they altered the damp forest of the Atlantic period by tree felling and selective burning and their browsing animals slowed down forest regeneration by the removal of saplings. These processes continued into the drier sub-Boreal period after about 2000 BC.

CROMLECHAU

The most spectacular achievements of the Neolithic folk were the megalithic burial chambers (dolmens or *cromlechau*) of various types, many of which can still be found in north Pembrokeshire. Among the best-known are Longhouse near Mathry (Fig 2), Carreg Coetan Arthur near Newport, and Ffyst Samson near St Nicholas. Tombs probably began to appear in the Welsh countryside only when family groups had developed the arts of agriculture to the extent of remaining for several generations in one locality. Then it became the custom to build permanent structures as burial places and perhaps as monuments for the veneration of ancestors. The family vaults in present-day churchyards are not so very different. The main structure of each tomb was made by placing one or more huge 'capstone' slabs on top of upright stone pillars. The spaces between these pillars were filled with dry-stone walling, and then the structural core of the chamber was covered with stones or earth to form a substantial mound or cairn. Originally most 'barrows',

Fig 2 A sketch of the fine cromlech at Longhouse, near Mathry. The capstone is supported by no less than seven vertical pillars

as they have come to be known, were round or elongated; but over the centuries the natural processes of erosion, helped by farmers and tomb-robbers and amateur antiquarians, have removed almost all of the covering materials. Nowadays there is little left to see of the remaining *cromlechau* except the grey lichen-encrusted pillars and the occasional massive capstone.

There are at least three different types of *cromlech*. The simplest is the 'sub-megalithic' type of chamber, usually set in a hillside where the uphill edge of the capstone is supported on a bedrock ledge and the downhill edge held up by vertical pillars. The two *cromlechau* on St David's Head belong in this category, perhaps representing a rather lazy style of building which seems to have been common among the Neolithic communities of St David's peninsula and Pencaer. More complicated were the round barrows with polygonal burial chambers in the centre and access provided by a passage through the mound. The Longhouse monument is of this type, and there is a variation on the theme at Cerrig y Gof, near Newport, where the original round barrow had no less than five chambers or recesses set around its circumference. Most impressive of all were the large long-barrows built with pillars and capstones weighing fifteen tons or more, and with elaborate curved forecourts and portals. Paradoxically, these technically advanced monuments seem to have been built before the smaller and rather decadent hillside tombs referred to above. One of the most famous examples of a megalithic long-barrow in the whole of the British Isles is the Pentre Ifan *cromlech* near Nevern. Here three tall pillars provide delicate support for a capstone measuring almost 17ft by 10ft. At the entrance portal the capstone was more than 7ft above the ground, and it sloped down towards the centre of the chamber. From the excavations undertaken at Pentre Ifan in 1936 it seems that the original barrow must have been over 130ft long, 65ft wide at its broadest, and at least 11ft high. Pentre Ifan, like the other remaining *cromlechau* of Pembrokeshire, shows a mastery of a simple yet impressive technology, and there can be no doubt that such a monument must have been built and used with great ceremony.

It is perhaps not surprising, given their obvious antiquity and their impressive proportions, that some of the megalithic monuments have been linked with legends of giants and heroes such as Samson and Arthur. Early antiquarians also mistakenly attributed them to the druids, referring to the capstones as altars on which the priests performed human sacrifices. Nowadays we take a rather more sober view of their origins.

Between 5,000 and 4,000 years ago, Pembrokeshire was the home of a mixed population with different and distinct cultural traditions. There were still many groups of Mesolithic people living around the coastline, which by this time was in approximately its present position. Inland there were tribes of Neolithic farmers and herders, and there were other groups of Neolithic immigrants who seem to have followed a way of life along the coast which was not far removed from that of the Mesolithic groups. As a result of contact with each other and with influences from the outside world, these groups gradually merged and evolved their material culture. Trade became increasingly important, and Professor Emrys Bowen has shown how the Pembrokeshire peninsula acted as something of a crossroads between the coastal routes running s–n through St George's Channel and those running e–w across the seaway between Ireland and Wales. There was much trade in stone axes, and axe factories came into being in sites which had particularly favourable rock-types. There may well have been axe factories in the Presely uplands, at least one manufacturing axes from rhyolitic tuffs, and another using the spotted dolerite derived from Carn Menyn and other nearby outcrops. Axes of these types are widely distributed in Pembrokeshire and elsewhere.

At about the dawn of the Bronze Age, the Mesolithic and Neolithic peoples of Pembrokeshire were just beginning to come under the influence of the Beaker people and were learning the skills of metal-working. There was a new flowering of culture throughout south-west Britain, and the greatest remaining symbol of this culture is the famous Stonehenge monument in Wiltshire.

THE STONEHENGE MYTH

Pembrokeshire has played a special part in the Stonehenge story since 1923, when the geologist H. H. Thomas proved that many of the 'bluestones' which form the inner circle at Stonehenge come from the county. Furthermore, he suggested that the three main types of bluestone (namely dolerite, rhyolite and volcanic ash) occur naturally close together only in a small area in the Presely uplands around Carn Menyn. Following these discoveries archaeologists evolved an elegant hypothesis to the effect that the bluestones, and other stones

43

such as the altar-stone, were deliberately transported some 180 miles from Pembrokeshire to Wiltshire. The hypothesis involved a great deal of imagination concerning land and sea routes, the 'sanctity' of the Presely area, and the desire of the Stonehenge builders to use stone-types with which they were already familiar from the stone-axe trade. In our minds this hypothesis has quietly turned into 'fact'. We all know the stirring tale of primitive men hauling the massive bluestones on sledges and then sailing them on rafts from Milford Haven along the Bristol Channel to the Avon valley, and taking them by sledge again, or on rollers, for the last triumphant part of the journey to the Stonehenge site on Salisbury Plain. This is all a part of our contemporary folk-lore, and when in 1954 a BBC experiment proved that the journey was indeed possible, the theory seemed confirmed.

However, the 'bluestone theory' has remarkably little archaeological or other evidence to support it, and it is only in recent years that anyone has pointed out how flimsy the theory really is. Mr Geoffrey Kellaway of the Institute of Geological Sciences has now suggested, perfectly reliably, that the Stonehenge bluestones may well have been carried to the innermost shores of the Bristol Channel by glacier ice. It has been known for many years that the great Irish Sea glacier which over-rode Pembrokeshire more than 100,000 years ago flowed southeastwards up the Bristol Channel, carrying with it erratics and till eroded not only from Presely but also from Ireland, the Lleyn Peninsula and Galloway in Scotland. But only recently has it been discovered that this glacier over-rode the Somerset coast and deposited part of its load in the Bristol–Bath region. This being the case, it is now much more logical to assume that the bluestones (in reality from quite a wide variety of sources both within and outside Pembrokeshire) were, at the time of the Beaker culture, conveniently littering the countryside less than thirty miles from Stonehenge. There is infinitely more evidence to support the theory of ice transport than there is in support of the great contemporary myth of long-distance haulage by the Beaker people.

THE AGE OF METAL TOOLS

The Bronze Age settlers who established themselves in Pembrokeshire about 3,800 and 2,500 years ago seem to have made much greater use than their predecessors of the centre and south of the county. They continued and speeded up the process of forest clearance, now with metal tools. It is thought that they depended less upon cultivation than the Neolithic people; but the cultural advances of this time may be seen as a sign of both increased trade and more stable settlement. The best-preserved traces left in the cultural landscape by the Bronze Age peoples are again linked with religious activities and with burials. Such are the stone circles of the Welsh uplands (of which there is only one in Pembrokeshire, near Mynachlog-ddu), the standing stones which are common in the north of the county (as at Rhos-y-Clegyrn and Henry's Moat), and some smaller single-chambered tombs. Many of the round barrows of the Presely area and the south of the county date from this time.

The Bronze Age was followed about 2,500 years ago by the dawn of the Iron Age. It came with the many groups of Celtic immigrants who followed the sea-trading routes northwards and westwards from Spain, France and the south-west peninsula of England. They spoke languages which were the forerunners of Welsh and Gaelic, and it was they who began to give Wales its imprint of Welshness. As they arrived the climate deteriorated, and the immigrant tribes had to contend with cool, damp conditions. Nevertheless, the density of their settlements in Pembrokeshire was greater than that of any of their predecessors and they must have been largely responsible for the removal of the remaining virgin forest. They were also the first great fort-builders. The Iron Age hill fort is termed by Frank Emery 'easily the most striking relic of any of the prehistoric landscapes in Wales'. Earth ramparts and ditches on clifftop headlands are commonplace on all the coasts of Pembrokeshire, as at Penpleidiau, Great Castle Head and St Ishmael's. Inland there is the great hill fort at Mynydd Carningli, and many more forts which are marked on the map as 'raths' or 'camps'.

45

Most impressive of all is the summit fort on Moel Drygarn (Plate 3a), occupying the most easterly hill of the main Presely range. Its stone ramparts contain three enclosures, and in addition to the three prominent cairns (probably of Bronze Age origin) there are traces of many hut hollows and platforms to suggest a large population. There is another fascinating site on the St David's headland, where the stone-built defences of the 'Warrior's Dyke' enclosed a compact settlement of perhaps a dozen round huts. Beyond the main defences another stone wall may have defined the home territory of the Iron Age community, and in the valley between Porth Melgan and Carnllidi one can still see the stone walls of the original small enclosed fields. The finds from the settlement suggest that even in this barren, windswept locality there was a mixed farming economy in which stock breeding played a part.

During the Iron Age the changing style of promontory fort and hill fort building shows that there were tribal rivalries in which raiding and open warfare were becoming more common. The earliest forts were protected only by single curved banks, but by 100 BC double- or even treble-curved embankments were characteristic. The embankments were probably faced with stone and protected with a bristling array of pointed stakes, and sometimes they enclosed areas large enough to maintain beleaguered communities together with their livestock during long periods of seige. Examples are the promontory forts at Bosherston Pools, Flimston Bay, Greenala Point and Linney Head.

During the Roman period (AD 43–AD 410), which coincided broadly with the end of the Iron Age, Celtic tribal society in Pembrokeshire evolved largely unmolested. In this remote western peninsula only one possible Roman camp site has been discovered, but the Romans knew enough of the area to record its people as the 'Demetae'. Gradually, through the distant mysterious millennia before the birth of Christ, the many tribal groups of immigrants had coalesced into one people.

4 THE WELSH, THEIR SAINTS AND THEIR STORIES

GRADUALLY the people of Pembrokeshire, and the landscape of the county, began to acquire the imprint of Welshness. The Celtic tribes grew, and their territories gradually emerged during the long period after the departure of the Romans from Wales in AD 383. Complicated trading movements and folk migrations linked Wales and Ireland, and because of its strategic position on the sea-trading routes of the Dark Ages, Pembrokeshire at this time was one of the great centres in the development of Celtic culture. Many large stones inscribed with the Ogam alphabet (as at Brawdy, Nevern and Steynton) bear witness to Irish secular influence before about AD 450, but of much greater importance for the geography of the county was the later growth of a distinctive Welsh culture. Often the political situation in south-west Wales was anything but quiet, but by the middle of the sixth century the kingdom of Dyfed had been established. It was ruled by the somewhat mysterious Verteporix, who was probably of Irish descent.

THE CELTIC SAINTS

Before looking at the effects of the Celtic secular settlement in Dyfed, it is worth examining the impact made by the Celtic saints. Their missionary activities probably began about AD 450. Gradually a network of religious cells was established through the area, based for the most part upon a belief in the spiritual benefits of individual withdrawal into the wilderness. Small churches were established in remote localities, and were particularly common in Pembrokeshire. Here, as elsewhere, they seldom became nuclei for later settlement; small churches with Celtic dedications can still be seen around the wild rocky coastline, standing against the elements in splendid isolation.

The Celtic saints (including St David and St Patrick) and their disciples travelled back and forth across the Irish Sea and St George's Channel on their missionary journeys. These 'peregrini'—as they are called by historians—used frail skin boats similar to the Irish curragh of today, and there is no doubt that the smaller Welsh coracle is another vessel which traces its ancestry back to these times. There can be no doubt either about the seamanship of the Celtic saints or about the seaworthiness of their fragile craft, for well before AD 800 they had reached and established settlements in both the Faroe Islands and Iceland. They were, nevertheless, very much at the mercy of winds and tidal currents, for their sailing techniques were primitive and their knowledge of navigation limited. Where possible they used wide sandy bays, but often they must have been driven ashore by chance on to more precarious rocky landing-places. Where this happened, as John Barrett has pointed out, '. . . their first thought was a thanksgiving for safe delivery. So from the start, little chapels began to appear along our coasts, dedicated to the saintly leaders.'

Typical of the coastal chapels of this time were those at St Justinian's, St Non's, Cwm-yr-Eglwys and St Dogmael's. Many of these chapels have disappeared; others stand in ruins or have been replaced by later buildings. The little limestone chapel at St Govan's (Plate 4a) is perhaps the best known symbol of this time of missionaries and monastic seafarers. It stands deep in a cleft in the white cliffs, approachable only by a steep flight of rough steps. The chapel, now dirty and empty, may have been a monastic cell as long ago as the fifth century; but probably only the rock-cut cell and the stone altar and bench date from this time. Most of the structure which we see today is no older than the thirteenth century. But it is a place shrouded in mystery. The holy well, which ran dry during the present century, is said to have cured eye troubles, and as such the little chapel was a medieval place of pilgrimage. No one knows who St Govan really was. Possibly the chapel is named after one Cofen, the wife of a king of Glamorgan; or possibly after St Gobhan who was a contemporary of St David. Most popular is the idea that he was Sir Gawaine, one of the Knights of the Round Table who turned hermit after the death of Arthur.

As the fame of David brought pilgrims flocking to this sacred corner of the western world, more and more beaches and small harbours were used by pilgrims and traders, and the beach at Whitesands was particularly widely used as a landing-place. Here the small chapel of St Patrick was established. Nowadays there is hardly any trace of it left, but it was excavated in 1924 and the skeleton of a young man was unearthed beneath the level of the old chapel floor (Plate 3b). It is not known who he was, but he was certainly not St Patrick, for Patrick was apparently quite ancient but very much alive when he set off from here on his last voyage to Ireland.

DEWI SANT AND HIS FOLLOWERS

Some of the early monastic cells in the county did attract settlement, and these grew into larger religious communities. Among these we can count Nevern, St Dogmael's, Penally and Caldey, but these never compared in importance with the community of Dewi Sant in the secluded valley of the River Alun. Like the others, the church of St David probably began as a monastic *llan*, about AD 520. However, as the reputation of the founder grew so did his church and the associated settlement, then called Menevia. Soon it was the most important ecclesiastical centre in South Wales, and it has remained so to this day (Plate 5a). By its very presence the cathedral and its community have had a profound effect upon the course of events during the medieval period and later centuries.

The area round about the cathedral city has a wealth of tradition about the man himself and his followers. Legend tells us that Dewi was born during a great gale at a spot later to be named after his mother, St Non. He was baptised, possibly at Porth-clais, by Elvis the Bishop of Munster, 'who at that instant by divine intervention was landed there from Ireland'. He was educated at Tŷ Gwyn, near the present city, but spent much of his missionary life far away from his monastery in other parts of the Celtic world. But he returned in his old age to Menevia, where he was visited by monks and disciples from other parts of Wales, Brittany, Cornwall and Ireland. The influence of his cult was so great that more than 100 churches and monasteries were established in his name. There is a jolly story about Dewi Sant and a heathen chieftain named Boia, who gave the famous rock of Clegyr Boia its name. Legend has it that Boia's wife told her maids 'to go where the monks can see you and with bodies bare, play games and use lewd words'. Although this display seems to have had the desired effect upon the monks, Dewi remained strong. As divine retribution against the family Boia's wife slew her stepdaughter and went mad, while the chieftain and the rest of his household and camp were destroyed by fire from heaven. When the saint died, probably on 1 March AD 588, a brilliant sun shone over his mourning and fasting disciples, and 'Jesus Christ bore away David's soul in great triumph and gladness and honour. After his hunger, his thirst, and cold, and his labours, his abstinence and his acts of charity, and his weariness, and his tribulation, and his applications, and his anxiety for the world, the angels received his soul, and they bore it to a place where the light does not fail, and there is rest without labour, and joy without sadness, and abundance of all good things, and victory, and brilliance, and beauty . . .' These words, written in 1346, must be among the most beautiful in early Welsh literature.

There are other legends associated with St Justinian, who was David's friend and confessor. He retired to Ramsey to escape the lax ways of the mainland monks. But he had too many visitors, and prayed that the rocky causeway to the mainland would be destroyed. A giant axe appeared, and chopped the causeway into a series of rocks called the Bitches. These rocks, submerged at high tide, force the tidal currents to run through them with great force; this must have been an effective deterrent to unwanted visitors. Poor Justinian was murdered by his own followers on Ramsey by having his head cut off, but showing great resilience he picked it up and then walked across the sound with it tucked under his arm. He laid it down on the opposite shore, and at that site he was buried and his chapel was built. The present ruins of the chapel at St Justinian's are of much later date, but the saint's well can still be seen.

A rather more worldly tale of the early Christians is reminiscent of 'the immortal drunkard' who precipitated the catastrophe of Cantref y Gwaelod. It concerns Pyr, the first abbot of Caldey who gave that island its Welsh name. According to a near-contemporary source, he came to a sad and soggy end. 'One dark night this same Pyr in an unseemly drunken bout . . . wandered alone into the precincts of the monastery and fell into a very deep well. He raised a shout of distress, but when he was rescued from the water by the monks he was almost dead, and so he died that night.'

THE CELTIC WAY OF LIFE

Although the saints and their settlements made a great impact upon the landscape of Pembrokeshire, probably of greater importance was the normal Celtic way of life, which gradually became based upon permanent settlement during the Dark Ages. As mentioned at the beginning of the chapter, the kingdom of Dyfed emerged as the forerunner of present-day Pembrokeshire. The kingdom was composed of seven districts or *cantrefi*: and in spite of the great political upheavals of the period 700–1093 there was a gradual progression towards an ordered society. A pattern of small scattered 'homestead' settlements and fragmented holdings appeared in the landscape. The homesteads were built by tribal freemen, and they provided security and protection for large family groups. Some of the small hamlets of north Pembrokeshire originated at this time, and the prefix *tref* (township) is a common place-name element throughout the north of the county. Many of the isolated upland farms of Mynydd Presely must have been founded as *hafodydd* or dwellings used only during the summer cattle grazing season. The enclosure of many small rectangular fields bounded by stone walls or thick turf banks may date from this time, as must the creation of the dense network of trackways. Arable farming, with an increased use of oats, became more important, and the clearance of the remaining forest land continued at an accelerating pace.

Since most of the family dwellings of the Dark Ages were made of wood, few traces remain. Many families must have continued to use the peninsulas which had been fortified in the Iron Age, and other fortified hilltop sites must also have continued in occupation for centuries after the Romano-British period. There are very many settlement traces on the OS maps referred to as 'raths', 'camps' and 'earthworks'. They are often difficult to date, but many of them must have been home to the freemen of Dyfed and their families. Old field enclosures and hut groups from the island at Skomer, which may have been used in the Dark Ages, have been described in detail by Professor W. F. Grimes, and there may have been a sizeable community living in the old settlement and tilling the fields on St David's Head during the lifetime of the patron saint. On Gateholm, off the Marloes peninsula, over a hundred rectangular huts set end-to-end or grouped around courtyards have been dated to the Dark Ages. There are a large number of oblong hut hollows (unfortunately never excavated) on the grassy slopes of Sheep Island off the Angle peninsula. These, like the mysterious traces of ancient buildings on St Margaret's Isle near Caldey, may also be the remains of Celtic settlements long since abandoned and forgotten.

If it is difficult to interpret the landscape of these hazy times, there is no shortage of wordage on its history. It is not a purpose of this book to analyse the complicated internal conflicts which shook the kingdoms of Wales, nor to discuss the effects of the early wars with the English; but it is worth recording that some of the romantic memories of the Celtic Dark Ages were written down, probably in Dyfed, during the tenth and eleventh centuries. The outcome was one of the gems of European literature —*The Mabinogion*. Through the romantic poetry of its strange tales there runs a thread of references to Pembrokeshire, and indeed much of the action of 'The Four Branches of the Mabinogi', the best of the tales, takes place specifically in Dyfed. The first legendary king of Dyfed, named Pwyll, is supposed to have had his fateful encounter with Arawn, the king of the underworld, while hunting amid the beautiful oakwoods of Glyn Cuch near Newcastle Emlyn. We learn that his court was accustomed to meet at Arberth or Narberth. Pwyll's son Pryderi and his companions were forced to stay on the enchanted island of Grassholm for eighty years while travelling from Ireland to London. In another story Pryderi and all the people of Dyfed disappeared through the work of a magician; we are told of mice devouring the corn crop and of pigs being taken from Dyfed to Gwynedd. Perhaps the most famous story is linked with the Arthurian legend, and occurs in the tale of Culhwch and Olwen. The great wild boar called Twrch Trwyth, having been attacked by Arthur and his knights, swam from Ireland to Dyfed and landed at Porth-clais. To avenge himself on Arthur the boar did enormous damage, 'slaying what men and beasts were in Daugleddau' before Arthur caught up with him. There followed a furious battle on the summit of Mynydd Presely before the great beast fled southwards to Laugharne and crossed the mouth of the River Tywi. After further battles in which the last of Twrch Trwyth's seven attendant boars were killed, he crossed from South Wales to Devon and Cornwall and eventually swam off into the Atlantic.

THE VIKING SEA-ROVERS

The later part of the Age of the Saints was much disturbed by the raids of the Vikings, who had little respect either for the magical properties of the princes of Dyfed or for the holiness of St David's and other ecclesiastical centres. Roving far and wide from their bases in Ireland and Scotland in their magnificent long-ships, the Vikings terrorised the coasts of Pembrokeshire between AD 844 and AD 1091. St David's was burnt on no less than eight occasions during this period. Mathry, too prominent for comfort on its hilltop site, also suffered greatly. We do not know which ports and harbours were used by the Vikings, but Professor Emrys Bowen feels that almost certainly there were a number of viking coastal trading bases or 'marts'. There is a tradition that Milford Haven was widely used as a temporary base. In the year 877, for example, a chieftain called Hubba is said to have wintered in the Haven with a fleet of 23 ships and about 2,000 warriors. Some authorities have believed that there was a substantial viking settlement in the centre of the county around AD 1100, and indeed south Pembrokeshire people have some blood-group affinities with the Scandinavian races even today; but there is no reliable archaeological trace of either an inland settlement or of any colonies on the coast. The only Norse 'find' is a small lead object with a brass inset of a dragon, found on the shore at Freshwater West. Probably it dates from the tenth or eleventh century. But there is much place-name evidence to prove that the Vikings were familiar with the Pembrokeshire coast and with some inland localities as well. There are at least twenty-one place-names of Norse derivation, mostly linked with major coastal landmarks and islands, and it says something for the viking imprint upon the local community that these names have persisted for a thousand years. Among these names are Fishguard, Skokholm, Grassholm, Ramsey, Skomer, Milford, Goodwick, and Gosker. There would undoubtedly have been more were it not for the coming of the Normans.

5 THE CREATION OF 'LITTLE ENGLAND'

IT is difficult to decide just when Pembrokeshire began to be split into its two halves, the Englishry and the Welshry. It has been suggested by Margaret Davies that a primitive settlement divide, a forerunner of the Landsker, split Pembrokeshire into two even during the prehistoric period. She believed that the damp forests of central Pembrokeshire discouraged settlement, and that the western peninsulas and the Presely uplands provided more suitable sites both for agriculture and pastoral pursuits. From the maps of Neolithic and Bronze Age finds there certainly seems to have been a little-used belt of country approximately in the position of the Landsker zone, but Iron Age settlement traces are so widely distributed that it would be unwise to talk of any 'cultural divide' at this time. Also traces of burials may survive best on the coast and in the uplands, because both have such stony thin soils that ploughing has been less intensive and has had less effect than in the centre of the county. In any case Pembrokeshire during the Age of the Saints and even during the period of viking raids was a single Celtic community organised in to *cantrefi* and *cymydau* and ruled by the princes of Dyfed. After about 950 the administrative units were governed according to the laws codified by Hywel Dda, one of the earliest kings with a real vision of a united Wales. In the year 1093 Pembrokeshire was, almost certainly, all Welshry. There was no Landsker and no Englishry.

THE CREATION OF 'LITTLE ENGLAND'

The death of Rhys ap Tewdwr, the last Prince of South Wales, in 1093, precipitated the most important event in the history of settlement in Dyfed. The Welsh tribes of Deheubarth, weakened by their own internal dissensions, were no match for the Norman armies which arrived with expansionist designs from England. The army of Roger of Montgomery overran south Pembrokeshire before the end of the year. However, the Welsh chieftains now had a common enemy, and repeated attempts were made to drive out the Norman intruders. Temporary stockaded earthworks were constructed by both sides, but eventually the Normans consolidated their control over the southern part of the county as a result of a number of determined military thrusts. Gradually the land was parcelled out among the invaders; part of the native population was displaced, but those who remained were absorbed by the Anglo-Norman settlers and continued to practice the arts of farming under new management.

During the first half of the twelfth century the stockaded earthworks evolved into more substantial motte and bailey forts, and later still substantial stone castles took their place. Major fortresses were established at Pembroke (Plate 10a) and Haverfordwest; and frontier castles were thrown up at strategic points approximately four miles apart as a front line of defence against the Welsh, who continued in control of the northern and eastern parts of Dyfed. These fortresses, at Roch, Wiston, Llawhaden, Narberth and Amroth, are thought to have defined the early Landsker as a military frontier bounding the landward sides of Anglo-Norman Dyfed. Little England was beginning to find its identity. In the north the Martin family established the Marcher Lordship at Cemais; it was administered initially from an older fortress at Nevern, and after 1191 from the garrison town of Newport. Here William Martin built the strong stone castle which was to be his headquarters.

It has often been claimed that the physical difficulties encountered in the northern part of Dyfed may have discouraged the Normans from attempting any large-scale settlement north of the Landsker. However, it is more likely that administrative, rather than environmental, factors determined the boundaries of the early Anglo-Norman enclave. The real Landsker passed along the southern boundary of the bishop's lordship of Pebidiog (Dewisland) in the west and along the boundary between Cemais and Daugleddau in the centre of the county. From near Llysyfran the medieval Landsker is more difficult to define, but it probably ran through the episcopal lordship of Llawhaden and thence the northern boundary of Narberth eastwards towards Whitland. Francis Jones, the Wales Herald Extraordinary, is in no doubt about the importance of this historical accident in preserving the 'Welshness' of Dewisland and Llawhaden. Concerning Dewisland, he writes:

> It is the only part of Wales that has never been conquered by either the English or the Normans. Its inhabitants are the oldest free folk in Britain. The Normans, pious if nothing else, respected the property of the Church, so that Dewisland was spared the battles and sieges that accompanied the annexation of other parts of Pembrokeshire. No stone fortress was built on its soil; no alien garrison stood ward and watch over its inhabitants. The fact that it was the land of Dewi, the patron saint, proved sufficient to preserve it from the grasping hands of ambitious invaders. [Here] an agricultural folk passed tranquil days, for here the Cross was even mightier than the sword. While all the Norman castles are in ruins, the cathedral of St David's remains an enduring monument to the arts of peace.

Nevertheless, the Welsh people of Dewisland and Llawhaden were very effectively under the control of Norman bishops and Norman knights in the twelfth century. At least eleven manors were established on the episcopal lands (for example at Letterston, Castle Morris and Pointz Castle), but there seems to have been no widespread immigration of Anglo-Saxons or any of the other racial groups who came in the train of the Norman invaders. The bishop retained one fortified residence, rebuilt in stone at Llawhaden about the year 1285, but his other residences, at St David's, Trefin and Lamphey, were unfortified.

THE CREATION OF 'LITTLE ENGLAND'

During the twelfth century, when it was clear that Welsh labour was not going to be sufficient to maintain the manorial system, the Normans had to import many foreign workers to consolidate their control of southern Dyfed. English and Saxon immigrants were encouraged to settle, as were the Flemish immigrants introduced by Henry I about 1108. More Flemings arrived in 1111 and 1156. They were settled for the most part in Rhos and Daugleddau where they served as farmers and traders within the feudal system, as well as making up part of the feudal armies. Many Flemish leaders rose to positions of eminence, and soon there were Flemish occupiers of the castles at Roch and Wiston. Anglo-Flemish villages and hamlets were established in Daugleddau on the southern foothills of Mynydd Presely up to an altitude of almost 700ft. These settlements can still be located by non-Welsh place-names on the OS map, as at Little Newcastle, Puncheston, Henry's Moat and Ambleston. Thus, by the thirteenth century, there existed in the centre of the county a substantial non-Welsh settlement well to the north of the original fortified Landsker. It seems that the line of frontier castles, if indeed we can talk about a line at all, had ceased to have any military or economic significance within a few decades of its creation.

The impact of the colonial settlement upon the landscape of the Landsker zone was slight compared with the fundamental changes which occurred further south. Here the Anglo-Normans introduced quite distinctive forms of landholding, settlement, and farming. At least 120 villages and hamlets (many of which were on the sites of earlier Welsh settlements) were established in twelfth-century Pembrokeshire during this intensive phase of settlement. Most of the new villages and hamlets have Anglo-Saxon names like Letterston, Hayscastle, Slebech, Rudbaxton, Monington and Picton. But there are also Flemish elements, as in Wiston (the *tun* of Wizo the Fleming); and even south Pembrokeshire still has an abundance of Welsh place-names which have survived in spite of centuries of anglicisation.

58

Examples are Llangwm, Pwllcrochan, Rhoscrowther and Begelly.

In the Englishry the typical manorial village generally consisted of grouped farmhouses and cottages, a castle or fortified manor house, a well if there was no stream, and a church and parsonage. Later the church was given a disproportionately high, castellated tower (Plate 6a), which served both as a watch-tower and as a last line of defence in case of attack by the 'unquiet Welsh'. Where possible the buildings were placed around a central green for defensive purposes, but often a village was forced by the dictates of site into an irregular outline. Great agricultural progress was made in the Englishry, where the dense alien settlement was organised on a feudal basis on the many new manors. Around the village were the open fields with their distinctive strip systems, which were gradually demarcated by earth banks and ditches. Traces of these strip field patterns still survive around many villages, for example Cosheston (Plate 1) and Letterston. Where the enclosures had to incorporate elements of earlier 'Celtic' field patterns they were irregular, but in the Englishry there are still traces of the original open fields (now subdivided) which may have been up to thirty acres in extent. The field pattern was interspersed with areas of woodland and moorland, some of which had common grazing rights. In addition to the larger villages the medieval parish landscape incorporated a number of smaller hamlets, often founded beyond the boundaries of village lands in response to the growing population pressure of the thirteenth century. Settlements of this type have self-revealing names such as Carew Newton, Manorbier Newton and New House. Many single farmsteads appeared on the scene, cleared or assarted from woodland or scrub and held by tenants often as a reward for military service. Examples are Bicton and Mullock near St Ishmael's.

Many of the immigrants arrived in Pembrokeshire by the sea route into Milford Haven, and now the great waterway assumed real strategic importance for the Normans, who needed it as a lifeline during many conflicts with the Welsh princes. Their defence system (although probably never planned in a co-ordinated way) was based upon the sea, and particularly upon the tidal waters of Milford Haven and the Daugleddau. Their early motte and bailey structures, and later their stone castles, show a distinct preference for easily defended bluffs overlooking tidal waters. Only four stone castles (Roch, Wiston, Llawhaden and Narberth) are inland, and as mentioned earlier these served originally as forward defences against the Welsh raiding-parties in the Landsker zone. The major stone fortresses at Pembroke, Carew, Haverfordwest, Cardigan, Manorbier and Tenby, and the other smaller fortresses, must have depended on many occasions during troubled times upon the transport of supplies and troops by sea.

THE ANGLO-NORMAN TOWNS

Later, as peace and harmony began to prevail and as agricultural surpluses began to flow from the prospering manors of the Englishry, Pembroke, Haverfordwest and Tenby developed into trading towns. By the thirteenth century sailing vessels were becoming large enough and seaworthy enough to make long trading voyages. Also, they could carry cargoes below decks where they were protected from both sea and weather. Sailing vessels were frequent visitors at each port, importing wine, salt, spices and luxury goods and exporting wool hides, grain and herrings and similar products. All three towns acquired substantial numbers of wealthy merchants, and many small craft industries sprang up. The mercantile importance of Haverfordwest can be gauged from the fact that the mayor was granted the extra title of 'Admiral of the Port', which survives to this day. Thus the ports of the south of the county began to prosper, and the full advantages of the sheltered waters of Milford Haven were at last realised. From this time onwards, the smaller ports on the rocky coasts of north Pembrokeshire were much less successful in comparison, although Newport did enjoy some prosperity as a market town and trading port.

Pembroke was the first important town to be established in the Englishry, and indeed it can claim to have been the first county town in Wales. It received its first privileges in the reign of Henry I (1100–35) and gave its name to the county palatine established in 1138. Even today it is a superb example of a Norman walled town. Its buildings are aligned along a single street on a narrow limestone ridge which runs eastward from the castle, and the original community was protected by an embattled wall defended by several bastions and entered by well guarded gateways. Some sections of the town wall are still intact, and within the medieval town there are several buildings whose white limestone masonry and projecting Tudor corbels attest to their age. But the crowning glory of Pembroke is its castle dominating the western end of the town and controlling, as ever, the approach from the Pembroke River. It stands on a rocky promontory, its limestone walls rising almost naturally from the grey-white cliffs of its base. The present castle was begun about the year 1190 by William Marshall. He built the round keep in the early inner ward, and the building was continued by his five sons until it was largely completed by about 1245. Although the castle has been damaged comprehensively and restored piecemeal during its turbulent history, it is still regarded as one of the supreme examples of an early medieval stone fortress. It is certainly the most spectacular castle in Pembrokeshire, and in the whole of Wales perhaps only Caernarvon and Harlech castles can compete in the magnificence of their sites and the strength and style of their buildings.

Beneath Pembroke Castle is a vast limestone cavern known as the Wogan. It is entered by narrow steps from the northern hall, and it has an exit to the river bank. Probably it was used by the castle inhabitants as a store-house and boat-house. In addition to the fortifications and interior buildings of the castle there are several other features of interest, including the Water Port in the south-west wall (where the piped water-supply was led into the castle) and the Mill Port which provided access to the flour mill and mill dam on the northern edge of the town. The dam which impounded the mill pond was defended by a drawbridge. To the west of the town is the ancient Monkton Priory, established in the Dark Ages but with buildings (including a dovecote) whose remains date largely from medieval times.

Pembroke, the proud stronghold and commercial centre of the early days of the Englishry, gradually declined because of its remoteness from the centre and the north of the county and because of the economic limitations of its own hinterland. As the strategic advantages of its site became less important the waterway of Milford Haven, which had been Pembroke's first line of defence, began to act as a real barrier to the aspirations of the town. Its port facilities were much inferior to those of Haverfordwest, and it began to lose more and more trade to its rival.

Located in the centre of Pembrokeshire, Haverford (as it was then called) received its first charter probably during the reign of Henry I, and this was renewed by Henry II in the later part of the twelfth century. The Anglo-Norman town, dominated by its impressive stone fortress and sited at the head of navigation and the lowest bridging point of the Western Cleddau river, expanded rapidly. At first it was entirely enclosed within its town walls; then, as the Englishry was developed and as Welsh raids from the north became less frequent, it spread through the adjacent parishes of St Martin and St Thomas, and later encompassed Cartlett and Portfield. Prendergast, to the east of the river, remained a separate village. During the Middle Ages the great advantages of site and situation became apparent. As the military functions of the castle declined the town came to depend more and more upon commerce and trade; the routeways which converge upon it demonstrate its success in generating business between the varied tributary areas of the Englishry and the Welshry. At the same time the town acted as a service, religious and administrative centre for a wide area and developed a variety of industries and trades; in the Middle Ages guilds of feltmakers, glovers, saddlers, tailors, carpenters and blacksmiths flourished, and later a guild of shoemakers appeared, emphasising the importance of the town's tanneries. Most of the later industries were located along the river banks, including three flour mills, two paper mills, two sawmills, a rope-walk, and a churn-works.

As the centre of the Flemish settlement of the Englishry Haverfordwest, with its port and markets, built up a considerable commercial tradition. To this was added, during the sixteenth century, the administrative functions of a county town at the expense of Pembroke; in 1543 a charter constituting it a county in itself guaranteed its continuing success.

Nowadays there are few traces of the medieval roots of Haverfordwest. The town walls have gone, but for occasional traces in gardens and back yards, and even the castle survives only as a battered shell frowning down from its leafy eminence above the main shopping centre. But the quays along the river bank remain, as do some of the ancient warehouses. The towers of the parish churches of St Mary, St Martin, St Thomas and St David (Prendergast) are all medieval, and St Mary's church at the top of High Street is renowned as one of the largest and finest parish churches in Wales. Down-river from the old quays are the sad ruins of a once-magnificent Augustinian Priory— one of many religious houses established by the Normans in their feudal lordships.

THE MEDIEVAL WORLD

Apart from the Anglo-Norman castles and battlemented churches, and the traces of their abbeys, priories and friaries, there are many other medieval features in the Pembrokeshire landscape which owe their origins to the Middle Ages. In the Englishry at least the distribution of villages dates back to this time, as does the road network and most of the features of the field pattern. The belt of large parishes across the country, stretching from Roch in the west to Amroth in the east, and coinciding with much barren moorland even today, is thought to coincide with the medieval *rhos* which separated the Welsh from the English. And everywhere, often in quite unexpected places, are the traces of medieval features in the domestic architecture of renovated halls and farmhouses. Some of the diagnostic features of these buildings are considered in a later chapter, but for the moment let us remember that the atmosphere of the Middle Ages is still very much a part of many Pembrokeshire towns and villages. Tenby (Plate 5b) and Newport have the feel of history about them. In hamlets like

Llawhaden, Lamphey and St Florence the visitor feels that he has strayed into another world; a medieval world of walled gardens and orchards, dovecotes, fishponds, mills, and tumble-down stone outbuildings. The area around Carew and Sageston is a microcosm of the Anglo-Norman world of the Middle Ages. At the head of navigation on the Carew River there is a magnificent combination of millpond, corn mill (Plate 8a), castle and road bridge, seen as a unity from the new picnic park on the north shore of the pond. In the village centre there are old limestone cottages, their ages given away by their squat, square chimney stacks topped with slate ledges. In a garden there is a 'Flemish' round chimney standing in splendid incongruous isolation. There are ripe blackberries on the hedgerows in mid-July, and the air is heavy with scent of newly cut hay. To the east there are some fine farm buildings at Sageston, but perhaps least affected of all by the passing of the centuries is the group of buildings around the fifteenth-century church at Carew Cheriton. The parish church with its corner steeple, the high stone walls, the chantry chapel and the old rectory with its square corbelled tower are all splendid symbols of the Anglo-Norman traditions of Little England. If it were not for the early Christian Celtic cross at the roadside above the castle one might believe that the Welshry was a thousand miles away.

6 GEORGE OWEN'S PEMBROKESHIRE

GEORGE OWEN of Henllys (1552–1613) was one of Pembrokeshire's most famous sons and perhaps its most delightful character. We see him today somewhat hazily but certainly larger than life; to us he seems far more appealing than his illustrious contemporaries Sir John Perrot of Haroldston and William Philipps, the squire of Picton. Owen was neither a particularly powerful politician nor a particularly wealthy member of the gentry, but his fame rests upon the fact that he was an inveterate scribbler. He wrote furiously on all sorts of topics, and much of his manuscript material has survived to this day. Most important of all are his writings about Pembrokeshire in general and about his beloved Cemais in particular. As a result of his magnificent *Description of Pembrokeshire* the county is the best documented of all the shires of Elizabethan Wales. There is no comparable achievement anywhere else in the Welsh literature of the time, and in the *Description* we have a unique record of Elizabethan life and manners. And yet, Owen's literary fame seems not to have spread very far during his own lifetime. When the work was published in 1893 under Dr Henry Owen's editorship, it became freely accessible for the first time. The Welsh press referred to it as 'an embarrassment of riches', and gradually its true worth was recognised. Somewhat belatedly, 280 years after his death, George Owen acquired a wide reputation as a scholarly antiquary and an accurate and learned historian. At last he was seen as a man fascinated by the environment, the customs, the economic life and the life-style of his own times. Also, as we have seen in Chapter 2, he was thoroughly deserving of the title of 'patriarch of English geologists'.

Before looking at some of the themes from the *Description of*

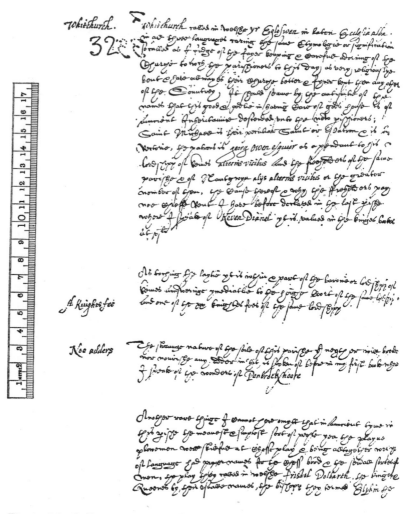

Fig 3 A typical page of George Owen's manuscript, from Book II of the
Description of Pembrokeshire

Pembrokeshire it should be stressed that George Owen was no more objective than anyone else in his assessments of history and of the scenario of late sixteenth-century Pembrokeshire. He does not seem to have been particularly well liked by the majority of his contemporaries, and Dr B. G. Charles, in his biographical portrait of the man, shows him to have been tough, determined and stubborn. He made many bitter enemies, but he was obviously well loved, too, for he fathered twenty-four children. Major Francis Jones has called Owen 'a conceited, learned, litigious, biased, and wholly delightful individual'. Much of his work was motivated by a desire to re-establish the past glories of the lordship of Cemais and to advance his own claims to the title of Lord of Cemais. His writings therefore contained much that was exaggerated or deliberately distorted, and his descriptions of Pembrokeshire localities and customs were very uneven. He described Cemais, his own home territory, in great detail: but other parts of Pembrokeshire (which he clearly knew almost as well) received almost cursory treatment. It is not surprising that he failed to keep up the early momentum of the *Description*, for even in its present form it is a monumental work.

The extracts on the following pages have already been published in *Elizabethan Pembrokeshire: the evidence of George Owen*. They do less than justice to the range of Owen's abilities as a writer, and it is a pity that there is no space to reproduce his descriptions of mountains and valleys, coasts and islands, hundreds and parishes, towns and villages. But the extracts do show something of Owen's affection for his county, his enthusiasm for poetic licence, his zeal for agricultural reform, his acute powers of observation, and his dry sense of humour. Much of what he wrote is very funny, and intentionally so. The extracts below are reproduced by kind permission of the editor, Dr Brian Howells. Together, they give us some fascinating glimpses of an Elizabethan world on the threshold of changing times. In 1603, when the *Description* was completed, the landscapes, manners and customs of the Middle Ages were finally giving way to a new order. But Owen described many survivals from medieval times in his sections on agricultural practices, the use of various fuels, and the catching of fish, shellfish and wild-fowl. In particular, his vivid and justly famous description of the game of *cnapan* showed it to be a survival of great antiquity.

THE ENGLISH AND THE WELSH

The said county of Pembrokeshire is usually called Little England beyond Wales and that not unworthily, and therefore I think good to show my opinion why the same was so called. Mr Camden calleth it *Anglia Transwallia*. The reasons why it took that name may well be conjectured, for that the most part of the country speaketh English, and in it no use of the Welsh. The names of the people are mere English, each family following the English fashion in surnames. Their buildings are English-like, in townreds and villages and not in several and lone houses. Their diet is as the English people use, as the common food beef, mutton, pig, lamb, veal and kid, which usually the poorest husbandman doth daily feed on. The names of the county places are altogether English as Wiston, Picton, Haroldston, Robeston . . . so that a stranger travelling from England and having ridden four score miles and more in Wales, having heard no English nor English names of people or of places, and coming hither to Pembrokeshire where he shall hear nothing but English . . . would think that Wales were environed with England, and would imagine he had travelled through Wales and come into England again.

This shire is taken to be divided into two parts, that is to the Englishry and the Welshry . . . The upper part of the shire, which I call the Welshry, is inhabited with Welshmen, the first known owners of the country, and are such as were never re-moved by any conquest or stranger that won the country. These are the people of the hundreds of Cemais, Cilgerran, Dewisland and part of Narberth, in which hundreds there are of divers ancient gentlemen that to this day do hold and keep their ancient houses and descent from their ancestors for 400, 500, 600 years and more . . . But the countries of Roose, Castle-martin, Narberth and most of Daugleddy hundred, the bishop's lordships excepted, were wholly put to fire and sword by the Normans, Flemings and Englishmen, and utterly expelled the inhabitants thereof and peopled the country themselves, whose posterity remain there to this day, as may appear by their names, manners and language, speaking altogether the English and

Plate 5 (above) Oblique air photograph of St David's Cathedral and Close. To the right of the Cathedral is the Tower Gatehouse; immediately to the left is St Mary's College; and in the left foreground are the remains of the splendid Bishop's Palace; *(below)* Five Arches, the best-known of the remaining gateways through the Tenby town walls

Plate 6 (left) A typical high castellated church tower of the Englishry. This one is at Johnston. The tower dates from the thirteenth century, but the rest of the church is largely rebuilt; *(below)* the church at Llanwnda in north Pembrokeshire, typical of the 'Celtic' style of this area

differeing in manners, diet, building and tilling of the land from the Welshmen.

What shall I speak here touching the constitution of the bodies of the people of this country must be understood of the general and common sort of people in the country . . . This kind of people I find to be very mean and simple, short of growth, broad and shrubby, unacceptable in sight for their personal service . . . so that of all the countries of Wales I find and speak by experience Pembrokeshire to be worst mannered . . .

The gentlemen, serving men and the townsmen of this country are not so serviceable, but very personable, comely and tall men . . . And of the common people of this country the Welshmen, whom the rest call the mountain men, are found to be the more personable, as men not so cloyed with labour as those that live by tillage.

Generally, for the inclination of the people as well gentlemen, yeomen, rich and poor, they all embrace peace, quietness and neighbourly love, hating contentions, troubles, brawls and factions entreated after an offence received.

COUNTRY LIFE AND AGRICULTURE

. . . this country of Pembrokeshire being almost environed with sea, bare, open, and naked of wood and shelter, is more subject to extremity of storms and sudden tempests and sea, gusts of wind and hail than other the inland countries are, and therefore there are few hedges or enclosures to be found, by reason whereof the husbandmen are forced to keep herds for their cattle and that in greater numbers than . . . they themselves need . . . For I have by good account numbered three thousand young people to be brought up continually in herding of cattle within this shire, who are put to this idle education when they are first come to be ten or twelve years of age and turned to the open fields to follow their cattle, when they are forced to endure the heat of the sun in his greatest extremity to parch and burn their faces, hands, legs, feet and breasts in such sort as they seem more like tawny Moors than people of this land. And then with the cold, frost, snow, hail, rain and wind they are so tormented, having the skin of their legs, hands, face and feet all in chinks and chaps . . . that, poor fools, they may well hold opinion with the papists that there is a purgatory . . . And when they have redeemed their liberty out of this purgatory by attaining to twenty or twenty four years of age, then are they held in such continual labour in tilling of the land, burning of lime, digging of coals, and other slaveries and extreme toils, as while they live they never come in shape, favour or comeliness to be accounted among the number of personable men.

There was in times past in some parts of this shire, especially where gavelkind was, a custom used called *rudwall custom*, which was that no action of trespass lay for pasture in open fields out of enclosures . . . This custom seemed somewhat reasonable among the gavelkind men, for that at every descent the lands were shared and so the whole land of the country grew into small pieces, so that of necessity the owners must graze in common . . . And this custom, although it be almost abolished, yet remaineth the name and term thereof very usual among the common people, for that time of the year after harvest when all the neighbours' cattle run together in the common fields they call 'rudwall time' . . .

This commodity of corn is the chiefest that bringeth in money to the country, being a country more apt for tilling than for breed, the soil being naturally dry and fit for the plough work, but this differeth much in some part of this shire from other.

The chiefest corn land in Pembrokeshire is the hundred of Castlemartin as that which yieldeth the best and finest grain and most abundance, being a country of itself naturally fit and apt for corn, having lime, sand, weed of the sea, and divers other principal helps to better the soil where need is. This country yieldeth the best wheat and greatest store, being found by experience to be better of yielding in the mill, and maketh the bread fairer than any other wheat of the shire. The next to Castlemartin for good and good store of corn is Roose, an open and plain country without much wood or enclosures. This although it may not compare with Castlemartin, is the next good soil and yieldeth great abundance of wheat, barley and other grain . . .

Next cometh in course the hundreds of Narberth and Dewisland. Which to prefer for their tillage I cannot well discuss, for although Narberth have the better land and better means of mending as lime, sand, seaweed, stone marl, yet by reason the country is woody and enclosed the inhabitants convert more of their land to pasture than Dewisland doth or can do, the country being all open champion and dry land . . . Dewisland [is in] many parts thereof very fruitful for corn, especially barley, but it is accounted oaty and not so fine as that of the other parts, which I take to come by the negligence of husbandmen in sowing of bad and oaty seed, for I have not seen better or finer land nor greater store of corn than I have seen growing about Saint Davids.

The second and next commodity that this county selleth is cattle, as oxen steers, bullocks, heifers and kine of the country breed, which of late years is greatly increased more than in times past as a commodity that particularly yieldeth profit with less charge to the owner, but generally not so commodious for the commonwealth as tillage, by reason it procureth depopulation and maintaineth less people at work. This trade of breeding cattle is sued much in all parts of the shire, but most in the Welsh parts and near the mountains where their land is not so apt for corn and where there is larger scope of ground.

The third commodity that helpeth this shire to money is wool, whereof there is great quantity yearly sold, beside that which is spent in the country for their necessary uses of clothing. The country aboundeth with sheep more at this present than heretofore, and yieldeth great profit with little charge, for in this country they feed not their sheep with hay in winter, as is used in divers parts of England, but let them get their living out themselves. Yet in some part of the country they house them by night, which they do to keep them from the fox and for making of dung for their land more than for any other cause, for fodder they never bestow on them, for in this country the snow never covereth the ground for any long time and therefore they are sure always of feeding. The sheep are but small of body and the wool coarser than the English wool . . . but the flesh of these muttons is found to be very sweet in taste, wholesome and good meat . . .

The fourth principal commodity that this country yieldeth is butter and cheese, whereof there is greater store made now in this shire than in times past and the same is uttered, especially the butter by sea, but this may not be known; so is the cheese to the countries adjoining, and sometimes to Ireland for provision of the Queen's garrisons there.

The manner of tilling the ground in this shire is in two sorts. The Englishmen use most sowing of wheat, rye, barley, peas and beans. The Welshmen, being the worse husbands, apply more to tilling of oats, and some cause there was which caused this in former times, which now being taken away the Welshmen are become the better husbands.

Now . . . I will speak somewhat of the natural helps which are found in the country to better the land and to make it more fruitful and apt to bear corn and grass.

The chiefest thereof I reckon the lime, for that it is most commonly and most used . . . This limestone, being dug in the quarry in great stones, is hewn lesser to the bigness of a man's fist . . . and being hewn small the same is put into a kiln [Plate 7a] made of walls six foot high, four or five foot broad at the rim but growing narrower to the bottom, having two loopholes in the bottom which they call the kiln eyes. In this kiln first is made a fire of coals or rather culm (which is but the dust of the coals) which is laid in the bottom of the kiln, and some few sticks of wood to kindle the fire. Then is the kiln filled with these small hewed pieces of limestones and then, fire being given, the same burneth . . . and maketh the limestones to become mere red fiery coals, which being done and the fire quenched, the lime so burned is suffered to cool in the kiln and then is drawn forth through these kiln eyes, and in this sort is carried to the land where it is laid in heaps. And the next shower of rain maketh it to moulder and fall into dust, which they spread on the land, and so sow wheat or barley therein as the time of the year requireth . . . This trade of liming hath been more used within these thirty or forty years than in times past and it destroyeth the furze, fern, heath and other like shrubs growing on the land, and bringeth forth a fine and sweet grass and quite changeth the hue and face of the ground and hath greatly enriched those that used it.

The next and chiefest kind of mending of the land is the clay marl, so called for the difference between it and the sea marl. This kind of marl is digged out of the earth where it is found in great quantity and thought to be in round great heaps and lumps of earth as big as round hills, and is of nature fat, tough and clammy, and must be cast and set on the ground very thick in small pieces close one by another, so thick that it must cover all the ground.

The fourth kind of amendment that this country yieldeth is the sea sand, which is found in many places but not in all parts of the sea coast. This is found in Newport, Dinas and about these parts and the people knowing these places do use upon spring tides, or after great tempests of the sea, at which time the sea will cast the same in more abundance together into great heaps, and lay it out of the high tide mark, and there hence fetch it in sacks on horseback and carry the same three, four or five miles and cast it on the land, which doth very much better the ground for corn and grass . . .

. . . As for the sea weed, or woad as some call it, which is very weeds growing underwater in the sea upon rocks and stones, and with tempest of the sea is torn and cast ashore with the wind and tide, and under the high tide mark may be gathered and cut off the stones, the same is used of many rather as muck or dung, serving but for one year only . . . This kind of ore they gather and lay it in great heaps, where it heateth and rotteth and will have a strong and loathsome smell. The same being so rotten, they cast on the land as they do their muck, and thereof springeth good corn, especially barley.

It is a saying among the countrymen of the continuance of these aforesaid amendments that a man doth sand for himself, lime for his son, and marl for his grandchild . . .

MARKETS

There are three market towns in Pembrokeshire, viz. Pembroke, Haverfordwest and Tenby, the second whereof, being seated in the midst of the shire and most convenient for trade, is greatly frequented of the country people, and therefore is the greatest and plentifulest market of the shire, and is kept once every week on the Saturday, wherein methinketh the town is very backward in their own profit in not suing for another market in the middle of the week, which would turn to the great good both of the town and country. Also they have but one fair in the year, whereas if there were more purchased from His Majesty it might be beneficial both for town and country. This market of Haverfordwest is thought to be one of the greatest and plentifullest markets, all things compared, that is within the Marches of Wales, especially for the plenty and goodness of victual, as namely for beef, mutton, pork, bacon, veal, goose, capon, kid, lamb, rabbit, turkey, and all sorts of wildfowl in their season, that it is a marvel to many where the victuals that are there to be seen at noon should be shifted away ere night, and for fish it passeth all others in Wales, without any comparison both for plenty and variety.

Pembroke market is also on the Saturday, and Tenby on Saturday for victuals and on Wednesday for corn. These two towns for their markets are much inferior for plenty of victuals and corn to that of Haverfordwest by reason those towns are seated, the one very near the lower parts of the shire and much hindered by reason of a ferry on the one side, and Tenby seemeth, as it were, a town running out of the country and stayeth on the sea cliff, by reason whereof they stand not so commodious for resort of people, which maketh less trade and utterance in their markets. But both these towns, being seated in a more fruitful soil than Haverfordwest is, for goodness of victual are nothing inferior if not better than Haverford, and so for goodness of corn, and for fish especially Tenby, where is a daily market thereof, passeth Haverford market . . .

There are also markets of victuals used in St. Davids and Newport, not worth the speaking of, partly for that they be so small and bad, but especially for the abuse for that the same is used every Sunday before service, even about sunrise. There hath been in times past divers markets used in divers other places, and by reason of the poverty of the towns and unaptness of the places altogether decayed, as at Cilgerran, Fishguard, St. Dogmael's, Rosemarket, Wiston, Llawhaden, where, by report of ancient men, markets have been kept in old time.

THE GENTLE GAME OF CNAPAN

I cannot overpass a game used in one part of this shire among the Welshmen both rare to hear, troublesome to describe, and painful to practise . . . This game is called *cnapan* and not unfitly, as shall be shown. The game is thought to be of great antiquity and is as followeth.

The ancient Britons being naturally a warlike nation did, no doubt for the exercise of their youth in time of peace and to avoid idleness, devise games of activity where each man might show his natural prowess and agility, as some for strength of the body by wrestling [and] lifting of heavy burdens, others for the arm as in casting the bar sledge, stone or hurling the bowl or ball, others that excelled in swiftness of foot to win the praise therein by running, and surely for the exercise of the part aforesaid this *cnapan* was prudently invented had the same continued without abuse thereof. For in it, besides the exercise of bodily strength, it is not without resemblance of warlike providence, as shall be here after declared.

Plays would oftentimes be by making of match between two gentlemen, and that at such holiday or Sunday as pleased them to appoint the time and place, which most commonly fall out to be the greatest plays, for in these matches the gentlemen would divide the parishes, hundreds or shires between them, and then would each labour to bring the greatest number and would therein entreat all his friends and kinsmen in every parish to come and bring his parish wholly with him, by which means great number would most usually meet. And therefore against these matches there would also resort to the place divers victuallers with meat, drink and wine of all sorts, also merchants, mercers and pedlars would provide stalls and booths to show and utter their wares. And for these causes, some to play, some to eat and drink, some to buy, and some to sell, others to see and others to be seen (you know what kind I mean) great multitudes of people would resort besides the players. They contend not for any wager or valuable thing, but for glory and renown—first for the fame of their country in general, next every particular to win praise for his activity and prowess, which two considerations ardently inflameth the minds of the youthful people to strive to the death for glory and fame, which they esteem dearer unto them than worldly wealth.

The companies, being come together about one or two of the clock after noon, beginneth the play in this sort. After a cry made, both parties draw together into some plain, all stripped bare saving a light pair of breeches—bare headed, bare bodied, bare legs, and feet, their clothing being laid together in great heaps under the charge of certain keepers appointed for the purpose, for if he leave but his shirt on his back in the fury of the game it is most commonly torn to pieces. And I have also seen some long-locked gallants trimmed at this game, not by polling but by pulling their hair and beards . . . This kind of trimming they all do bestow freely without asking anything for their pains.

The foot company thus meeting, there is a round ball prepared of a reasonable quantity so as a man may hold it in his hand and no more. This ball is of some massy wood as box, yew, crab or holly tree, and should be boiled in tallow for to make it slippery and hard to be held. This ball is called *cnapan* and is by one of the company hurled bolt upright into the air, and at the fall he that catcheth it hurleth it towards the country he playeth for. For goal or appointed place there is none, neither needeth any, for the play is not given over until the *cnapan* be so far carried that there is no hope to return it back that night, for the carrying of it a mile or two miles from the first place is no losing of the honour so be it still followed by the company and, the play still maintained, it is oftentimes seen the chase to follow two miles or more in the heat of course both by the horse and foot.

The *cnapan* being once cast forth you shall see the same tossed backward and forward by hurling throws in strange sort, for in three or four throws you shall see the whole body of the game removed half a mile and more, and in this sort it is a strange sight to see a thousand or fifteen hundred naked men to concur together in a cluster in following the *cnapan* as the same is hurled backwards and forwards.

If the *cnapan* happen to come to the hands of a lusty hurler he throweth the same in a wonderful sort towards his country, further than any man would judge the strength of the arm were able. If it happen to the hands of a good footman he presently singleth himself and runneth and breaketh out of the body of the game into some plain ground in the swiftest sort he can which, being perceived, all the company followeth, where the good footmanship of all the company is plainly discerned, being a comfortable sight to see five or six hundred good footmen to follow in chase a mile or two as greyhounds after a hare, where shall see some gain in running upon his precedents, some forced to come behind those that were once foremost, which greatly delighteth the beholders and forceth them to follow likewise to see the pleasure of the chase. And thus the one seeketh to win honour by his footmanship until he be overtaken by a better runner or encountered by one of the scouts which will not fail to meet with him, and when he seeth himself near surprised or that his breath or legs fail him, he hurleth the ball forward towards his country, with a great violence, and perchance it lighteth to some of his fellows, who carry the same as far again which, notwithstanding, is not given over as long as the main body is anything near at hand: and when the ball happeneth to one of the contrary party it cometh back again as fast.

It is strange to behold with what eagerness this play is followed, for in the fury of the chase they respect neither hedge, ditch, pale or wall, hill, dale, bushes, river or rock or any other passable impediment, but all seemeth plain unto them wherein also they show such agility in running, such activity in leaping, such strength and skilful deliverance in hurling, such boldness in assaulting, such stoutness in resisting, such policy in inventing, such skill in preventing, as taking them out of their game they are not able to perform or invent half the prowess or devices shown in the same, a thing much noted of men of judgement.

The horsemen have monstrous cudgels of three foot and a half long, as big as the party is well able to wield, and he that thinketh himself well horsed maketh means to his friends of the footmen to have the *cnapan* delivered him, which being gotten he putteth spurs and away as fast as the legs will carry. After him runneth the rest of the horsemen, and if they can overtake him he summoneth a delivery of the *cnapan*, which should be thrice by law of the game, but now they scarce give it once till he be struck. And if he hold the *cnapan* it is lawful for the assailant to beat him with his cudgel till he deliver it. The best of foot troops also will follow the horse, who are so well trained by the often exercise of the game, as that when the horsemen miss to fetch up the *cnapan*, the foot will oftentimes recover the same and will in heat of chase follow the *cnapan* when it is out of sight and past hope . . .

You shall see gamesters return home from this play with broken heads, black faces, bruised bodies and lame legs, yet laughing and merrily jesting at their harms, telling their adversaries how he broke his head, to another that he struck him on the face and how he repaid the same to him again, and all this in good mirth, without grudge or hatred. And if any be in arrearages to the other they store it up till the next play and in the meantime will continue loving friends.

This play of *cnapan* seemeth to be an ancient exercise described to us Welshmen from our first progenitors the Trojans . . .

7   CHANGING FORTUNES

T HE three centuries which followed the death of George
Owen proceeded quietly enough in Pembrokeshire. For
the most part Pembrokeshire was a remote rural back-
water largely by-passed by the great events of Britain and
Europe. But occasionally events in Pembrokeshire came to the
attention of the outside world, as during the turbulent years of
the Civil War, or during the farcical 'last invasion of Britain'
near Fishguard in 1797, or during the Rebecca Riots of the
early 1840s. And during this whole period, slowly but surely,
the landscape evolved with the changing fortunes of agriculture,
with the rise and fall of the great landowning families and the
minor gentry, and with the great religious revivals which swept
across Wales. The modern period was being ushered in, slowly
but surely, and in the following paragraphs we examine some
themes from the period 1600–1900.

THE CIVIL WAR

The Civil Wars of 1642–8 made but a minor impact upon the
Pembrokeshire landscape, for the county was spared the most
vicious and destructive of the military campaigns. But some of
the results of the fighting can still be seen, and several of
the famous events of the later part of the war took place in the
area. For the most part the Welsh-speaking section of the
county was loyal to the King, but many townsmen and some
squires in south Pembrokeshire embraced the Parliamentary
cause. In 1644 the royalist Earl of Carbery (of Golden Grove, in
Carmarthenshire) attempted to reduce Pembrokeshire, but he
was repulsed by Rowland Laugharne of St Bride's, who was 'one
of the ablest tacticians thrown up during the unhappy conflict'.

Laugharne, the Parliamentary leader of the day, took Tenby, Haverfordwest and Carmarthen from the Royalists. This stirred the Royalists to replace their leaders in West Wales, and during a determined assault they recaptured Haverfordwest and Carmarthen. However, Tenby and Pembroke held out as a result of the superiority of the Parliamentary fleet. It controlled the waters of the Haven, relieved the beleaguered garrison of Pembroke, and was able to support various land operations. Now the tide was turning against the Royalists, and as troops were withdrawn to England Laugharne again took most of Pembrokeshire and the town of Cardigan as well. In 1645 Charles Gerard returned and made good these losses for the Crown, but by this time much of Wales was alienated from the Royalist cause by insensitive military control of the King's armies and by the plundering of the countryside. When Laugharne turned to the offensive again there occurred the most famous local battle of the Civil War, on a patch of moorland between Wiston and Llawhaden. This was Colonel Laugharne's greatest hour, thereafter termed the 'Colby Moor Rout'. It was 1 August 1644, and the decisive Parliamentary victory signalled the beginning of the end for the Royalist cause in Wales.

During this first phase of the Civil War the focal points of the armed campaigns were the old medieval fortresses, now hopelessly out-of-date from a military point of view and quite inadequate to withstand a battering by heavy guns. Nevertheless, they were used and strengthened, and they served to hold off attacks from lightly-armed forces and even to resist prolonged sieges. The castles at Tenby, Pembroke, Haverfordwest, Roch, Cardigan, Laugharne, Carew and Picton all figured prominently in the ebb and flow of the complicated military campaigns of 1643–5, changing hands frequently.

The so-called 'Second Civil War' of 1648 made a much greater impact upon the castles of Pembrokeshire. The fighting began because of a variety of dissensions and partly because of disappointment and resentment against the disbanding of the Roundhead army. The local Parliamentary commanders, who had served their cause well, were disappointed with the rewards paid for their efforts. Mayor John Poyer of Pembroke refused to give way to a new governor, and he was joined in his rebellion by Colonel Rice Powell and Major-General Rowland Laugharne. All three had previously been staunch Parliamentarians. Powell and Laugharne joined the Glamorgan Royalists. Their army of about 8,000 men advanced eastwards through Carmarthen into Glamorgan, taking Swansea and Neath on the way. They were defeated by a smaller but highly trained Parliamentary army under Horton at St Fagans on 8 May 1648, although the renegade leaders managed to escape back to Pembrokeshire.

But now the net tightened. Cromwell had had enough, and he decided on a show of strength in South Wales. He advanced with Horton into Pembrokeshire, taking Tenby on 31 May and capturing its chief defender Powell. Poyer and Laugharne, with their garrison, were established in Pembroke, protected by the town walls and the great stone fortress itself. Cromwell decided to starve out the garrison, for he had only his light artillery with him and could make no impression on the defences. He sent to Carmarthenshire for shot to be made in the iron furnaces there, and he ordered his big guns to be sent by sea from Gloucester. Various attempts to scale the town walls failed. The big guns arrived and finally opened fire on 11 July, and after a seven-week siege Poyer was forced to surrender. He and Laugharne joined Powell in captivity. The three renegades were taken to London, where they were tried by court martial and sentenced to death. As a gesture of clemency it was decided that only one of them should die. According to legend they were asked to draw lots, but they refused. So three slips of paper were given to a child, one of them blank and the others bearing the words 'Life given by God'. The child gave a slip to each of the prisoners and the hapless Mayor Poyer received the blank one. He was shot at Covent Garden by a firing-squad.

Now the castles of Pembrokeshire had seen their last military action. They had proved an unexpected nuisance to Cromwell during the 1648 rising, and he ordered them to be destroyed. He commanded that towers should be blown up and lengths of curtain wall demolished. He seems personally to have ordered the destruction of several of the towers and wall sections of

Pembroke Castle. Tenby and other fortresses also suffered sadly as a result of his edict. Within days of the surrender of Pembroke, Cromwell wrote to the mayor and corporation of Haverford- west leaving them in no doubt as to his intentions. He demanded that they 'forthwith demolish the works, walls and towers of the said Castle, so as that the said Castle may not be possessed by the enemy, to the endangering of the peace of these parts. We expect an account of your proceedings with effect in this business by Saturday, being the 15th of July instant.' There followed a menacing footnote: 'If a speedy course be not taken to fulfil the commands of this warrant, I shall be necessitated to consider of settling a garrison.' The threat was enough, and the municipal authorities set to work with their explosives to such effect that the castle was largely destroyed. To this day only the sorry rem- nants of the walls of the once-great fortress remain, although renovations are afoot and the Castle Museum is housed here in a substantial restored section of the castle buildings.

FARMING

The effects of the Civil War were soon past, and Pembroke- shire returned to more tranquil times with agriculture and trade occupying most of its inhabitants. The gentry remained in con- trol of the large estates which had evolved from the manors of the Middle Ages, and they consolidated and improved their properties. Farmers and peasants benefited from agricultural advances, and the merchants and craftsmen of the main towns grew rich through the improved marketing of larger and larger agricultural surpluses. As in the time of George Owen, arable farming was important in the south of the county, and Castle- martin and Rhos continued to produce good crops of wheat, barley and oats. On the St David's peninsula the main grain crop was oats, while in the eastern and northern parts of the county landlords and tenant farmers devoted more attention to livestock farming. Sheep were plentiful everywhere, and there were large surpluses of wool.

The old open-field style of farming was gradually giving way, and as the larger landowners increased the size of their estates after the Civil War more and more of the county was affected by enclosures. Not only were the open fields enclosed, but much of the old common land was incorporated in to the estates, causing much hardship among the poorer farming classes. Gradually the landscape of open fields and strips around nucleated villages and hamlets gave way to a landscape of smaller enclosed fields, separate farmsteads, and consolidated farm buildings. Over a period of 300 years or more, farming became more efficient as new methods of crop rotation and animal husbandry were introduced. But eighteenth-century innovators like Charles Hassall were frustrated by the reluctance of Pembrokeshire farmers to accept change. He wrote in 1794 'The inhabitants of this county are not forward in receiving improvements in agriculture. I mean the middling and lower orders of them. A general prejudice seems to pervade the people against anything new or differing in any respect from the old and beaten track in which they and their forefathers have trod . . .' Other observers were particularly disturbed by the lack of progress in the Welshry, where conditions were often harsh and where efficient land management was most necessary. Even the agricultural societies founded in the later eighteenth century failed to make any great impact.

As the rural population grew many people were forced to take to the roads. Squatting became a real problem, for many poor people falsely believed that if they could clear waste land and build a cottage in a day and a night, so that smoke could be seen issuing from the chimney next morning, then the cottage became their freehold by law. Whole groups of cottagers were evicted, and serious riots often resulted. While the rich became richer, the poor became poorer.

THE DROVERS

Between the medieval period and the middle of the nineteenth century Pembrokeshire figured prominently in the overland trade in livestock. Mostly this was a one-way trade, with herds of cattle, sheep and pigs being driven along the network of drovers' roads towards the Welsh borderland and beyond to the fattening pastures, markets and fairs of central and southern England. Many of the 'great herds of black cattle' from the Castlemartin peninsula and other parts of the county ended up in Smithfield market in the heart of London. The livestock were delivered by farmers to the drover and his helpers in one of the collecting centres. Haverfordwest was the main centre in Pembrokeshire, but there were others at Eglwyswrw, Boncath, Crymych and Whitland. Here the animals were shod before setting off along one of the traditional routes eastwards. Cattle could be driven at a rate of up to twenty miles a day, but pigs travelled only about six miles a day; the journey from Pembrokeshire to London could take almost two months. Many of the resting-places along the route had inns to house the drovers —hence the frequently encountered inns named 'Drover's Arms'. The drovers' routes kept clear of the main highways as far as possible; thus they avoided the payment of tolls on the turnpike roads and avoided coach traffic and town centres. Many of the routes involved considerable river crossings by the livestock droves. Traces of the old drovers' roads can still be seen, particularly in the north of the county where they have been preserved from the assault of agriculture in the quiet hills of Mynydd Presely. But few of these roads have been used during the past hundred years, for the coming of the railways effectively destroyed the droving trade.

Seen in their proper context, the drovers' roads played a relatively minor part in the total trade of Pembrokeshire. Above all the fortunes of the county have been irrevocably tied to the use of the sea for fishing and, as we shall see in the next chapter, particularly for coastal trading.

THE RELIGIOUS REVIVALS

While life in town and country developed quietly during the seventeenth and eighteenth centuries the church made relatively little impact. But from about 1730 onwards there was a series of 'evangelical explosions' throughout Wales, collectively known as the Methodist Revival. As elsewhere in Wales, this revival made a considerable impact upon Pembrokeshire life and landscape. The roots of nonconformity go back well into the seventeenth century, for the 'Green Meeting House' (now Albany Chapel) in Haverfordwest was founded in 1638 and maintained a faithful congregation even during the time of persecution prior to the 1689 Toleration Act. There were groups of Quakers and other dissenters in the other towns also. And while the nonconformists slowly built up a following, another impetus for the intense religious experience of the 1730s was provided by the 'educational revival'. In this respect Pembrokeshire was particularly fortunate to have received the patronage of Sir John Philipps of Picton Castle, who as a leading member of the SPCK founded several schools entirely at his own expense. By 1712 a visitor was able to report that 'Pembrokeshire, though it be one of the smallest counties in South Britain, out vies most of the largest counties in the number of Charity Schools.' Sir John played an active part in the founding of the famous 'Circulating Schools' of Griffith Jones, which did so much to encourage adult literacy and the survival of the Welsh language through the medium of religious instruction. By 1760 there were twenty-three charity schools in Pembrokeshire, with a total of 837 pupils, and there must have been thousands more who received some teaching in the Circulating Schools.

The religious movement gathered momentum. Griffith Jones made himself rather unpopular with authority (frequently requiring the support and protection of his brother-in-law Sir John Philipps) by his insistence upon itinerant evangelism. His bishop complained that he was 'going about preaching on week days in Churches, Churchyards, and sometimes on the mountains to hundreds of auditors.' These activities were not only frowned upon but actively discouraged by the established church, which signally failed to appreciate the spirit of evangelism which was now abroad in the countryside. Griffith Jones was a powerful preacher, and one of his converts, Daniel Rowland, also began the life of an itinerant evangelist in 1735. In the same year Howel Harris began independently to preach beyond the confines of his native Breconshire, and in 1738 William Williams joined the evangelical campaign. These three were the first real leaders of the Methodist Revival. Rowland

Plate 7 (above) The lime-kilns at Solva, which functioned very much as described by George Owen until recent times; (below) remnants of the old stone quay in the 'blue lagoon' slate quarry at Abereiddi. Small vessels were able to enter the quarry through a narrow channel at high tide

Plate 8 *(above)* The renovated corn-mill at Carew. The mill was present at this site in 1558, but it has probably been greatly modified since then; *(below)* the face of an industrial token of the Carmarthen Iron Co, showing what the inside of the Blackpool forge must have looked like, about 1792

was one of the most famous of all Welsh preachers; Harris was
above all a tireless itinerant organiser of religious societies in all
parts of Wales; and 'Williams Pantycelin' was the poet and
hymn-writer whose music became as powerful a factor in the
religious revival as the sermons of his contemporaries.

Intense religious experience was felt in Pembrokeshire as elsewhere, and the county had its own great revivalist in Howell
Davies. However, because the greater part of the evangelical
campaign was conducted through the medium of Welsh, its
impact upon English-speaking south Pembrokeshire was less
marked than in the north. Conversely, John Wesley himself
appears to have made a greater impact in 'Little England', and
he did little preaching north of the Landsker during his various
visits to the county. He visited Haverfordwest on fourteen
different occasions between 1763 and 1790. He recorded his first
visit thus: 'I rode over to Haverfordwest. Finding it was the
Assize Week, I was afraid the bulk of the people would be too
busy to think about hearing sermons. But I was mistaken; I have
not seen so numerous a congregation since I set out of London;
and they were one and all deeply attentive. Surely some will
bring forth fruit.' By the time of his visit of 1772 he was able to
write 'There is a considerable increase in this Society, and not in
number only. After preaching on Wednesday evening, we had
such a meeting as I have seldom known. Almost everyone spoke,
as well as they could for tears, and with the utmost simplicity:
and many of them appeared to know "the great salvation", to
love God with all their heart.'

Within fifty years of the beginning of the Methodist Revival
the Pembrokeshire landscape was dotted with chapels. Generally
these were built in the towns and villages, although some served
as the centres for scattered rural societies and were built in
isolated spots just like the original small Celtic churches of a
thousand years before. Most of these chapels were built without
the support of the local gentry; with the exception of the Bowen
family of Llwyngwair they remained loyal to the established
church. In Haverfordwest the Moravian church dates from this
time (1773) as does Wesley Methodist chapel (1772), Tabernacle (1774) and Bethesda (1789). Ebenezer chapel (1817) and

F

Hill Park Baptist chapel (1885) followed after a while, and many of the chapels of Haverfordwest and other parts of the county were extensively restored or rebuilt during a later religious awakening in the period 1870–90. At this time Welsh nonconformity was at its height, and the villages and towns of Pembrokeshire were enlivened by active religious societies whose congregations far surpassed those of the established church.

In style the new chapels were very different from the older churches with their stone exteriors, their arched windows and their medieval battlemented towers or simple bell-cotes. They were functional buildings, paid for by the subscription of ordinary folk rather than with the endowments of landed gentry. They were constructed on a simple rectangular plan with sparse furnishings and, as often as not, an unprepossessing façade. There were exceptions, like the fine chapels of Tabernacle and Bethesda (Plate 4b) in Haverfordwest and Hermon in Fishguard, but often these are later rebuildings by larger and more prosperous congregations. The new chapels were the homes of Baptists, Wesleyan and Calvinistic Methodists, Congregationalists, Moravians and Presbyterians, and their sheer density on the ground still causes amazement. In Haverfordwest, for example, there is a distinct cluster of churches and chapels on the old western edge of the town, with three large medieval parish churches and six substantial nonconformist chapels providing total accommodation for several thousand worshippers. In addition to the chapel buildings themselves, many of the nonconformist societies built school halls and large vestries adjacent to their places of worship, for Sunday School and week-night activities have always been a strong part of local nonconformist tradition. In the towns few of the chapels were built on sites large enough for graveyards, so burials were performed in the parish graveyards on the outskirts of the towns; but in the countryside many chapels have their own adjacent graveyards, as at Llanddewi Velfrey and at Bethesda near Llawhaden. Often the chapels have magnificent biblical names: Hermon, Tabor, Zion, Bethel and Tabernacle crop up time and again.

But while the face of town and country changed as a result of the Methodist Revival, society was changed even more by the inspired preaching of the evangelists. Wynford Vaughan-Thomas writes 'the Church could not possibly hold such enthusiasts. The final break . . . was devastating for the Church of England when it came. The new Methodist church took with it great numbers of the Welsh people. The chapel, not the church, now held the loyalty of the people. The Church stood for the gentry, the landowners, the alien traditions of England and Toryism. The Chapel sprang from the people. It was democratic in form, radical in politics, and Welsh in thought and speech.' The chapels acted as the new social centres, and they provided new leaders. In the Welsh-speaking areas the language acquired a new status. 'But,' says Wynford Vaughan-Thomas, 'there were losses, too. Wales after the revival was a sterner place. The dancers, the fiddlers, the carefree interlude players, the laughter in the ale-houses died before the strict admonition to men that their first duty was to save their souls from Hell.'

THE LAST INVASION OF BRITAIN

The 'Last Invasion of Britain' was more of a farce than a threat to national security, but it is still very much a part of local folk-lore. And at the time (1797) it caused great alarm, not only in Pembrokeshire but in Westminster also. The invasion arose out of a French theory that forces landed in Ireland and Britain might provoke a widespread 'peasants' revolt' of the poor against the rich. It was planned that 15,000 troops should land in Ireland, and 1,400 near Bristol or in Cardigan Bay. As it happened, the Irish invasion never took place, and the Bristol expeditionary force was forced by unfavourable winds to sail around the tip of Pembrokeshire towards Pencaer. The four ships of the expedition carried a motley and undisciplined force of ex-convicts and grenadiers under the command of an American named Colonel Tate. Tate was no great leader of men, and he must in any case have been somewhat confused by the complex details of his military instructions. The ships were sighted off St David's on 22 February 1797, by Mr Williams of Treleddyn, who decided that they were French in spite of the fact that they were flying English flags. Soon the alarm was raised, and by the time the ships reached Fishguard Bay the Fishguard Fencibles were ready for them. A single shot from the fort warned off the French commander, Castagnier, and he withdrew his vessels eastwards out of sight of Fishguard. The day was uncommonly hot for the time of year, and the sea was calm, so after some deliberation Castagnier and Tate decided that the expeditionary force should be put ashore immediately, at the foot of the inhospitable cliffs of Carreg Wastad. During a calm moonlit night all the men and supplies were ferried ashore, and by morning everything had been carried up the cliffs. Soon Tate had established his headquarters at Trehowel Farm, Castagnier and his ships had left for home, and French troops were in charge of Carnwnda rocks, the highest point in the area.

From this point on, the successful military exercise deteriorated rapidly into farce. There was no organised body of professional soldiers to oppose the French, and for a while the local military leadership was in a state of panic. However, the defences were soon organised, and Lord Cawdor (who had studied military tactics but never been involved in conflict) assumed overall command of his motley army of 575 volunteers. The army was made up of members of Lord Cawdor's Yeomanry Cavalry, the Cardigan Militia, Captain Ackland's Pembroke Volunteers, the Fishguard Fencibles (Plate 9a), and a party of Royal Navy sailors. The local force reached Manorowen and, after almost walking into a French ambush on Carnwnda, Cawdor withdrew to Fishguard and Goodwick for the night of 23 February.

Meanwhile the French force was showing its true colours. Tate himself seems to have been remorseful at his involvement in the invasion, his officers were rebellious and angry at having been abandoned by the ships, and the men were undisciplined and rowdy. Tate needed transport and food for his men, and sent out foraging parties in all directions. As the day wore on the invasion turned into a fiasco. Small groups of soldiers wandered far and wide, making no attempt to hide their movements. They looted all of the farms they came across and slaughtered calves, sheep and poultry for food. A number of local people and French soldiers were killed or injured in isolated incidents throughout Pencaer, for the locals were united in their opposition to the invader; there was never the slightest chance that a 'peasants' revolt' would be the outcome of the action. As luck would have it, in January a Portuguese coaster had been wrecked on the nearby coast and there was hardly a farmhouse in the vicinity which did not have a plentiful supply of Portuguese wine. Soon both soldiers and officers were drunk and even less capable than they had been when sober. On Thursday evening Tate was forced by his officers to write a surrender note. Following a stern reply from Lord Cawdor, the surrender terms were signed on Friday morning 24 February 1797, on the small table that stands in the bar of the Royal Oak inn. Tate probably signed the agreement later at Trehowel Farm, and during the afternoon the French troops (less twenty-five or so who were recovering from the effects of alcohol and eating uncooked poultry) marched down to Goodwick Sands to lay down their arms. They were later taken to Haverfordwest and imprisoned for a while in the castle and in the churches of St Thomas, St Martin and St Mary. The great invasion was over.

Inevitably, various incidents connected with the invasion have entered into local folk-lore. One story concerns the local women dressed in 'scarlet mantles and round hats' who crowded the hills on the Fishguard side of Goodwick Sands, looking from a distance like soldiers. Tradition has it that Lord Cawdor had them march round a rocky knoll, giving the enemy the impression of a seemingly endless line of troops and striking terror into their hearts. There is probably little truth in this, for Tate had almost certainly decided to surrender before most of the local women had appeared on the scene as spectators or volunteers.

All good stories need a hero, a heroine and a villain. Lord Cawdor was certainly the hero of the moment, but the local heroine was Jemima Nicholas, 'a tall stout Amazon masculine woman who worked as a cobbler in Fishguard.' She marched out with a pitchfork and captured twelve Frenchmen in a field near Llanwnda. She herded them to the guardhouse in Fishguard and then went back for more. She died in 1832 at the age of eighty-two, and today her tombstone stands at the front of Fishguard church. It bears the inscription:

> In memory of
> JEMIMA NICHOLAS
> of this town.
> THE WELSH HEROINE
> who boldly marched to meet
> the French Invaders
> who landed on our shores in
> February 1797

The villain of the piece was James Bowen, who had been a servant at Trehowel Farm on Pencaer but had been dismissed by his master, Mr Mortimer, and transported for horse-stealing. It is uncertain how he came to be involved in the invasion, but probably he found his way by chance to Brest, and was enrolled there by Tate as a guide before the departure of the troopships. Perhaps he hoped to use the expedition as an opportunity to return home and regain his freedom by deserting, or perhaps he was bent on vengeance against his local community and against his old employer in particular. Whatever Bowen's motives, it must have been largely due to his presence that the French landing was made at Carreg Wastad, on a piece of the coastline with which he must have been very familiar. In addition, he must have encouraged Tate to use Mortimer's farmhouse as his expedition headquarters. Probably, were it not for Bowen's presence on board Tate's ship, the last invasion of Britain would not have taken place near Fishguard at all.

THE REBECCA RIOTS

It has often been said that the French invasion killed all sympathy in Wales for the French Revolution and removed any possibility of a revolt of the local peasantry against the ruling classes. This may be so, but South Wales at the onset of the nineteenth century was a region of discontent. There was great hardship among the poorer people of the towns and villages of the coalfield; the suppression and exploitation of industrial workers eventually led to attempts to organise labour representation, and the discontent boiled over in the terrible clashes in Merthyr in 1831 and the Chartist encounter in Newport in 1839. There were many other clashes in the industrial areas.

There were problems on the land too. Agriculture was passing through a depression, and the rural population was increasing rapidly. The large landowners were enclosing more and more land in West Wales, and pushing the limits of cultivation higher and higher into the hills. Life was hard for the small farmer and the agricultural labourer; rents were high, agricultural prices were falling, and there was great resentment against new Poor Law legislation. Life became even harder as the turnpike roads were improved and as greater stringency was exercised in the collection of tolls. In West Wales there were many small turnpike trusts, each one controlling a part of the road network and operating its own toll-gates.

In the area between Narberth and St Clears most of the roads were owned by the Main and Whitland trusts. In 1839 the latter trust decided to erect new toll-gates on its roads, which were in a very poor state of repair. One of these gates was at Efail-wen in the foothills of Mynydd Presely. The gates were brought into use just as the lime-carting season was about to begin. This was the last straw for local farmers, who had suffered extreme hardship because of a succession of bad harvests. On the night of 13 May, scarcely a week after it had been opened, the gate at Efail-wen was destroyed and the toll-house set on fire. The gate was re-erected and provided with seven special constables for its protection, but on the night of 6 June 1839 a mob of about 400 arrived on the scene, drove off the constables and smashed down the gate and the toll-house. All were disguised; some wore women's clothes and had blackened faces. A week or so later another mob, similarly disguised, smashed down another new gate at Maes-gwyn north of Whitland. On 17 July, this time in broad daylight, a crowd of 'black-faced women' again smashed the Efail-wen gate, and the leader was referred to as 'Becca'. Whoever she was—and she was probably Thomas Rees, a pugilist who farmed at Carnabwth in the parish of Mynachlog-ddu—Rebecca won a remarkable victory, for the riots were followed by an order from the Whitland Trust for the dismantling of the four new gates. So the legend of Rebecca and her daughters was born.

In 1842–3 there was more rioting over the toll-gates, and this time it started at St Clears. Here, near the junction of roads owned by the Main and Whitland trusts farmers, cattle drovers and other travellers had to pay tolls twice within a mile as a result of a new gate built to prevent toll avoidance. In November and December 1842 the gates in St Clears were destroyed by Rebecca and her daughters on three occasions. At Pwll-trap in Carmarthenshire the destruction of the gate was accompanied by a little pantomime which frequently thereafter became a part of the rioting. Approaching the gate, Rebecca would say in Welsh, 'My children, this gate has no business to be here, has it?' The reply would come, 'No, it has not!' Then she would ask what should be done with it. On receiving the reply that it should be destroyed, Rebecca and her daughters would remove the chain and cut off the gateposts (Fig 4).

Fig 4   Rebecca rioters attacking one of the turnpike trust gates during the troubled years 1839–44

Now the rioting spread like wildfire. There was no shortage of men inclined to play the role of Rebecca, and no shortage of followers. Gates were destroyed at many places in Pembrokeshire, for example at Prendergast in Haverfordwest, Narberth, Robeston Wathen, and Scleddau near Fishguard. It spread further afield, with gates being destroyed in the Teifi and Tywi valleys and eventually in the semi-industrial area of south Carmarthenshire. Local militiamen, professional troops and special constables were pressed into service to quell the rioting, and eventually the open riots were replaced by greater secrecy and by more sinister activities on the part of Rebecca and her daughters. They transferred their attention to other grievances besides the toll-gates, and at the culmination of the rioting in 1843 matters occasionally got out of control and the original objectives of Rebecca were largely forgotten. In the country north-west of Llanelli a gang led by Shoni Sgubor Fawr and Dai'r Cantwr represented the lunatic fringe of the movement. David Williams, the historian of the Rebecca Riots, writes 'By day the countryside seemed quiet, but at night fantastically disguised horsemen careered along highways and through narrow lanes on their mysterious errands. They developed uncanny skill in evading the police and the infantry, and although their mounts were unwieldy farm horses, they also succeeded in outwitting the dragoons.' Although a number of 'Rebeccas' were captured, tried and even deported, the riots which began in Pembrokeshire achieved their objectives, for a commission which met in 1844 resulted in legislation which removed many of the turnpike grievances. By their somewhat grotesque activities, Rebecca and her daughters gave a jolt to authority and made their own life on the land a little easier to bear.

8 SEAFARING AND LIFE BY THE SEA

T HE influence of the sea pervades every part of Pembrokeshire. Because of its very irregular coastal outline, and especially because of the presence of the ancient drowned river-system of Milford Haven and the Daugleddau, no part of the county is more than ten miles from the sea. In addition, the wide variety of coastal environments provides literally hundreds of good landing-places for vessels of all types, ranging from muddy creeks and narrow tidal inlets to open sandy beaches, and from sheltered rocky coves to splendid natural harbours like Solva and Milford Haven. Pembrokeshire people have always lived in rare intimacy with the sea; only one Pembrokeshire town (Narberth) is located away from tidal waters, and the visitor is just as likely to find families with long seafaring traditions in Haverfordwest or Llangwm as in Solva, Fishguard, Milford or Saundersfoot. Even in the 1700s and early 1800s the land traveller from England could only reach this remote western peninsula after a long and wearying road journey; no wonder, then, that the sea has always been Pembrokeshire's great highway.

COASTAL TRADING

The seventeenth and eighteenth centuries were exciting ones in the lives of the Pembrokeshire ports. Coastal trading developed rapidly, and storehouses and limekilns as well as stone quays and jetties were constructed wherever there was a need for the export and import of goods and wherever coastal conditions were suitable. The road network of the county, and of the rest of South Wales, was quite inadequate to cope with the long-

98

distance transport of bulky loads, and almost everything was moved by sea. Such roads as there were in the coastal districts converged on the nearest small port. Manufactured goods became more and more prominent as items in the shipping registers, and minerals such as coal, limestone and slate became important as the value of the woollen trade gradually declined. Whereas coastal trading in George Owen's day had been organised and financed by the local gentry and the merchants of the main towns, now to an increasing extent local farmers, fishermen, townspeople and joiners shared in the ownership of small vessels. They shared, too, in the profits as their ships traded in a vast range of commodities with an ever-increasing number of British and foreign ports. For example, in 1603 almost all of the overseas trading contacts were with Ireland and France, but a century later there were many links with Spain, Portugal, Holland, Germany, and ports across the Atlantic. Whereas in 1603 most of the coastwise shipments were to and from Bristol, Barnstaple, North Wales and South Devon, the port books for the later part of the seventeenth century show that the number of trading links had increased and diversified greatly. The volume of trade was substantial; for example, in 1680 alone there were no less than 793 shipping movements in and out of Pembrokeshire ports. In addition, there must have been many more movements which were deliberately or 'accidentally' omitted from the port books and registers.

SHIPBUILDING

There was a thriving local shipbuilding industry, and by about 1800 small vessels were being built at thirty or more coastal sites. Only in a few places (such as Fishguard, Newport and Lawrenny) were there proper shipyards, and most vessels were simply constructed on temporary slipways on the beach just above high water mark. But there was considerable local craftsmanship involved; some of the ships' timbers were cut in the county, and sails, fittings and ropes were generally made by local craftsmen. Most of the early vessels built were ketches and sloops (fore-and-aft rigged) of less than twenty tons and often less than forty feet long; but in the later part of the eighteenth century larger sloops of twenty to forty tons were being built, as well as schooners and square-rigged vessels of 100 tons or more.

Most of the memories of those ship-building days have been dimmed with time, but many of the old 'shipyards' can still be located by reference to old maps and through conversations with the older inhabitants of coastal communities. On an old map of about 1856 'shipyards' are shown at Whalecwm (Cosheston), Lawrenny and several other sites in the inner reaches of Milford Haven. There are some details of the shipyard at Cosheston in the writings of Florence Howell, one of the literary sisters who lived at Blackpool Mill and Whalecwm. The shipbuilding business there was owned by David Morgan and Thomas Howell. Many ships were built to order for Liverpool shipowners, and it was the custom in the late 1800s for the ships' captains to stay at Cosheston during the final stages of building in order to supervise the details of fittings, rigging and sails. Up to thirty men and boys were employed at the yard, and there was an apprenticeship of seven years. Local oak was widely used, and the ships' seams were caulked with 'oakum and pitch'. The larger ships took two years or more to build, and they were launched down the greased slipway with due ceremony, often by the new owner's wife. This was followed by a launch dinner: 'a fine spread on the mould loft; and that night we had singing and dancing until the early hours of next morning'. Then came the fitting-out process, with the erection of the masts, the construction of the superstructure, the fitting of the rigging and the making up of sails. Then, again in the words of Florence Howell's old shipwright, '... when she was ready for sea, everybody on the place went aboard, and the Minister come, and we had a service aboard the new ship, prayers and singing and a short sermon. After that, we went ashore, her crew up anchor, her sails was hoisted, and down the Haven she sailed. We watched her till she was out o' sight, on her road to the sea.'

WRECKING

Some idea of the excitement of Pembrokeshire coastal life during this era of sea-trading can be gained from the old port books and from contemporary ships' logs and other records; but some people enjoyed more excitement than others. Several remote coastal communities indulged in wrecking activities, and the historian Richard Fenton (writing in 1811) tells us that Llanunwas, near Solva, 'had the reputation of hanging out false lights to decoy the wandering mariner in order to benefit from his misfortunes'. Ships driven on to the rocky coasts during storms were rapidly relieved of their cargoes, often with the energetic help of the local customs officers. Several coastal localities have names connected with flotsam and jetsam, or with particular shipwrecks, or with smuggling. For instance, we have Brandy Bay and Dutch Gin near St Bride's Haven, Driftwood on Ramsey, and Ogof Tobacco near Solva. A report of 1668, concerning the fate of the cargo vessel *Amity*, reads: 'The ship being at anchor in Ramsey Sound was by a violent storme put from her anchors and nothing to be expected but death, the men deserted her and went ashore on Ramsey Island in their boats: the ship ran ashore near St David's Head where the country people were soe barbarous that they staved the wine casks in so much the master saved not anything considerable only some fruit which we indemnified.' In his book, *The Sounds Between*, Roscoe Howells tells another story handed down by the older boatmen of St David's. Apparently several casks of strong drink were washed ashore on Ramsey Island where they were found by the men working on the farm. They drank well, and then hid the remaining casks. However, they were so drunk at the time that they failed afterwards to rediscover the casks. That, at any rate, was the story which they told to the enforcement officers, whose repeated searches proved fruitless. . . .

It is natural that those Pembrokeshire folk who live by the sea should have an instinct for looking for wreckage. It is also natural that those communities inhabiting the western tips of the county's peninsulas should have developed this instinct most strongly, for the areas around the islands of Ramsey and Skomer have always been extremely dangerous to shipping. Ramsey Sound, Jack Sound and Broad Sound (between Skokholm and Skomer) have been the scenes of many shipwrecks, and the people of St David's, Solva and Marloes have been involved in many epic rescues. However, even into the present century newspaper comment about local priorities has not always been kind: 'This coast, we believe, has in the ancient times past, enjoyed, or rather been credited with a rather dubious reputation as to whether life saving or property salving comes first in the correct order of things . . .' In 1908 the Austrian steamer *Szent Istvan* went ashore on Ramsey Island in dense fog. It was carrying general cargo worth £200,000, and much of this was washed ashore in St Bride's Bay after the ship went down. The newspaper report says 'Parts of the shores of St Bride's Bay were literally strewn with wreckage. From St David's to Little Haven the people were busily engaged on Sunday in salving it . . . At Solva the "wreckers"—if that term is permissible—included deacons, and respectable tradesmen, publicans and sinners, cobblers and hooligans, all bent on the same errand.' Naturally enough the deacons and other good people of Solva were deeply offended by this report, for they all knew that the real wrecking activities of the community were long since over.

There is another delightful tale of a Marloes parson who had one of his church services disturbed by a messenger with news of a newly wrecked vessel beneath the nearby cliffs. The service could obviously not continue under such circumstances; after imploring his congregation to show moderation in all things he appealed to them to give him a head's start since he felt he had lost something of his youthful turn of speed.

SMUGGLING AND PIRACY

During the seventeenth and eighteenth centuries smuggling was officially frowned upon, but it was aided and abetted by local municipal officials, JPs and customs men alike. During this sea-trading era, thousands of profitable voyages to and from Pembrokeshire were made as deliberate smuggling enterprises. Many remote coves and creeks were used, sometimes by 'free enterprise' smugglers who simply appeared out of the blue, sold their exotic duty-free goods to local people, and then disappeared again. A document dated 1611 records that 'great quantities of wine' were brought by French merchants into Pembrokeshire ports and discharged 'without paying any impost'. Quite respectable ships'

masters, who normally operated legally, used to carry the occasional illicit cargo just to provide a little extra income and a
little extra excitement. Major Francis Jones records that an
eighteenth-century ancestor was engaged in the coastal trade,
carrying legal cargoes of grain and illegal (and possibly more
profitable) cargoes of salt. An old inhabitant of Abereiddi relates
that his great-grandfather was the leader of a smuggling gang
until he was eventually caught red-handed with a consignment
of smuggled tobacco. For his sins he was put away in Ports-
mouth Jail for a while. In Solva a number of houses have secret
cupboards and shafts which may well have been used for con-
cealing smuggled goods.

Piracy, although less prevalent in Stuart than in Tudor times,
was still by no means a thing of the past. In the year 1633 a
pirate vessel captained by a Breton anchored in Ramsey Sound,
and twenty-seven of the crew, armed with swords, half-pikes,
muskets and pistols raided the island and made off with assorted
cheeses, lambs and sheep. This caused a great stir locally, since a
number of local men were thought to have been co-operating
with the pirates. During the Civil War and later wars (such as the
Napoleonic Wars) piracy was common in St George's Channel
and the Bristol Channel, and French vessels were often involved.
During the American War of Independence the famous John
Paul Jones paid at least one rapid visit to Pembrokeshire. His
vessel *Black Prince* entered Fishguard Bay and he demanded a
ransom for a merchant vessel which he had seized. There is some
doubt about whether the ransom was paid, but Jones fired two
broadsides on Lower Fishguard and succeeded in damaging a
few chimney pots and in injuring Richard Fenton's sister Mary.
In the south of the county Jones Bay is the place where Paul Jones
reputedly went ashore for water. Pembrokeshire's own favourite
pirate was Bartholomew Roberts, born in the hamlet of Little
Newcastle in 1682. In 1719 he turned pirate, earning the name
'Black Bart'. Within two months he was captain of his own ship,
and within three years he was dead. But in his brief career he
captured more than 400 ships on the high seas, and became
known as the terror of the Spanish Main.

THE PEMBROKESHIRE LIGHTHOUSES

The difficulties of navigating on the Pembrokeshire coast have led to the construction of a number of lighthouses on rocky head-lands and islands. The lighthouse at St Ann's Head, at the entrance of Milford Haven, was built largely through the efforts of the Allen family. There are other lighthouses at Strumble Head and on Skokholm Island and Caldey Island. But the most valuable lighthouses of all are those which guard the Bishops and Clerks, off Ramsey Island, and the Smalls, far out beyond the gannet island of Grassholm. The Bishops and Clerks were dreaded by ships' masters in the days of sail, and their evil reputation elicited this poetic and much-quoted statement from George Owen:

> The Bishop and these his Clerks preach deadly doctrine to their winter audience, such poor seafaring men as are forced thither by tempest. Only in one thing they are to be commended, they keep residence better than the rest of the canons of that see are wont to do.

The South Bishop Light was built in 1839, but it was preceded by some sixty years by the famous structure built on the Smalls rock by Henry Whiteside.

The Smalls lighthouse was the brainchild of one John Phillips, a Cardiganshire man who was a docks manager in Liverpool. Having scraped together sufficient funds for the construction work, he engaged Henry Whiteside as his engineer. Whiteside evolved a plan by which the lighthouse could be built on a sub-merged rock and yet provide minimal obstruction to the passage of fierce currents and violent storm-waves; it was to be an octagonal house of timber mounted on nine legs, three of which were to be of cast iron and the other six of wood. This was a revolutionary design, and it was greeted with scepticism by most authorities. Nevertheless, Whiteside set to work with the con-struction, using Solva as his base. The great timber pillars and all the other materials were shipped the twenty-two miles to the desolate hidden rocks of the Smalls and, in spite of bad weather during the first season of construction, the light was lit for the first time on 1 September 1776. The vibrations and movement of the structure during gales caused the lighthouse keepers to suffer from sea-sickness, so in January 1777 Whiteside determined to stay there himself with a blacksmith to effect repairs and improvements. They were stranded during a period of severe storms and, with almost all of their fresh water gone and no fire to warm them they desperately cast three similarly worded messages (bottled inside wooden casks) into the sea. By incredible good luck, one of the casks was washed up only a few days later near the home of Thomas Williams of Treleddyn. He was acting agent for John Phillips and it was he who, a few years later, was to raise the alarm at the time of the 'Last Invasion of Britain'. Being a man of action, he had the stranded lighthouse builders rescued in no time.

After further modifications the original Smalls lighthouse stood for eighty years before being replaced by a more modern stone structure completed in 1861. Again the community of Solva was involved in the construction work, providing homes for the workmen and experiencing much activity associated with the import of Cornish granite, the dressing of the stones, and the transport of the shaped blocks by steam tugs and barges out to the Smalls.

Locally perhaps the most famous story relating to the original Smalls lighthouse dates from the year 1801. It is a slightly gruesome tale, but it marks another crucial development in British lighthouse history. Two men were keeping the lighthouse when one of them, Thomas Griffiths, died during a violent storm. His companion Thomas Howell was afraid lest he should be suspected of foul play, so he decided not to cast the corpse into the sea. Instead he made a wooden box from some of the interior fittings of the house, and placed the body in it. Then he lashed it to the lantern rail. Although various passing ships noticed this strange object none of them stopped, for the light was still working and there was no obvious cause for concern. When Howell was relieved at the end of his four-month tour of duty he was half demented, and since that time Trinity House has insisted

G

that all lighthouses should be manned by three keepers working together.

THE COMING OF THE RAILWAY

The nineteenth century was a time of accelerating change in Pembrokeshire as elsewhere, and if we can point to one event which signalled the end of the sea-trading era it was the coming of the railway to Haverfordwest in 1854. From this year onwards bulky goods could be transported rapidly and cheaply overland, and soon there were rail termini at Neyland (1856), Milford (1863), and Pembroke Dock (1864). Within a few years the Pembrokeshire sea trade was suffering a slow, lingering death and by 1900 there were few local vessels participating in it. In addition to the effect of the railways, the road network was now much improved, so that the remnants of the coastal shipping trade were forced by competition to concentrate on the few largest and most efficient ports (eg Haverfordwest, Fishguard and Milford). As hard times came, ship-owning also became concentrated in the hands of fewer large ship-owners who could afford larger and more efficient vessels, sometimes with steam engines and screw propulsion. The days of the small port and the small ship-owner were over.

9 MILFORD HAVEN AND ITS 'NEW TOWNS'

IN earlier chapters we have referred on several occasions to the magnificent waterway of Milford Haven. Undoubtedly it is one of the finest natural harbours in the world. It is a long, sheltered *ria* about a mile wide at its entrance and over half a mile wide all the way to Pembroke Dock. In its lower parts it is mostly more than thirty feet deep, and there is an even deeper central channel. On both shores there are broad embayments such as Dale Roads and Angle Bay. About nine miles inland the character of the waterway changes dramatically near Neyland and Burton. Upstream from here, the Daugleddau is a beautiful tidal estuary with many small inlets and branches to remind one that the whole waterway is one large river-system cut millions of years ago, and later drowned as the sea flooded in. At Picton Point the Daugleddau branches into two, the Western Cleddau and Eastern Cleddau still being tidal as far inland as Haverfordwest and Canaston Bridge respectively. In spite of the great mud-banks to be seen in the Daugleddau at low tide, silting is no problem in Milford Haven. There is a tidal range of up to twenty-five feet but tidal currents are not too strong. The local climate is relatively mild, and compared with almost all other ports in the UK there is remarkably little fog.

All manner of men have praised the qualities of the waterway. Shakespeare wrote: '. . . how far it is to this same blessed Milford; and, by the way, tell me how Wales was made so happy as t'inherit such a haven.' Daniel Defoe, on his famous tour, described Milford Haven as one of the greatest and best inlets of water in Britain. And he added 'Mr. Camden says it contains 16 creeks, 5 great bays and 13 good roads for shipping, all distinguished as such by their names; and some say a thousand sail of ships may ride in it and not the topmast of one be seen from the other.' Most famous of all is the pronouncement of Lord Nelson, who said in 1803 that Milford Haven was the only seaport for commerce on the west coast of Britain, and that it rivalled Trincomalee in Ceylon as the greatest harbour he had ever seen.

While the Vikings and the Normans seem to have appreciated both the strategic and economic possibilities of the Milford Haven waterway, it was never properly developed as a port until the nineteenth century. There had been abortive plans during earlier centuries, and indeed Thomas Cromwell had stressed the need for fortification and survey in 1539. In addition Henry VIII had, in the later sixteenth century, embarked on an ambitious plan to fortify both shores. Two blockhouses were built on the north and south sides of the Haven entrance, but they seem never to have been effectively maintained or used for the defence of the waterway.

THE NEW TOWN OF MILFORD

The first of the major maritime developments within the Haven was linked with the growth of Milford. The town was founded in 1793 and grew rapidly as a result of the energy of Charles Greville. Among the earliest inhabitants were a group of Quaker whalers from Nantucket, who continued their whaling activities for only a few years before turning to an easier life of manufacturing and trading. Unfortunately the Navy abandoned the dockyard at Milford in 1814 following a dispute over land purchase. But the small fishing industry was healthy enough, and the town progressed quickly. The Irish steam packet service was based here until 1836, but following its removal to Pembroke Dock there was a period of stagnation, and the population even declined. After many delays Milford docks were completed in 1888, almost a century after the founding of the town. A journalist in the *Financial News* commented 'Milford Haven has been the port of the future for so long that it is surely time that the future should merge itself with the present.'

But still the development of the town was slow. After 1888

there were dreams of a great shipbuilding industry and of the town becoming a transatlantic passenger terminus, but these dreams never materialised. The real growth of Milford came largely by accident, arising out of the rapid improvements in the design of fishing vessels and out of the discovery of rich fishing-grounds in the western approaches to the British Isles. Between 1900 and 1914 the proximity of Milford to these fishing-grounds, the excellence of Milford Haven as a port and the size of Milford docks themselves led to remarkable growth in the fishing industry. By 1904 there were 66 trawlers and 150 smacks based at the docks, which were also used by many vessels from other ports. By 1914 about 2,000 local people were employed in the fishing industry, and Milford was in the top league of fishing ports. However, the boom could not last and the fortunes of the industry fluctuated violently after World War I as a result of national economic factors and over-fishing in the western fishing-grounds. World War II allowed the fishing-grounds to recover somewhat, and a record catch of 59,286 tons was obtained by the Milford fleet in 1946. But then a slow decline started and gradually catches have become smaller and smaller and the number of trawlers has fallen drastically.

In 1972 there were only twelve trawlers registered at the port, with only 3,160 tons of fish landed during the year. Since then, the crisis in the fishing industry has become even more severe. Reduced catches and rising operating costs have placed the trawler owners in great difficulties, and throughout 1974 there was a desperate attempt by local politicians, union officials and businessmen to save the industry and the jobs of about 100 trawlermen and 300 ancillary workers. The organised chaos of the docks basin and the fish market, which was a part of Milford life until the mid 1950s, has disappeared.

But Milford is by no means a dead town. The fishing industry has known periods of depression before, and the town has diversified its interests greatly since 1900. The Royal Naval Armaments Depot at Newton Noyes (opened in 1934) provides employment for 300 men, and until recently there was an old-established shipbreaking yard nearby in the muddy creek of Castle Pill. Increasingly the town depends upon light manufacturing, and the Thornton industrial estate has six factories providing employment for over 600 people. The oil industry has made an enormous impact upon the town, bringing with it an influx of construction workers during each of the refinery-building projects and many new jobs both in the refineries and in the various services which the oil industry requires. This will be looked at in greater detail in a later chapter.

As a town, Milford still retains much evidence of its planned and graceful origins. Sir William Hamilton (husband of Lord Nelson's famous Emma Hamilton) was the owner of Milford, and it was his money which financed the port developments and the building of the town. But his nephew Charles Greville was the planner and builder. He adopted a gridiron layout, with three principal streets running parallel with one another and intersected by side streets. Hamilton Terrace, closest to the shore, was given the most stylish houses. Behind that Charles Street was designed as the main shopping thoroughfare, while Robert Street, the third and highest terrace, was given the least pretentious housing. The main public buildings are at the east end of Hamilton Terrace: the Town Hall, the public library and St Katherine's Church dating from 1801–8. Other links with the past can be seen in the Hakin Observatory, the Friends' Meeting House in the town centre and the old row of cottages on Cellar Hill above Castle Pill. Most of the newer developments have taken place to the east and north of the original town centre, and this can be seen quite clearly in both the irregular street patterns and post-1850 style of much of the housing. The old villages of Hubberston, Hakin and Steynton have now been incorporated into Milford, and they have many of the newer housing estates of the post-war era.

NEYLAND

Further up the Haven but still on its northern shore, the little town of Neyland also started life as a deliberately planned settlement. It was conceived during the railway era of the mid-nineteenth century by the illustrious Isambard Kingdom Brunel. He chose the site (previously a small fishing-port) as the terminus for the South Wales railway, to connect with the Atlantic passenger service and the Irish packet service. The railway line was completed to the port of 'New Milford' (as the town was christened) in 1856, and the huge Great Western Hotel was built on the water-front. Now the future seemed secure, and local people felt that great times lay ahead. Sure enough, the town enjoyed a brief period of prosperity, with much house-building, a rapidly rising population, and even some ship-building. A wagon-works was established at the railway terminus on the broad flat coastal terrace beneath the eastern edge of the town. This provided much local employment. The fishing industry boomed, and a refrigeration factory was built to provide ice for the rapid rail transport of the fish catch towards the towns of the South Wales coalfield.

But the good times did not last. Comparatively little shipping used the port. Atlantic vessels were few and far between, and in 1906 even the Irish service was transferred to Fishguard. There was competition, too, from the other towns of Milford Haven which had greater natural potential for growth. On the opposite shore of the Haven, Pembroke Dock acquired its railway link in 1864 and was rapidly developed as a naval dockyard after that date, and by 1863 Milford had its own railway line as well. These developments meant that Neyland's advantages were much reduced, particularly since the Admiralty blocked any schemes for further development so as not to congest the upper reaches of the Haven. The little town declined gradually, losing its fishing industry and its ice factory, losing its shipbuilding and later its wagon-works. Although the rail depot kept some wagon-repairing facilities until the post-war era, these disappeared with the rail service in 1955. In 1971 the track was lifted. Now the little town finds itself increasingly isolated. In 1974 the car ferry service between Neyland and Hobbs Point was still running, but with the completion of the new Haven Bridge more and more traffic will by-pass the town. Nevertheless, it still survives happily enough. It has its technical college, it provides shopping facilities for a wide local area, and the old railway yard is a valuable industrial site. There is more land with industrial potential just across Westfield Pill at Barnlake. Local people enjoy living in the town, and they feel that the good times will come again.

PEMBROKE DOCK AND ITS DOCKYARD

Pembroke Dock thrived on the early failures of the other two new towns of Milford Haven, and it is the only town in the county ever to have acquired a real industrial image. Its early growth occurred after 1814, when Paterchurch was selected as the site for the new naval dockyard. The site was sheltered and spacious, and there was deep water close inshore. There was a long tradition of local ship-building and a pool of skilled labour. Moreover, the Haven was remote enough from the troubles of the European mainland to serve as a strategically safe base for major techno-logical developments in naval shipbuilding. For this was indeed an exciting time; there were experiments with steam propulsion, with paddles and with screw propellers, and with iron cladding. Warships were increasing rapidly in size. Once established, the dockyard was the scene of many innovations in shipbuilding, and it is not often realised that for most of the century Pembroke Dock was the most advanced shipbuilding yard in the world. The year 1834 saw the launching of *Tartarus*, the first steam man-of-war; in 1846 *Conflict* was launched, being the first warship fitted with a screw propeller; and in 1847 *Lion* was launched, being then the largest warship in the Royal Navy. Five years later there followed *The Duke of Wellington*, the largest three-decker ever built. Five royal yachts were built and there was a long line of naval barques, brigantines, cruisers, gunboats and battleships. By 1875 the Chief Constructor of the American Navy was able to report that 'Pembroke Dockyard is the finest shipbuilding yard in the world.' In all, the dockyard saw the construction of more than 250 naval vessels, and at its height in the later years of the nineteenth century it employed over 3,000 men. Many employees travelled daily to the dockyard by rowing-boat from other parts of the Haven. Some came from as far afield as Llangwm.

In the early years of the present century Pembroke Dock was still one of the main industrial centres of West Wales, and during World War I the dockyard worked at full pace, specialising in the building of small, swift cruisers. But its remoteness was beginning to count as a disadvantage, and in the hard inter-war years the

Admiralty began to think of it as something of an expendable luxury. In 1926 it was abruptly closed, and the town was thrown into despair. The whole community suffered a great deal of hardship, and the bitter memories of this time have still not entirely disappeared. Hundreds of families left the area, and the unemployment rate approached 25 per cent. Since 1926 there have been various attempts to improve the employment situation and to improve the town's image of poverty and depression.

During World War II the town was made the main Atlantic Sunderland flying-boat base, and part of the dockyard was again used as a naval base for ship-repairing. Innumerable Atlantic convoys in the dark years of the war were assembled here, in the sheltered waters of the Haven, and much minelaying, minesweeping and escort work was co-ordinated from the dockyard HQ. It has been estimated that during the course of the war some 17,000 cargo vessels sailed from the Haven. The town became an important fuel storage depot, and there was a sizeable garrison. But these wartime activities were a mixed blessing, for the town attracted enemy bombing attacks and suffered greatly from air raids. Although its sheer distance from the continent provided some protection from enemy bombers at the beginning of the war, Pembroke Dock enjoyed no immunity from aircraft with a longer range. There are still bitter memories of the great destruction and loss of life in the town, particularly during the twelve months between July 1940 and June 1941. The main enemy targets were the oil storage tanks at Llanreath, the Llanion Barracks, the dockyard, and the military airfield a short distance away at Milton (Carew Cheriton).

During the summer of 1940 the attacks built up in intensity, but the event which brought the plight of Pembroke Dock to national attention was the 'Great Tanks Fire' of 19 August 1940. A single enemy bomber scored a direct hit on one of the oil storage tanks. An immense fire raged for eighteen days, destroying eleven tanks and 132,000 tons of fuel oil. Six hundred firemen from twenty-two fire brigades helped to fight the blaze, and there were five fatalities and 1,148 other casualties. Mr Arthur Morris, Pembroke's Fire Chief, who was among the first on the scene of the fire, did not go to bed for seventeen days; afterwards there was great local indignation that his heroic efforts received no real recognition from officialdom.

The most severe air raids of the whole war occurred on 11–12 May and 11 June 1941. The first of these was an intense attack with high-explosive bombs, while the second was referred to locally as 'the fire blitz', being largely an incendiary attack. The death toll on the night of 11–12 May was at least thirty-six, and nearly 2,000 houses were damaged. Pembroke Dock was never very well defended, and it was inevitable that after the tragedy of that night a flood of refugees left the town. W. L. Richards, the historian of Pembrokeshire's air raids, described the scene as follows:

> Down over the hill from Pembroke Dock they came in an end-less stream, in cars, lorries and overloaded buses, on motor-cycles, bicycles, and horse-drawn carts and waggons. Hundreds came on foot, weary mothers with infants in arms and little boys and girls hardly of school age running behind, wonderment written plain on their faces; old men on sticks, young men with grim expressions, subdued boys and frightened girls. Dusk fell and still they came . . .
>
> There were those who, with no friends or relatives outside the town and no money to pay for a roof over their heads, had to face the night in Pembroke Dock or flee to the open country. It is a fact that many people slept in the open in Bush woods and the surrounding fields and hedges for nights after May 12th.
>
> Pembroke Dock was a dark, deserted, dismal town that night . . . And so it was the next night and for many nights after until gradually with the general slackening of the air attacks, people began to return to their shattered homes.

The unfortunate town, which had suffered cruelly after the closure of the dockyard in 1926, had borne the brunt of the enemy assault on Pembrokeshire. Haverfordwest, Milford, Neyland and Tenby escaped largely unscathed.

Since the end of the war the Navy has maintained a small presence at Pembroke Dock, but the dockyard itself has been used largely by small private ship-building and repairing concerns. The town continued to be used as a base for the Sunderland flying-boats of RAF Coastal Command until 1958, and many people have fond recollections of the cumbersome white aircraft in the skies above Pembrokeshire. Although the flying-boat base was the largest in the world there is now little evidence of this. The last Sunderland was taken (in pieces) from Pembroke Dock to the RAF Museum at Hendon in 1971, where eventually it will go on permanent display.

Now Pembroke Dock is largely rebuilt, still preserving its original gridiron plan and still bearing many traces of its military history. The oil storage tanks are still there. They are fed from the sad floating bulk of *Warrior*, the first of the ironsides. In addition to the dockyard there are the Defensible Barracks and Llanion Barracks and the other fortifications dating from the Napoleonic era. But the town cannot look to the past for its prosperity. It has no tourist attractions to compare with the medieval towns of Pembroke, Haverfordwest and Tenby, and its prosperity must be based on industry and services. There are two government 'advance factories' on the outskirts of the town. Sadly, one of them has been empty for several years, but the other is now a thriving woollen mill. The most successful local enterprise is the Firth Cleveland factory nearby, with a floor area of 200,000 square feet and employment for about 300 men. It produces extruded nuts and bolts, including nearly all the fixings for the UK car industry.

Through its suffering Pembroke Dock has acquired resilience and hope, and it has grown used to a seesaw existence of booms and depressions. Like the other towns of Milford Haven, its fortunes have always been linked with the sea. Now all eyes are turned to the sea again; this time it is the Celtic Sea and the search for oil, and the townspeople are witnessing the conversion of the dockyard area into a major centre for the exploration activities of the oil industry.

THE PROTECTION OF THE HAVEN

During the nineteenth century, with the great investment in the new towns of Milford, Neyland and Pembroke Dock, the Haven became a harbour of great strategic importance. Before 1820 there had only been very few half-hearted attempts to fortify the waterway, but now proper plans were put into hand. The first large building project was connected with the defence of the Royal Naval Dockyard. Between 1844 and 1857 the Defensible Barracks were built (to hold a garrison of 500 men), together with two martello towers to protect the waterfront around the dockyard. Further down the Haven impressive new forts were built between 1850 and 1870 at Dale Fort, Popton Point, Chapel Bay, South Hook Point and Hubberston, and in the waterway itself on Thorn Island and Stack Rock. There were plans to defend the landward approaches to Milford Haven, too, and a number of inland sites were selected. However, only two of these additional forts were ever built—at Fort Scoveston and on St Catherine's Island, Tenby. The strongest of the forts, at Popton Point and Hubberston, were designed to hold garrisons of more than 200 men, and they were each armed with about thirty heavy guns. In all, the forts could accommodate a total garrison of about 1,900 men, defending the Haven with 220 heavy guns. The cost of constructing all of the defences was about £1 million —a considerable sum in those days.

Some of the forts are now in ruins, but they are well worth looking at in any case. Others have been preserved and are put to good use. The Thorn Island fort (built between 1852 and 1859) is used as a hotel; Dale Fort is a popular field studies centre; the Defensible Barracks are used as a golf club house; the South Hook Point fort is used by Esso Petroleum, lying as it does within the refinery periphery; and the Popton Point fort is used as the headquarters of the BP Angle Bay ocean terminal. St Catherine's Fort in Tenby is used, even more exotically, as a private zoo.

10 COAL, STONE, SLATE AND IRON: PEMBROKESHIRE'S INDUSTRIAL REVOLUTION

LONG before the building of the new towns on Milford Haven, there were small industries scattered about Pembrokeshire. Few people realise how rich the county's industrial past has been, but just like the more densely populated parts of Britain this remote corner of Wales was affected by the Industrial Revolution. Pembrokeshire's own coalfield, specialising in high-quality anthracite, had an exciting history of successes and disasters. The county had its own metal mines and metalworking industries, and at Stepaside there was a combined coalmining and iron-working industry similar in many respects to the larger concerns which changed for ever the way of life of the South Wales coalfield. Pembroke Dock, between 1814 and 1926, was one of the world's most famous naval dockyards. In the previous chapter we saw how many of its innovations revolutionised shipbuilding in the days when steam replaced sail and iron replaced wood.

In addition to these relatively large industries the county has, from the Middle Ages to the present, supported many smaller enterprises. Slates, building stone and road stone have been produced in hundreds of quarries in the countryside. Most of these are forgotten and overgrown; some, like Rosebush, Porthgain and West Williamston, remain impressive to this day. All around the coast there are limekilns to remind us of the past practice of burning lime to improve the land. In the towns there have been tanneries and rope-works. Corn mills and woollen mills were once widespread, and brick-works and paper mills were thriving local industries. And on the smallest scale village craftsmen have for centuries been making farm implements, coracles, furniture and a host of other useful or decorative items which found their way into local homes.

Most of the traces of these industries have been lost over the years, but there is still much to see, and this chapter attempts to describe some of the industries based on the county's mineral resources of coal, stone, slate, iron and other metalliferous ores.

THE COAL INDUSTRY

The Pembrokeshire coal industry has a fascinating history. The landscape still bears some of the scars of coal extraction, although most of them are now healed. Traces of the spoil-heaps, railway tracks and pit-head buildings can be found by anyone who knows where to look, but these are not clearly marked on the OS maps and many visitors are unaware of their existence. The small coalfield is the western part of the South Wales coalfield, being made up of thin and disturbed seams of anthracite. Although the coal has been very difficult to work, there is a long history of mining going back to the fourteenth century at least. Prior to 1500 coalpits seem to have been concentrated on the western part of the coalfield, especially west of Roch and in the Little Haven area, but by 1600 there were more pits inland of Saundersfoot Bay and around the confluence of the Eastern Cleddau and Western Cleddau. It seems from the writings of George Owen that on the Pembrokeshire coalfield the value of coal for domestic heating purposes was realised earlier than elsewhere in Wales, and during the seventeenth century production for the home market rose sharply. By 1700 Pembrokeshire anthracite was also in great demand further afield, and was renowned for its low ash content and excellent heating properties. Now it had become the chief item of shipment from the Pembrokeshire ports, and for two centuries it was also the basis of most of the industrial activities of the county.

Production on the Pembrokeshire coalfield reached its peak in the later years of the eighteenth century, when annual totals of well over 150,000 tons were achieved. For the next fifty years or so the Pembrokeshire collieries remained prosperous, but in the face of increased competition from the major British coalfields output fell gradually through the latter half of the nineteenth century. Among the factors which caused this decline were the lack of capital investment in mining plant by the colliery owners, the working out of the uppermost seams, the increasing difficulty of deep working in the shattered and faulted lower seams, and the impossibility of loading coal direct to large vessels in the tidal reaches of the Daugleddau. By the 1890s Pembrokeshire had become a high-cost region at a time when competition was intensifying, and at a time of national depression. As many of the smaller mines closed larger and more efficient units appeared in more favourable localities; but as costs rose inexorably they, too, were forced to close.

The section of the coalfield which was centred on the confluence of the Western and Eastern Cleddau rivers depended greatly upon the export of coal from small quays and jetties. One of the earliest areas which shipped out coal and culm in barges and little sailing vessels was the Landshipping area. Before 1844 there were five working collieries here, and Landshipping village was a thriving mining community. There were quays at Landshipping Ferry and Picton Point which were connected by a ferry service. The main quay was at Landshipping itself, and from here over 10,000 tons of coal and culm were exported annually at the beginning of the nineteenth century. The Garden Pit colliery, very close to the quay, was quite famous locally; but in 1844 it hit the national headlines. Water from the river broke into the workings, and more than forty men and boys were drowned. The mine was closed and the community never recovered. Many families emigrated, and by 1867 all the other collieries in the area had also closed. Further south, the collieries around Yerberston, Cresselly and Jeffreston were running down, and after 1850 little coal was exported from Cresswell Quay. Surprisingly, the quay is still in a good state of repair.

On the other side of the river the Hook district was much more successful, and over the years shallow workings, drifts and deep mines were worked. For about a century, from the mid-1800s until 1948, Hook was a real mining community, and there were many mining families in Freystrop as well. There were at least sixteen substantial collieries in the area, besides a number of smaller ones which only worked for a few years before being abandoned. Most of the collieries around Hook were closed by 1910, and until 1930 production figures fluctuated around 10,000 tons per annum. Several small quays in the area, such as Black Hill Quay, Little Milford Quay, Hook Quay, Lower Hook Quay and Sprinkle Quay, were used for exporting coal. Of these, we can still see the remains of Little Milford Quay, and Hook Quay is a prominent industrial relic.

About 1850 cargo vessels became too large for the smaller quays. More and more barges came into use for carrying the coal to Llangwm Pool and Lawrenny, where it was transhipped. But this was an expensive and time-consuming operation, and Hook Colliery could not have survived were it not for the construction of the Hook Colliery Railway in 1929 to join the GWR at Johnston. At last the Hook Colliery no longer had to depend upon the small coal barges using Hook Quay, and could export coal promptly direct to the major markets. In 1932 a screening plant was built, giving Hook Colliery a selling advantage over its local competitors, and later £10,000 was spent on a plant for patent fuel. A further stroke of luck was the closure of the Bonville's Court Colliery near Saundersfoot, enabling Hook Colliery to capture its markets. Production rose sharply to a peak of 42,000 tons in 1934, falling to 15,000–25,000 tons per annum during the war years; but rising costs, the NCB takeover in 1947, and a severe flood in the Hook West Drift led to the ending of all mining activities in 1948.

By far the most important colliery district in the county was that around Kilgetty and Saundersfoot. Before 1900 there were several quite prosperous collieries at work, including Bonville's Court Colliery, Grove Colliery and Kilgetty Colliery (both at Stepaside), Begelly Colliery and Moreton Colliery. At first the coal was transported by horse and cart and by bullock waggon to the beaches at Wiseman's Bridge and Saundersfoot, where it was loaded on to sailing vessels at low tide. During the eighteenth century there were sometimes thirty vessels or more being loaded at the same time on Coppet Hall beach, served by over 100 carts. Everything changed after 1829 when the fine harbour at Saun-

A FISHGUARD FENCIBLE

Plate 9 (left) A hero of the 'campaign' against the French during the 'last invasion' of Britain. One of the Fishguard Fencibles, caricatured in a contemporary print; *(below)* the poster which was used to attract tourists to the delights of Rosebush—the holiday resort that never was

THE RESORT OF THOSE WHO SEEK SCENERY HEALTH & REPOSE

THE STUDY OF NATURE

TOURIST SEASON   MAY TO SEPTEMBER

PEMBROKESHIRE   SOUTH WALES

MAENCLOCHOG RAILWAY

BOOK FOR CLYNDERWEN   FREQUENT TRAINS   THENCE TO ROSEBUSH
                                        ALSO
                              SPECIAL
                           ARRANGEMENTS
                              BY LETTER FOR
                              SCHOOLS &
                           LARGE PARTIES

VISITORS TO PRECELLY MOUNTAINS CONVEYED ANY DAY AT TOURIST FARES
ONE SHILLING   RETURN JOURNEY

Plate 10 (above) An air photo of the Norman fortress at Pembroke. Behind it can be seen the old walled town aligned along the single main street; (below) an old print showing work in progress on the reconstruction of the Porthgain Harbour, about 1903

dersfoot was built and the various mineral railway lines came into use. One line ran inland to Begelly and Thomas Chapel, and it was used for taking the miners to work as well as for the export of coal. The other branch ran northwards towards Wiseman's Bridge to the Stepaside area, where it served several local collieries and the local iron industry. The line ran along the coast and needed several short tunnels, which are still in a good state of repair. Coal could now be exported quickly and efficiently, and by the middle of the century the industry prospered. Several new collieries were opened up, and by 1864 over 30,000 tons of coal were being exported from Saundersfoot Harbour each year. New industries, such as the fire-brick works at Wiseman's Bridge, appeared on the scene. But as the best seams were worked out and as high transport and drainage costs began to affect the collieries, they closed one after another. By 1900 Bonville's Court was the only large working colliery in the area. It remained open until 1930, employing some 300 men and producing over 30,000 tons of coal in most years. Several other collieries opened during the twentieth century, including Reynalton Colliery (1914–21), Broom Colliery (1934–9), and Loveston Colliery (1932–7). At Loveston there was a flood disaster in 1936 in which seven miners died. Until recently one could see the remains of Kilgetty Colliery at Stepaside, which worked from 1935 to 1939. With the closing of Broom and Kilgetty collieries at the beginning of World War II the long coal-mining traditions of the Saundersfoot area came to an end.

On the St Bride's Bay coast, where there were sandy beaches close to the coal-mining districts, it was difficult to build proper quays. Instead, the coal was always exported in small vessels which were beached on the sand at high tide, loaded amid hectic activity from horse-drawn carts at low tide, and then floated off again on the next tide. The safest loading beaches were at Nolton Haven and Little Haven, but Newgale, Druidston and Broad Haven were also used occasionally. The only real loading-quay seems to have been built at Nolton Haven. Here, at the northern corner of the beach, there is an embankment where the coal was stored and then either loaded direct on to beached vessels or on to horse-drawn carts. There are still signs of the old tramway running down past the Counting House, from which the coal exports were controlled. The Nolton and Newgale coalfield had six main collieries and many 'levels' and 'slants'. Some of the buildings of Trefrane Cliff Colliery remain, and there are also a few traces of Southwood Colliery. In addition, several levels can be seen in the Coal Measures in the cliffs between Nolton and Little Haven. The collieries were not successful enough to compete with those further east, and by 1900 only Trefrane Cliff Colliery had survived. Even this was closed in 1905, having originally exported coal via Haverfordwest and then via Nolton Haven after haulage in trolleys pulled by traction engines. There were plans to re-open the Nolton and Newgale coalfield after 1915, using a railway line to Milford to export the coal. But these plans came to nothing.

So ended the most important of Pembrokeshire's industrial adventures. After a long history of exploitation, this small coalfield was forced to end operations through a combination of environmental and locational factors. During the present century the physical problems of mine drainage and the working of shattered and discontinuous seams raised production costs, and it is a tribute to the quality of Pembrokeshire anthracite that mining was still deemed worthwhile until 1948. However, the locational disadvantages of the county had become increasingly apparent in the slow adoption of new mining techniques, the reluctance of colliery owners to invest in exploration and new workings, and the rising costs of bulk coal transport by sea and rail. After centuries of national renown prior to 1800, the coalfield suffered increasingly from competition, for its larger rivals were located much closer to the major markets. Perhaps, in the long run, this was no bad thing for the economy of Pembrokeshire.

QUARRYING

The varied geological character of Pembrokeshire has ensured a plentiful supply of a number of different types of stone for domestic use and export. For example, slate has been quarried for several centuries, particularly in the north of the county where the most suitable varieties are found. The local slates vary from silver-grey and black to blue, green and red. Slate was widely used for roofing purposes, but slate slabs were also used for flooring and house-building. In the later 1800s many loads of slate were exported from the 'blue lagoon' quarry at Abereiddi (Plate 7b) and from Parrog (Newport) in small sailing vessels. The best-known slate quarries were in Mynydd Presely. Rosebush Quarries had brief success, and slate was exported between 1876 and 1906 by rail, using the North Pembroke and Fishguard Railway. This extraordinary line, and the little settlement of Rosebush to which it gave birth, had an adventurous life which is worth recounting.

The railway started life as the Narberth Road and Maenclochog Railway which was constructed between 1872 and 1876 between Clynderwen and Rosebush to export slates from the Rosebush slate quarries. The line somehow attracted sufficient passenger traffic to Rosebush station in the wild Presely foothills to encourage six years of development. Artificial lakes were dug out and stocked with fish, a coach service to Fishguard was inaugurated, stables were built adjacent to Rosebush station, and extensions to the value of £30,000 were carried out in the quarry. The 'Precelly Hotel' was built to accommodate tourists (Plate 9b), and twenty-six cottages were built for quarry workers. Sir Hugh Owen provided signposts for the tourists and built a gymnasium for the nearby Maenclochog school. By 1880 the population of Rosebush had risen from four families living in squalid conditions to a total of 179. The slate quarry was thriving, but its good fortune did not last long.

After a series of financial escapades Rosebush was linked to Fishguard in 1899 by a line which enjoyed only a short period of prosperity. It was taken over by the GWR which determined, as part of its plans for the development of Fishguard Harbour, to run down the difficult (and badly constructed) line through the uplands and to concentrate instead upon a link from Clarbeston Road to Letterston junction. After 1906 all the boat trains used the new main line, and the north Pembrokeshire branch became just one more of the vast network of branch lines run by the GWR. The Rosebush slate quarries closed, and apart from intermittent passenger services the line was little used. The track was lifted in

1914 as part of the war effort, but re-laid again by 1923. Now the GWR itself attempted to attract tourist traffic to the Presely Hills, but no more than 50–100 passengers per week could be induced to use the line, and passenger services ceased in 1937. In 1949 the last goods train ran on the north Pembrokeshire branch, and in 1952 all the track was lifted.

Today Rosebush still retains an air of fascination. The little settlement, dominated by its abandoned quarries, still inhabited, and still served by the Precelly Hotel, is a fascinating relic of the county's industrial past. The row of quarrymen's cottages is still in excellent repair. Many of the homes have traditional cement-washed slate roofs, and some have colour-washed outside walls in pastel shades. At the end of the row is the substantial house once used by the quarry manager and adjacent to it is the post office and general store. Nearby is the site of the old railway station, and across the track is the solid memorial erected in honour of Edward Cropper, the Hon Mrs Owen and J. B. Macaulay, all of whom were involved in the establishment of the settlement. The old lily-ponds are still there, and the multitude of planted conifers, rhododendrons and other exotic shrubs gives a hint of what the place could have become if circumstances had not combined to plot its downfall.

Away from the village the sweep of the old railway line can still be followed, running through the coniferous plantations which are gradually covering the floor of the broad Rosebush depression. Further away still one can still trace the cuttings, embankments, stations and halts of the railway, for example at New Inn, Puncheston, Beulah and Letterston, and the course of the track is marked on the OS 1:50,000 map. But most impressive of all to the visitor with time on his hands are the slate quarries themselves. There are four main pits, in one of which there is a deep dark pool. The main pit is very beautiful, with its dark slate staircase of gigantic steps, each one up to thirty feet high. The galleries and the vertical rock faces are now becoming well covered with grasses, lichens, mosses, ferns and heather. Here and there fresh rock falls remind one that the pits are not yet quite dead. Black tunnel entrances show one where work was driven through behind the face. The main pit is like a hanging garden, and on its

126

floor is an inaccessible paradise of lush ferns, heather, bilberry, moss and rushes. Specks of cotton grass thrive on the water which trickles down from invisible springs. In July there are foxgloves, and plump bilberries ripe for the picking. The sounds in the air are of sheep and skylarks and distant barking dogs and the alien sounds of traffic on the main road below. Here and there are the remains of old quarry buildings, and below the pits the massive ugly spoil heaps of discarded slate slabs and chippings contrast starkly with the lushness of the new green plants. Rosebush may be an industrial relic, but it has its own peculiar beauty.

Rosebush was not by any means the county's only slate quarry, nor even its most important. There was another large slate quarry at Tyrch, whence came the slate for the County Hall in Carmarthen. The quarry at one time employed over 100 workers, and it was working until 1939. There were other slate quarries at Glogue, Cilgerran and Sealyham. Slate from the Gilfach quarry roofed part of the Palace of Westminster.

The best road stone in the county came from the hard igneous rocks which were quarried and then crushed down to various sizes. Typical quarries are those at Trefgarn, Penbiri, Middle Mill and Bolton Hill, and there are older quarries at Brawdy and Gignog.

Possibly the best-known of all the north Pembrokeshire quarries was at Porthgain. Here Porthgain Village Industries Ltd operated a thriving quarrying and brick-making industry between 1878 and 1914. Following the rebuilding of the harbour in 1902–4 (Plate 10b) the little port was a hive of activity, and in some years there were more than 100 shipments of stone to ports as far afield as south-east England. After World War I, however, high costs made it difficult to operate the company efficiently and it was forced to stop working at Porthgain in 1931. The stone quarries were on the cliffs to the west of Porthgain, and between them and the harbour one can still see several quarry buildings and the route of an old railway track. The stone was crushed and graded and then stored in hoppers on the west side of the harbour for loading direct into sailing ships and steam cargo vessels. The remains of these hoppers are still prominent features of the local landscape. Despite its air of dereliction Porthgain has its own peculiar charm, and it is certainly one of the most important of Pembrokeshire's industrial monuments. Thankfully, plans for the 'development' of Porthgain were met by strong local protests, and the harbour and quarry buildings are now protected by a preservation order.

Many other quarries in the county were worked for building stone. In the north the beautiful purple sandstones for St David's Cathedral were quarried from the cliffs above Caerfai Bay, and these quarries have recently been used again. There were many small quarries in the centre and north of the county where shale was extracted for building purposes. It was mixed with clay (and sometimes straw) to make 'clom', which was for centuries the cheapest building material available.

The hard grey and white limestones exposed in the south of the county have always been of great importance as building materials. The stone was also used, along with coal or culm, for conversion into lime. Most of the limestone was quarried from the outcrops on the coasts of south Pembrokeshire, and it was shipped in small coastal sailing vessels (or on barges within Milford Haven) to most of the small Pembrokeshire ports and further afield. Originally there were hundreds of limekilns around the Pembrokeshire coast, even in localities such as Caerbwdi and St Bride's. In 1908 there were still eight kilns in Solva, eleven in Haverfordwest, and seventeen in Tenby. The last 'draw kilns' still operated in Haverfordwest in 1930, and in Tenby as late as 1948. A few culm and limestone barges were still operating around Milford Haven at the onset of World War II. In most coastal localities ships dumped their cargoes of limestone on the beach, and horses and carts were used for transferring the stone to the nearby kilns. Cargoes were also dumped on the river bed at Haverfordwest.

While there is now an interest in preserving the best of the lime-kilns in the county (as at Solva and Tenby), little interest has been shown in the old quarries themselves. On the open coast there are old quarries at Flimston, Bosherston, Lydstep and on Caldey Island, where vessels were loaded directly from the quarry workings. But in the Daugleddau district more elaborate procedures became more necessary as the quarries were worked back from the shore, and at several localities (as at Garron Pill and just south of Haverfordwest) little docks were cut into the limestone so that barges could have access to the flooded quarry interiors at high tide, to be loaded and then floated out later. The quarries at Garron Pill were cut in about 1814, and the stone used for building the Pembroke Dockyard quays.

The most magnificent complex of all is at West Williamston, where there is a maze of old 'docks' and quarry workings, now largely overgrown. The site is well off the beaten track and is no tourist attraction, but like Rosebush and Porthgain it has its own peculiar atmosphere. Perhaps this derives from the very lushness of the vegetation, with smooth grassy banks where stone was once quarried, a wild tangle of blackberry around the old crushing and grading machinery, and reed beds, trees and bushes fighting to keep the tide away from the old docks.

METAL-WORKING

Another group of mineral resources in Pembrokeshire is made up of metallic ores. Not many people realise that such ores have been mined in the county on a small scale for many centuries. For example, copper ore may have been mined on the cliffs overlooking Ramsey Sound and on the south coast of the St David's peninsula from pre-Roman times, and traces of the old workings can still be seen. Copper was once mined near Dale, and manganese ore near Fishguard and at Ambleston. More recently several attempts were made to extract silver-lead ores, particularly during the later part of the Industrial Revolution. The most easily worked ore deposits were in the north-east of the county, and at Llanfyrnach there was a silver-lead mine which was at one time locally quite famous. At the time of its peak production, from 1880–5, it was producing more than a thousand tons of ore per year.

There was a fine example of an early metal-working industry near Llechryd, beside the River Teifi. Here, because of plentiful water and charcoal, the Coedmore forge was established, perhaps as early as the seventeenth century. The forge was a thriving concern in the early 1700s, depending on imported pig iron and limestone (carried up-river in horse-drawn and man-hauled barges) in addition to its own local resources. The plant, its watercourse, and its workers' cottages were all located on the north side of the River Teifi, but now few traces remain. The forge closed before 1750. It was followed by the Penygored Tinplate Works, opened in about 1765 and sited on the other side of the river near Castell Malgwyn. There was great investment in plant for the works and on a watercourse and several bridges. Two bridges—the Hammett Bridge and the Castell Malgwyn Bridge—and the remains of the watercourse and some works buildings can still be seen. As in the days of the Coedmore forge, materials were imported on horse-drawn barges by river from Cardigan, and at one time 300 men were employed at the works. But the enterprise was too remote to succeed, and in 1806 it was forced to close.

Most of the other metal-working industries in the county were small smithies and iron forges making tools, domestic and agricultural equipment, and wrought iron railings. There was probably a little forge at Blackpool Mill during the sixteenth century, but the main furnace and forge were built between 1620 and 1630. In its heyday it used limestone shipped up-river and local timber for charcoal. The Barlow family of Slebech sold much wood to the Carmarthen ironmasters who owned the forge. One of the industrial tokens of the Carmarthen Iron Works (Plate 8b) shows what the interior of the Blackpool forge must have looked like in about 1792. On the left is the furnace where the pig-iron was reheated before being worked, and the man is holding a piece of iron on the anvil where it is being subjected to blows from the massive water-powered hammer. Elsewhere in the county the foundries at Neyland and Woodside (Wiseman's Bridge) were well known. Perhaps the best-known of all was the Marychurch works at Haverfordwest which earned great renown for the quality of its agricultural machinery during the later 1800s. It earned even greater renown for the spectacular boiler explosion which brought its working life to an end in 1910. Other foundries, as at Milford and Pembroke Dockyard, specialised in castings for the local ship-building industry.

In the valley below the small village of Stepaside there was once an important iron-working industry. The ironworks was opened in 1849 by the Pembrokeshire Iron and Coal Company. Anthracite mined at Grove Colliery, on the hillside above, was used as fuel in the smelting process. Iron ore and limestone for the furnaces were also found locally. The remains of the colliery can still be seen, together with part of the railway track which connected it to the works. Near Coppet Hall the 'levels' of the old iron ore mines (now very unsafe) are still visible in the cliff face. Stepaside Iron Works itself is now in a ruinous state, but we can still see something of its architecture. The old casting shed is the most impressive building, and nearby are old workshops now becoming very dilapidated. At the foot of the hillside are the remains of two blast-furnaces. At the time of its greatest success, in the 1860s, the works also had an enormous blowing engine and a line of limekilns. Up-valley from the works is a fine Thomas Telford causeway with a road arch and a tramway arch. On the valley floor there are traces of an old canal and of the mineral railway lines used for importing raw materials and for exporting pig-iron. Most of the shipments used Saundersfoot Harbour, which was reached by an extension of the mineral railway through Wiseman's Bridge and Coppet Hall. In some years over 4,000 tons of pig-iron were exported, in addition to large quantities sold locally, but production ceased in 1877. After that date only the workshop was kept open to provide a service for the local coal industry.

OTHER WORKS AND FACTORIES

Another industrial activity which was widespread in the county was brick-making from local raw materials. There may have been about a dozen brick-works in the county. There was one at West Angle which used clay from a brick-pit immediately behind the beach. The bricks were originally made by Staffordshire workmen, and the works had its own small tramway. The red brick buildings still stand near the beach café, but the old brick-pit is now filled in. There was a brickworks at North Johnston until 1935 and others at Penally, Haverfordwest gasworks and Llanddewi Velfrey. Apart from the firebrick works at Wiseman's Bridge there were others linked with the coal industry. The brickworks at Templeton made silica firebricks between 1885 and 1924. After World War I the works employed thirty people, and many thousands of bricks were despatched by rail each week. The main buildings of the brickworks are now used as a council depot, but there are no traces of the four kilns. There are much better traces of the brick industry at Porthgain, where we can still see the shell of the brick-works and the brick-pit which was connected to the harbour by a tunnel. The Goodwick brick-works closed down only in 1969. It met much of the local demand for building bricks, using shale from a large open quarry behind the works. Now the buildings are demolished, and the site is occupied by a modern housing estate. Another interesting site is at Flimston, where, until about 1880, the old clay-pits produced 'pipeclay' for the making of silica bricks and earthenware.

Several other types of factories existed in various parts of the county. Many of the small mills (such as woollen mills and furze mills) were located in remote areas deep in the rural hinterlands of the main towns, for they depended on agricultural products and supplied agricultural communities with some of their needs. Furze mills were quite common, producing chopped gorse for animal feed. Little sawmills were widespread, often run by one man and using water-power to drive the saws. However, they declined as local timber resources became scarce and as imported timber became cheaper. Some of the towns had larger sawmills. The remains of one of these, together with the leat used to supply its water-power, can be seen in Haverfordwest below Crow Hill. The county town had a number of other water-powered industries along the river, including five paper-mills. The most important of these was built at Prendergast in 1766, originally as a cotton-mill. This substantial mill gave employment to 150 persons, and was reputed to be the largest industrial concern in the county at that time. A number of cottages were built in Prendergast to house the workers, many of whom were brought from Lancashire. By 1791 the mill had been converted to the manufacture of rough paper, and in the nineteenth century a water turbine was installed to supplement the power obtained from several water-wheels. Rags were collected from all over the county for use in the mill, and they were made into a coarse kind of packing paper similar to that formerly used in sugar bags. Eventually the import of cheap foreign paper killed the trade of the paper mill, and it was closed down and some of its machinery sold as scrap. Now, although the mill is in a ruinous state the leat, the remains of the vertical turbine, and some of the architectural features of the mill can still be discerned.

Another famous Haverfordwest industry was Llewellyn's Churnworks, which started life in about 1790 as a timber-importing business. The factory exported butter-churns of prize-winning design throughout the world in the 1800s and early 1900s. Many coastal villages had industries making barrels, nets and fish-boxes, and at Milford docks some of these crafts survived until quite recently. At Neyland and Milford docks there were ice factories. At Whalecombe, not far from Cosheston, a chemical factory produced naphtha for explosives, and other products for the linen industry. The factory, in a beautiful setting on the banks of the Daugleddau, is still in good repair.

From the brief summary of industrial activities in this chapter, there is ample evidence to show that Pembrokeshire experienced a miniature industrial revolution of its own. However, it was spared the worst effects of industrialisation because it was too remote from the major markets of England, and in any case its mineral resources were by no means abundant. Hence the gradual decline of the coal industry and other industrial activities was not accompanied by large-scale depression in the county, for industry had always been rural; colliery owners and other industrialists were often landed gentry who also maintained their agricultural interests. On the coalfield many of the miners worked part-time on their own smallholdings. Thus the era which transformed the face of the South Wales valleys and brought their exploited working populations close to revolution did relatively little to alter either the face of Pembrokeshire or the way of life of its people.

11   TOWN AND COUNTRY

MOST of the man-made features of the Pembrokeshire landscape have been created by groups of people with widely differing interests. In earlier chapters we have seen how our ancestors modified the face of the land to meet their own simple needs. We have seen how, later on, townsmen and countrymen and industrialists and farmers continued this process into the present century. The process of landscape change goes on, at an ever-increasing rate, as our technology allows us to achieve more and more in a shorter and shorter time.

The communities which are altering the landscape most effectively in Pembrokeshire today are those of the towns, for as the population of the county has grown (to 97,295 in the 1971 census) the towns have spread outwards, consuming areas of farmland and sending suburban tentacles along the main roads. At the same time the pattern of life on farms and villages has changed. Many people, especially in the Welshry, have left the land, and many of the old northern parishes now have ageing populations. As more and more people have become car owners so rural bus services have declined. Life is becoming ever more 'efficient', and in the district of Preseli there is now a policy to concentrate rural people in existing villages. Many farms will survive, of course, but many more will be forced to close, so allowing land to be farmed in larger units. The country cottage will survive, too, if it is there already. But the provision of services to small cottages is now an expensive luxury, and few new country cottages will appear.

In the countryside and in the villages cottages are being sold at an increasing rate to non-residents who keep them as holiday homes or as future retirement nests. This causes great local resentment, but there is no easy way to halt the trend. The seller wants the best possible price for his property, and more often than not the best possible price is paid by a 'foreigner'; young married couples have little chance of competing with the industrialist looking towards peaceful retirement in the country. Some hamlets and villages have evolved into summer settlements, busy during the summer season when cottage owners are in residence, and virtually dead during the winter. This problem is of course most severe in the national park.

Pembrokeshire life, whether lived in town or country, cannot try to remain aloof from change. Pembrokeshire has changed, with the rise of tourism, the coming of the oil industry to the shores of Milford Haven, and greater affluence on all sides. The community has to adjust itself to these changes, even though the adjustment is at times painful. The following paragraphs are an attempt to summarise some of the means by which present-day Pembrokeshire is trying to adjust itself to changing circumstances.

MODERN HAVERFORDWEST

The old county town of Haverfordwest has remained largely unaffected by the booms and depressions experienced by the Milford Haven towns during the past 150 years. The advantages of its central position in Pembrokeshire were already apparent in the Middle Ages, and George Owen was in no doubt about its status as one of the chief market towns of Wales during Elizabethan times. During the seventeenth century it became a great social centre for the landed gentry, many of whom built fine town houses in High Street and Hill Street. Later growth was linked with its administrative and service functions as county town, and there has been irregular expansion of the built-up area along all of the major radial roads. The arrival of the railway in 1854 produced a prompt decline of sea trading and a century of economic stagnation, but nevertheless the population almost doubled to a total of about 8,000. Today the town is still an important market centre with a 1971 population of 9,101 and a wide range of services. There is a large cheese factory at the satellite settlement of Merlin's Bridge, and a small trading estate. There are large areas of new housing for the families of men stationed at RAF Brawdy.

The prosperity of the town at the present day is of course helped by the industrialisation of Milford Haven. There were real fears that the reorganisation of local government and social services would lead to the removal of many of the town's administrative and service functions. Already several government offices have been removed to Carmarthen and elsewhere, but the local impact of these changes has been relatively slight.

A much more serious talking-point in the town is the impact of planned development, particularly in the town centre. The riverside area, potentially a most attractive shopping centre and amenity between the two bridges, has suffered from a variety of schemes. The building of a weir near the old quay, downstream of the New Bridge, has had wide consequences. It has upset migrating fish and indigenous fishermen. It has also created an attractive lake in the very heart of the town, but this resource has still not been properly used by the planners. On one side of the lake is the unattractive rear view of Bridge Street, the main shopping thoroughfare, and on the other side is a car-park in the shadow of a monstrous new white supermarket. For years there has been talk of a 'Riverside Development' including a new shopping-centre and many new amenities, but it has been held up by opposition from local tradespeople. Renewal of parts of the town goes on slowly, but sometimes it is difficult to feel any enthusiasm for the new buildings, roads and roundabouts which modern life has forced upon the fabric of the medieval town. The most comprehensive scheme of all for the future of Haverfordwest was a vastly expansive town plan, entitled 'Haverfordwest 2000' and produced in 1973 by the old County Planning Department of Pembrokeshire County Council. This contained all sorts of proposals for the future fabric and life of the town. The planners obtained little response from the townspeople until it was realised what a vast impact the proposed new 'circulatory system' would have on the town, with new dual carriageways and roundabouts, fly-overs, sliproads and new bridges appearing at the cost of several areas of old housing. Even worse, the planners planned to demolish Bethesda chapel, perhaps the most attractive of the town's nonconformist places of worship. This would indeed have been an unforgivable crime. So the plan is now in cold storage, consulted by visiting geography students as an interesting historical document.

ROAD AND RAIL

At the present day, the pattern of communications in Pembrokeshire is changing in some respects, but in its main outlines there is little new. For example, the surprisingly dense network of major and minor roads in the county goes back to Tudor and Stuart times at least, although the main trunk roads are of course the products of the last century or so. Also, if we look at a road map of the county we can see how Haverfordwest is clearly the central point, attracting roads from all directions. This again is an old-established feature. Another point which must be borne in mind is the influence of the Milford Haven waterway, effectively cutting the south of the county into two and explaining why road and rail services have had to be duplicated for places only a mile or so apart as the crow flies. But now the new Haven Bridge (Plate 15b) is beginning to affect the links between the towns and country districts of Pembrokeshire, and it is worth investigating these links in a little more detail.

The density of the road pattern is perhaps due to Pembrokeshire's remoteness and its 'peninsulated' coastal outline. Consequently, there was little ordinary through traffic as in the inland counties of England, and no development of main communicating roads. Life in the numerous small settlements was largely self-contained, each farm producing or obtaining by exchange from neighbouring farms or at one of the many local fairs all or nearly all the necessities of daily life. For commodities which could not be produced locally and for the export of surplus goods, water transport was generally available. Many of the little roads in the south of the county must have originated during the centuries of medieval settlement, but if we look at the OS map we can see that the road pattern of the Welshry is no less dense. The Welshry does, however, have a less organised system of tracks and small roads; this is because of the area's 'patterned dispersion' of small farms, with few townships or villages which have acted as growth points. Obvious exceptions are St David's, Mathry and

Croesgoch, and Puncheston and Little Newcastle in the east; in the latter two cases the lords of the manor may have been responsible for some at least of the local roads.

Pembrokeshire's maritime traditions have had a great effect upon roads, particularly near the northern and western coasts and in the innermost parts of Milford Haven. For example, the poor road links of such settlements as Trevine, Llanwnda, Nolton, Marloes and Llangwm show that these villages grew up as independent and isolated communities using the sea for contact with the outside world. No less than thirty-six small ports or hard beaches on the open coast and on the Milford Haven waterway have been used for coastal trading, each one acting as a local centre for traffic from the immediate vicinity.

Haverfordwest has always been the natural focus of an agricultural community. The passage of statesmen, diplomats, clerics and pilgrims to and from the city of St David's must have helped Haverfordwest to grow as a routeway town, but the tracks and roads converging upon Haverfordwest carried little except local traffic until the beginning of the nineteenth century when, as we have seen, the town became the most important western collecting centre on the principality's network of drovers' roads. Later on, the growth of Milford and Fishguard as ports led to the building of better through-roads to maintain contact with the outside world, and it was these roads (the trunk roads of the present day) which more than anything else helped Haverfordwest to become the main distribution centre for the county.

The original railway network of the county was made in the great railway era of the middle of the last century. The South Wales Railway reached Haverfordwest in 1854, and was extended to Neyland by 1856. South of the Haven the rail link from Whitland to Pembroke Dock, via Tenby, was completed in 1866. Milford was given its own rail link in 1863. In the north of the county the railways were built at a much slower pace. The earliest line was the Narberth Road and Maenclochog Railway which reached the Rosebush slate quarries in 1876. This line, then known as the North Pembroke and Fishguard Railway, was extended to Fishguard in 1899, but it was badly constructed and was destined to fail. This was hardly surprising, for it ran through

Plate 11 (above) A grey seal pup on one of the sealing beaches of Pencaer, near Strumble Head; *(below)* part of the Grassholm gannetry, showing the great density of birds using the nesting area

Plate 12 (above) Manorbier Castle, the home of Giraldus Cambrensis and probably the best preserved of all the Pembrokeshire castles; (below) the stately mansion of Orielton, set in its own parkland in south Pembrokeshire. This was one of the centres of social life for the gentry of the county during the eighteenth and nineteenth centuries

very difficult country in the Presely Hills, and it could not compete with the new line built from Clarbeston Road via Letterston to Fishguard Harbour in 1906. In that year there were four main rail termini in the county, and the railway network was quite substantial. It included the lines of the Saundersfoot Railway in the coal-mining district of the south-east, and the line transporting slate from Rosebush and other quarries in the hills below Mynydd Presely. Later on (1926) the Hook Colliery Railway was also added.

The last forty years have seen several changes in the rail network. Branch lines were run at the beginning of the last war from Letterston junction to the armaments depot at Trecwn, and also from Milford to the armaments depot at Newton Noyes. In 1965 the service to Letterston was discontinued, and we have seen how Neyland also lost its rail link and its depot and workshop. On the other hand new tracks have been laid in recent years from the Milford-Johnston line to the Esso Refinery at Hubberston and the Gulf Refinery at Waterston. A new spur has also been laid for the Amoco Refinery, near Hakin. The refinery traffic more than compensates for the decline in fish traffic on this line since the last war. Without a doubt the presence of four rail termini in the county in the 1950s led to unnecessary duplication at a time when freely available road transport was already a fact of life. The present rail service, much reduced, is based upon the two main termini at Milford and Fishguard, which supply enough freight traffic to justify their existence; but the future of the Pembroke Dock branch is still very much in doubt, particularly since the opening of the new Milford Haven bridge has brought the Pembroke area into the communications network centred upon Haverfordwest.

The long, branching waterway of Milford Haven and the Daugleddau has always presented a social and economic barrier between the south and south-east of the county and that part centred on Haverfordwest. The road link from Pembroke to Haverfordwest via Canaston Bridge is over twenty miles long. Although the Burton–Pembroke ferry and the Picton ferry once shortened this journey considerably, both have been closed now for many years. The same is true of the other ferries which served

I

the various waterside communities. Examples were the Cosheston–Lawrenny ferry, the Landshipping–Llangwm ferry, and the Lawrenny–Picton Point ferry. The only ferry service operating at the beginning of 1975 was the vehicle ferry with a daily schedule of about thirty crossings each way between the precarious Hobbs Point slipway and the pontoon jetty at Neyland. It was a vital part of the county's road network, but it was no adequate alternative to a road or rail bridge between the north and south shores of the Haven.

There have been innumerable plans for such a crossing. In 1921 Sir Frederick Meyrick put forward an ambitious scheme for a barrage from Hobbs Point to Neyland, to be crossed by road and railway and to be equipped with turbine generators and locks to allow shipping to pass upstream to Haverfordwest. In 1945 the county council commissioned a report which suggested a high-level suspension bridge across the Haven between Pembroke Ferry and Barnlake, with a supplementary bridge crossing of Westfield Pill. This, like several other schemes, came to nothing, and it was eventually decided to improve the Neyland–Hobbs Point service with a new ferry boat.

In 1956 the Esso Petroleum Company was examining the possibility of a refinery on Milford Haven, but it required assurance of a water supply of 5 million gallons per day (mgd) by 1970. This led to renewed discussion of a barrage scheme, and the local authorities enthusiastically supported a firm proposal. Investigations were completed at five alternative sites and a private bill was introduced in the 1958–9 parliamentary session for a rubble masonry dam across the Daugleddau from Jenkins Point to Williamston Mountain to carry a road, double-track railway, and footpaths. The potential water yield was calculated at 56mgd, and the cost £2½ million. The advantages of the scheme were many, but amid great local disappointment a Commons Select Committee turned down the proposal, on the published grounds that the barrage would provide an amount of water far in excess of demand. The real reason for the decision may have been that a nuclear power-station was at that time being considered for Carew Cheriton, not far away from the proposed barrage site. Since 1959 the great developments on the shores of the Haven have shown just how short-sighted the government decision really was. The Pembrokeshire Water Board had to construct a pumping station on the Eastern Cleddau to meet the rising demand for industrial water, and was further involved in a £5 million reservoir scheme at Llysyfran (Plate 16a) for the provision of up to 19mgd to meet forseeable demand. In addition, the government has had to accept the need for a road link between the two shores of the Haven.

Work on the Milford Haven High Level Bridge started in 1968, largely as an act of faith by Pembrokeshire County Council. The estimated cost was £3 million, and the bridge was to be a box girder structure more or less on the site originally proposed in 1945. Work proceeded well at first. However, after the disastrous collapse of a section of the bridge in June 1970 and the Government investigation of box girder structures, the project was much delayed, and the Milford Haven High Level Bridge did not open to traffic until 1975. By this time the cost had quadrupled, to almost £12 million, and the local authority had no option but to impose toll charges higher than those of any other major road bridge in the British Isles. Little wonder that the people of Pembrokeshire, when faced with this long saga of indecision, expense and misadventure, are somewhat cynical about national planning decisions.

The various roadworks connected with the bridge are bound to make a great impact upon communications in the county. Already the roads on the north shore of the Haven are much improved, and the trunk road between Haverfordwest and Milford has been reconstructed to dual carriageway standard in places. There have been other improvements on the A40 trunk road between Whitland and Haverfordwest, and between the old county town and Fishguard. These have been necessary because of increased tourist and commercial traffic, and because of the great volume of heavy traffic carrying loads to the Milford Haven refinery sites. Around the refineries themselves access roads have also been widened and straightened. Now that the new southern by-pass of Haverfordwest is completed, through traffic to Milford, Neyland and the Esso, Amoco and Gulf refineries will no longer need to pass through the town's shopping centre, much to the relief of local people. But an eastern by-pass is still needed, to keep the increasing volume of heavy container traffic out of the town on its way to and from the Fishguard harbour Irish freight depot. Most important of all, perhaps, is the fact that local people can now travel more quickly between the north and south shores of the Haven than ever before.

FARMING TODAY

Agriculture is still the most important industry in Pembroke-shire in terms of employment and general economic importance. The 'standard output' of farming in the county is near £20 million per year and about 15 per cent of the total agricultural output of Wales. In 1973 there were about 3,000 farmers in the county working some 3,300 holdings. In addition there were 1,840 full-time employees on farms, and altogether no less than 3,840 persons find employment on farms either on a regular, part-time or seasonal basis. This figure is much lower than the figures of around 6,000 recorded for the late 1940s, but we should not forget that many other people are employed in activities connected with agriculture—for example in sales and deliveries of fertilisers and foodstuffs, milk collection, dairy work, and land drainage. Together with farmers' and workers' wives and families, the total work-force dependent upon agriculture in Pembrokeshire must be about 20,000.

The success of farming depends upon many different factors. Weather and climate are perhaps of the greatest importance, and it is not surprising that farmers become preoccupied with sunshine and cloud, wind and rain, frost and snow. On the whole the local climate is favourable to agriculture. Its main characteristics are its equable and maritime nature; its mild winters and its cool, changeable summers; its abundant and well-distributed rainfall; and its exposure, particularly to winds from the south-west. At St Ann's Head the minimum temperatures fall below freezing point only on three or four exceptional nights during winter, and for ten months of the year the average monthly temperature is above 5·6°C; this means that ordinary crops and grasses can continue to grow throughout most of the year, and that livestock can generally be kept in the open even during the winter months. Professor Emrys Bowen has pointed out that many hedgerow plants are in flower in Pembrokeshire by 27 April in most years, as early as the Scilly Isles and the south coasts of Devon and Cornwall. On the coast annual rainfall totals may be no more than thirty-five inches, and sunshine totals 1,700 hours; however, rainfall increases sharply inland, and the average annual rainfall for Mynydd Presely is more than sixty inches. Thus the climate gradually becomes less favourable as one moves from west to east across the county. Perhaps the biggest problem of all is the wind. Trees carved by the westerly gales into grotesque distorted forms are very much a part of the Pembrokeshire scene, and the outer coasts are bleak and occasionally treeless not just because of the wind but also because of the effects of salt spray. This spray kills natural vegetation and it can kill crops, and a stormy spring and summer can present a real danger to the livelihoods of farmers whose fields line the clifftops. In most years more than thirty gales are recorded at the coast, and in a stormy winter (such as 1974–5) gale-force gusts may be recorded on average every other day.

Another important factor in Pembrokeshire farming is the nature of the soil. Sometimes the nature of the soil is determined largely by the character of deposits left during the Ice Age; till and fluvio-glacial sands and gravels are particularly common in the northern part of the county and around the shores of St Bride's Bay. Where sands and gravels or sandy till occur they give the soil a stony, open texture and high fertility; such soils in Dewisland were believed to retain heat, and were much valued for cereal production. On the other hand soils which occur on sticky clay till are generally thin and rather acid as a result of heavy leaching, and fertility is much reduced in the moorland commons around St David's and also in the Fishguard–Dinas area where pockets of Irish Sea till are found. Other types of soils which are not particularly closely related to bedrock geology are the lowlands peats and the alluvial and sand-dune soils in some river valleys and coastal embayments respectively. In the uplands (above 400ft) 'gley soils' are much more common, with wide expanses of hill peats in the higher areas and many occurrences of 'mountain soils'. Some of these soils occur very close to sea-level in Pembrokeshire as a result of the county's oceanic location, its exposure and its heavy rainfall.

Most often the soils of the county can be related quite closely to the underlying bedrock type. Over much of the north of the county the rocks of the Lower Palaeozoic outcrops have produced medium to heavy silty loams of brown or greyish-brown colour containing many shale or 'rab' fragments. In the south of the county the best soils are encountered on the outcrops of Carboniferous Limestone and Old Red Sandstone; soils which have formed on the former are fine deep ferruginous loams, and on the latter deep red loams with much sand and silt. Both soils are among the most fertile in Wales. The Coal Measures and Millstone Grit outcrops in the centre of the county give rise to thin, shaly, grey-brown soils of low or moderate fertility.

As a result of all the various combinations of relief, climate and soils, a wide variety of environmental conditions faces the Pembrokeshire farmer at the present day. Naturally enough, the potential of the land varies greatly from place to place, and the pattern of farming is made even more complicated, when we look at it in detail, because of local farming expertise, or local traditions, or local shortages of capital. The environment is suited above all to various types of grassland, or a poorer type with rushes in the north and with ryegrass in the centre and south of the county. In the uplands the environment favours heather moorland and fell, with some areas of special mountain grassland. There are several distinct farming regions in the county, each specialising in slightly different combinations of farming activities.

Around the eastern, northern and western margins of the Presely Hills there is mixed farming with the rearing of cattle and sheep alongside arable agriculture. Farms are generally of medium or small size. To the east of the uplands dairying is rather more important, while barley is grown in greater abundance on the St David's peninsula. Oats and mixed corn are widely grown throughout the region as animal feedstuffs.

In the south-west of the county, bounded by a line running approximately from Newgale via Trefgarn to Saundersfoot, arable farming is an essential part of the way of life, with stock raising or dairying to a lesser degree. Here the greatest effects of the oceanic warming of climate are felt, for the Milford Haven–Daugleddau waterway allows sea water to penetrate far inland. In addition, this area has a lot of fertile land, so that cereals (particularly barley), and potatoes and other root vegetables are popular among farmers.

The eastern dairying region, occupying an arc of land from the southern foothills of Mynydd Presely as far west as Haverfordwest and thence eastwards along the lowland towards Whitland, experiences rainfall totals in excess of 50in. Consequently, there is a true pastoral way of life, in which dairy herds are more common than stock herds and where mixed corn is the major cereal crop.

Up in the mountains, including the detached moorlands of Mynydd Carningli, Mynydd Cilciffeth and Mynydd Castlebythe, sheep rearing is the main occupation, although cattle are often kept on the lower slopes. Where cultivation is possible, grass crops, oats and mixed corn are again most important.

If we examine some of the trends in Pembrokeshire farming since the last war we see that oats has become less popular as a crop while barley has increased its acreage. Mixed corn, after more than twenty years of unpopularity among farmers, is now more widely grown than it was in 1947 partly because of the availability of new, hardy and productive strains and partly because of subsidy payments. Trends in dairy farming show that while the number of milk producers has fallen since 1947 the dairy herd of the county has risen to more than 70,000 animals and milk sales to a record level of almost 50 million gallons a year. These figures show that Pembrokeshire farming has become much more efficient over the last thirty years, but it has not become much more specialised. Farming in the county remains variable in character, with the greatest part of the arable acreage each year devoted to grass crops of various types. There are still about 71,000 sheep in the county, and pig farming is locally important, although it must be remembered in the case of livestock that, as with arable farming, government subsidies and EEC policies can have a great influence. The serious fall in cattle prices during the winter of 1974–5 showed what a drastic effect a market slump can have on livestock producers, for it resulted in much hardship.

The major specialised crop in Pembrokeshire is early potatoes. Before 1937 early potatoes were not grown on a large scale in the county, but after experimental planting had proved successful around the Pembrokeshire coast, over 4,000 acres were devoted to early potatoes in 1944. Since 1947 acreages have been maintained at a level of approximately 7,000 acres per annum, according to demand and price fluctuations. Peak production was in 1963, when there were 8,954 acres of early potatoes, as against 1,549 acres of maincrop potatoes. The early crop is still much the more important when measured in terms of acreage. Nevertheless, increasing specialisation is evident on the coastal farms; out of the 780 growers participating in the early potato trade in 1962, only 370 remained in 1971. And in 1974 the rising cost of early potato production had forced even more growers to concentrate on less risky ventures. In that year the early potato acreage was down to 5,326 acres.

Early potato growing and marketing follows a set pattern. Planting begins on some farms in January, and goes on elsewhere until March. Given a good spring, the crop is well advanced by early May. Lifting is generally started at about the beginning of June, although in an exceptional year (such as 1971) it may be as early as 24 May. Casual labour is employed, with teams of 'spud bashers' moving from farm to farm. During the lifting season (which usually lasts for about six weeks) merchants from many parts of Britain visit Pembrokeshire and negotiate purchases individually with growers. Some growers consistently sell to the same merchants while others deal on a day-to-day basis. Growers may start lifting at a yield of only 3½ tons per acre, for the price at this time will be between £110 and £120 per ton. After a fortnight the price per ton is more than halved, and it falls to an average of £35 on the thirtieth day. On the other hand yields may be as high as 15 tons per acre at the end of the lifting season and growers acquire great skill in planning their lifting programme each year in order to obtain the maximum benefit. In particular, they have to try and assess the market impact of early potato imports from abroad. Nowadays the greater part of the early potato crop is exported by road, and the potato lorries are a common sight on the A40 trunk road during early June. Most of these lorries are destined for the South Wales and Midlands markets, although some travel as far afield as Lincolnshire, Lancashire and Yorkshire.

Other cash crops are not of great importance at the present day, although wartime production of flax rose to a level of 3,172 acres in 1944, and there were 1,684 acres of sugar beet in 1942. Although there was talk of a specialised sugar beet industry in the post-war years, this came to nothing because the nearest beet-processing factory was at Shrewsbury. Similarly, market gardening and flower growing have never become popular, even though the coastal environment is as favourable as that of Cornwall or the Scilly Isles. Currently a number of enterprising farmers are entering the flower-selling and bulb-growing business, for they find that the disease-free Pembrokeshire bulb fields have a marked advantage over the traditional bulb-growing areas such as Lincolnshire. One grower is entering the export market with considerable success, and he is also using the freezing plant and large refrigerators at one of the turkey farms to store cut daffodils and other flowers for winter and early spring sale in London and elsewhere just at the time of year when flowers from elsewhere are very scarce. There is considerable potential for this type of activity, for farm plant and buildings can be used during part of the year for turkey breeding and during the rest of the year for potato, bulb and cut flower storage and even cattle fattening. Turkey breeding is less popular in Pembrokeshire than it used to be but, nevertheless, about 30,000 birds are reared each year on large turkey farms for the Christmas market. Pig farming fluctuates greatly in popularity according to market conditions, and the pig population is usually around the 20,000 mark. Cauliflower and broccoli growing is becoming more and more popular, and in 1974 over 150,000 crates of cauliflowers were sent to the main vegetable markets. At present there are about thirty growers in the county, but more farmers are being attracted into early vegetables as a sideline, and the current area planted with cauliflowers is about 700 acres.

MILITARY ESTABLISHMENTS

Military establishments of one sort or another have been very much a part of the Pembrokeshire scene ever since the prehistoric period. The promontory and hill forts of the Iron Age were followed by motte and bailey castles and then by the mighty stone fortresses of the Normans. Later there came the forts planted on the shores of Milford Haven during the Napoleonic era, and garrisons such as the Defensible Barracks (1843) and then the Llanion Barracks in Pembroke Dock. Then there were the other structures dating particularly from World War II—airfields, gun emplacements, concrete coastal defences and radar stations. Many of these still remain as derelict and dangerous ruins, particularly along the coastline where they spoil the beauty of several sections of the coastal footpath. There were no less than twelve military airfields in the county; many of the buildings have been removed from these sites now, but the runways remain as crumbling expanses of concrete and tarmac, used only by farm vehicles and increasingly colonised by encroaching weeds.

The Army, the Air Force and the Navy are still present in force. Their establishments and their activities arouse strong feelings, particularly because they make a great impact upon the peace and quiet (not to mention the freedom of access) of several sections of the national park. But they provide employment and bring a great deal of money to the main towns, and Pembrokeshire people would be loth to lose them. The Ministry of Defence currently holds over 6,500 acres (about 5 per cent) of the national park, 24 per cent of the Pembrokeshire 'heritage coast', and eleven miles of the long-distance coastal footpath. At Castlemartin, in the south Pembrokeshire section of the national park, the Ministry of Defence tank range occupies some 5,880 acres of what used to be good farm land. In the middle of it stands the ghost settlement of Flimston, with only its chapel maintained in a good state of repair. The firing range, criss-crossed by tank tracks and in places littered with great piles of scrap metal, prevents summer access to what is probably the most magnificent stretch of limestone coast in the whole of Britain, and firing shatters the peace of much of south Pembrokeshire. On the other hand the range provides grazing for some 12,000 livestock (mostly sheep) from the Presely Hills during the winter months. In the north-east corner of St Bride's Bay, on the fringe of the national park, Brawdy is now the home of the RAF Tactical Weapons Training Unit, and also houses a US oceanographic survey base. At least 1,500 servicemen and other personnel are employed at Brawdy, and about 350 service families are housed in Haverfordwest. Just as the traders of Pembroke and Pembroke Dock benefit from the custom of NATO personnel from Castle-martin, so the tradespeople of Haverfordwest and Fishguard value the business generated by RAF Brawdy and its service families. At present one helicopter flight and three squadrons of Hawker Hunter jets are based at Brawdy. With a great deal of low flying over the St David's peninsula, the surrounding area is now much less peaceful than it was. Villages such as Llandeloy suffer a great deal of noise as a result of jets landing and taking off directly over them, and after complaints from residents sound-proofing of many homes has been undertaken at government expense.

Since the last war the number of Ministry of Defence establish-ments in the county has been greatly reduced, but some remain as valuable employers. Most of the wartime airfields and other bases were closed soon after the war, but HMS *Harrier* at Kete remained open until 1960, and the AA gunnery school at Manor-bier closed just a few years ago, releasing most of its 276 acres on a valuable coastal site in the national park for possible holi-day development. Of greater importance for the community is the release for local use of ninety-eight ex-ministry houses nearby. The most important of the remaining military sites are at New-ton Noyes, just east of Milford, and at Trecwn, in the deep Nant-y-bugail valley in the western foothills of the Presely Hills. Both of these are Admiralty depots concerned with the manufacture and storage of armaments, and between them they provide em-ployment for more than 1,300 local people. With the cut-back in defence expenditure during the mid-1970s there were, how-ever, real fears that the Newton Noyes and Trecwn establish-ments, like the small naval base at Pembroke Dock, would be closed as economy measures.

12

THE ENGLISH, THE WELSH AND THE LANDSKER

EVERYONE in Pembrokeshire knows that the county is divided into two regions of approximately equal size. Those regions are, according to Professor Emrys Bowen, 'sharply distinct from one another in language, race type, place-names, traditions, ecclesiastical architecture and general culture'. In the south is the Englishry, created by the Normans and still referred to as 'Little England beyond Wales'. In the north is the Welshry, a region which has evolved over many centuries of Welsh settlement as a stronghold of Welshness. And between these two halves runs a vaguely defined frontier known, in recent times at least, as the Landsker. The Englishry, the Welshry and the Landsker have been referred to earlier, particularly in Chapter 5, but it is of interest to examine the regions and their people in a little more detail, for Pembrokeshire's split personality is something which intrigues natives and tourists alike.

THE ENGLISHRY

The south of the county is, for many people, a land of castles and small nucleated villages, of small green fields and high wooded hedgerows, of winding, sunken, flower-fringed lanes, of English place-names and English speech. Some of the features of the landscape and culture of the area have already been explained in Chapter 5, where it was noted that towns, village distributions and individual village layouts, field patterns and many other features can be directly attributed to the Norman genius for organisation. This organisation of a new type of society created a new type of landscape.

By trying to map some of the features of this landscape one can appreciate just how fundamentally the Englishry differs from the Welshry. Margaret F. Davies has shown quite impressively, for example, how place-names and church types can be mapped in order to emphasise the character of the Englishry and to show its approximate northern border. The place-name evidence is difficult to interpret because there is so much doubt about what the earliest forms of present village names really were; but church types are easier to define. Margaret Davies recognised an 'Anglo-Norman' church type as characteristic of the Englishry. This type has a high, battlemented tower which is often quite out of proportion with the rest of the church. In many villages the church served not only as a place of worship but also as a place of sanctuary in case of attack by Welsh raiding parties; the tower would have been used often as a watch-tower and perhaps as a beacon, even as late as the Civil War. Architecturally there need not be anything particularly 'Anglo-Norman' about these churches, but they are quite different from their simple counterparts in the Welshry (Plate 6b) because they were built to serve prosperous village communities. In addition, the various medieval manorial lords looked upon church building as a means of demonstrating their prestige. There was no such tradition in the Welshry, and the churches there were built for the most part by dispersed farming communities which had few resources available for the construction of lavish places of worship.

Language is now, as in George Owen's day, the most obvious measure of the Englishness of south Pembrokeshire. Pembrokeshire English has evolved over a long period of time in an isolated enclave, cut off from direct contact with England by the Welsh-speaking areas of Cardiganshire to the north-east and Carmarthenshire to the south-east. Nowadays, of course, a standardised English prevails, but until quite recently south Pembrokeshire people spoke a strong regional dialect which included a great number of words not used in the other English-speaking parts of Wales. Some of these words are still in use today, and the regional accent is, thankfully, still strong enough to allow a south Pembrokeshire man to reveal his origins whenever he opens his mouth.

153

In his *Guide to the Place Names and Dialects of Pembrokeshire*, Valentine Harris argues that many of the words of the Pembrokeshire dialect are pre-Chaucerian, and that they are related to the vocabulary of the Danelaw in eastern England. Many more words have resemblances with words used in the Welsh Borders and the West Country, while others appear to have come from County Wexford. Again, there is a strong Flemish element, as suggested by Douglas James in his list of words and phrases used in old Haverfordwest. In contrast, relatively few words of Welsh origin have infiltrated into south Pembrokeshire, although Welsh influence is felt in intonation and in the construction of sentences. Typical is the Pembrokeshire habit of using 'trousers' and 'scissors' in the singular instead of the plural.

Some of the old south Pembrokeshire words still in use are as follows:

aclush—all in pieces	moory hen—a water hen
beauty—beautiful (as an adjective)	now just—a moment ago
caffled—entangled	to pile—to throw
to clanch—to beat or thrash	pill—a pool or creek
couple—a few, several	rab—broken stone or shale
drang—a narrow passage	siggy-wiggy—a blue tit
dull—foolish, silly	to take—to bring
lake—a brook or stream	tamping—exceedingly angry
to lam—to beat or thrash	tidy—good, first-rate
maid—a young girl	trash—cuttings from a hedge
	tump—a small haycock

The old towns of the Englishry, because they grew as self-contained communities over the past few centuries, developed strong corporate personalities. Douglas James considers that this may have been due to the overall lack of emigration or immigration, so that the histories of most families were common knowledge. There was 'an intimate knowledge of the diverse idiosyncracies of most of the townfolk, and hence the application of many a nickname'. Some nicknames were handed down through three or four generations. The nicknames of Haverfordwest at the turn of the century were no less magnificent than those collected by Trevor Fishlock from South Wales and recorded for posterity in his book *Wales and the Welsh*. In Douglas James's list of old

Haverfordwest nicknames are the following, most of which are self-explanatory:

Davy Seven Waistcoats	Hairy Mary
The Missing Link	Quick Dick
Satan	Unconscious
Drips	Marvel
Beattie Blackdrawers	Georgie Fourpence
Billie Flappers	Davy Daft
Butter Jaws	Cold Feet
Georgie Lovely	Quarter of Lamb
Klondyke	Hell Cat
Life and Death	Johnnie Wee Wee
Vest and Drawers	Tootsie
Full Moon	Cold Pudding
Billie Lumpy	Hamlet's Ghost

Concerning the physical and other characteristics of the people of south Pembrokeshire, it is difficult and perhaps dangerous to generalise. Much has been made of the fact that south Pembrokeshire people have blood-group characteristics which are rather different from those of north Pembrokeshire folk. The high frequency of blood-group A in the Englishry is probably due to the import of Scandinavian blood via Normandy, and certainly there do seem to be more tall, fair-haired people of Nordic type in the south than in the north. But south Pembrokeshire people are very mixed racially, for the present population is the result of intermarriage taking place between Normans, English, Welsh, Flemings, Irish and many other groups over the last thousand years. Typical family names of south Pembrokeshire are Philpin, Reynish, Gambold, Bateman, Gibby, Warlow and Skyrme; but there are many typically Welsh surnames as well. It should not be forgotten that the original Welsh population of Little England was never entirely replaced by immigrants. Very many Welsh surnames have survived, and parts of the Englishry appear never to have been settled with foreigners. One such area was the Amroth–Narberth–Canaston Bridge area, which at the beginning of the fourteenth century was still largely populated by Welsh people. Elsewhere, too, as we have seen in Chapter 5, the church lands around Llawhaden and Lamphey retained many

Welsh inhabitants, although by the Middle Ages these populations were speaking English rather than Welsh.

Comparing the people of south Pembrokeshire with the Welsh, R. M. Lockley described them as 'undoubtedly more open-hearted, smiling, easy-going, even indolent. They like music but sing badly. They talk excessively . . . They drink much, are amiable when drunk. They are fond of children and animals. Illegitimate children are numerous and not regarded with disfavour.' Others have described the people as conservative in politics, orthodox in religion (meaning that they prefer not to go to church at all), unemotional, adaptable, resentful of outside interference, and hyper-sensitive of criticism. But however they can be described, south Pembrokeshire folk cannot be described as English; they are proud of their Welshness, and they will tell you that they are as fanatical in their support of the Welsh rugby XV as the people of the Welshry. But they will insist that their Welshness is different from that of other Welshmen . . .

THE WELSHRY

The Welshry of the guide-books is a land of Celtic mystery, of wide, windswept vistas of rocks and moors and stunted trees. Its people live on farms or in small hamlets which sometimes nestle in deep wooded valleys. As noted earlier, simple churches predominate; often these are not in villages at all, but stand in isolation on the sites of old monastic cells. Similarly, many of the nonconformist chapels dating from the religious revivals were built in remote sites, as if their builders were determined to continue the lonely traditions of the ascetic Welsh saints. There are few castles. Farms are smaller than in the south, and more widely dispersed. In some areas the field pattern has remained unchanged since the days of Celtic tribal society, and often field boundaries are stone walls or low treeless hedges. As shown in Map 3, place-names are for the most part Welsh. Using landscape features alone, it is still possible for the practised eye to distinguish between Welshry and Englishry.

To some extent the Welshness of north Pembrokeshire has declined, particularly during the present century as agricultural

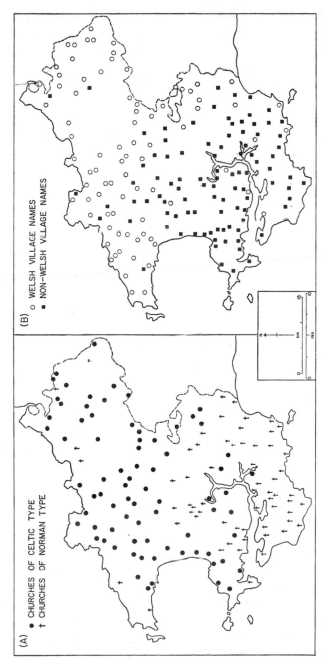

Map 3 Maps showing how church types (A) and village names (B) can be used to distinguish between the Englishry and the Welshry

practices, systems of land-holding and the overall way of life have all evolved towards the English model. But the Welsh language is still strong, and many features of Welsh life retain their importance. Menna Gallie, in an amusing and perceptive study of *Little England's Other Half*, writes 'Perhaps it is because they still feel themselves to be a last, threatened remnant of Celtic culture in Pembrokeshire that the [people of the] Welshry sometimes seem aggressively Welsh, as if still motivated by some ancient challenge, some urge to defiance.'

Pembrokeshire Welsh, like Pembrokeshire English, has developed somewhat differently from the mother tongue. Dr B. G. Charles has studied the local dialect, and he has traced its evolution along its own peculiar lines in vocabulary and pronunciation. Today it is a dialect apart and often far removed from standard or literary Welsh. There is also a considerable English element in its vocabulary. He believes that English words have been finding their way into the language for many centuries—probably an inevitable consequence of a long period of intercommunication between the two halves of the county. Many of the English words in the Pembrokeshire Welsh dialect have become almost unrecognisable, for their original spellings and pronunciations have been adapted to Welsh and have evolved along with the rest of the language. Menna Gallie says that Pembrokeshire Welsh has 'its own macabre beauty', and it has been the medium of many works of prose and poetry. North Pembrokeshire still produces far more literary men to the acre than south Pembrokeshire does to the square mile, and among the well-known poets born here are T. E. Nicholas, Dewi Emrys, J. Brynach Davies, James Nicholas and Edgar Phillips, otherwise known as the Archdruid Trefin.

Concerning the personality of the Welsh people of north Pembrokeshire, opinions vary. Writing in 1957, R. M. Lockley compared them with south Pembrokeshire people as 'more cautious, introspective (not to say inhibited), dour and reserved . . . They have outwardly a stricter religious code, attend principally chapels, and do no work on Sundays. They drink less intoxicating liquor. They are better singers. They live simply and efficiently on land where an Englishman might starve.' Others refer to their nationalist politics, their rich folk-lore, their open and generous hospitality, their love of food and drink. In outward appearance, it has been said that they are mostly dark-haired, stocky folk having much closer racial affinities with the Celtic people of north and central Wales than with their neighbours in Little England.

Surnames in the Welshry are as familiar as they are limited in number. Rees (Rhys) and Evans (Ifan) are of real Welsh origin, while surnames such as Thomas, Jones, Williams and Morris are alien Christian names which became Welsh surnames only in modern times. In those areas colonised by the Normans surnames such as Martell, Miles and Reynish belong to families which are now thoroughly Welsh; and there are a number of old English surnames, too. But generally the Welsh-speaking community has had to put up with its scarcity of surnames in the usual manner, by providing extra specifications. Hence:

Jones the loaf	Jones Great Western
Jones the Kremlin	Jones pop-bottle
Jones that won the war	Jones King's Arms

and many more appreciated only by those blessed with the gift of the Welsh language. Even more common are family names embellished by the names of places of abode, as in Emlyn Pontiago, Morse Good Hope, and Richards Llanwnwr.

THE LANDSKER TODAY

In earlier chapters there were descriptions of the changing course of the Landsker from medieval to Elizabethan times. Since George Owen, with perhaps a touch of poetic licence, described the Elizabethan Landsker so vividly, it has undoubtedly ceased to be a strong racial and cultural divide. But the Landsker has continued to separate two distinct communities. In 1888 Edward Laws wrote that there was still little intercourse between the Welsh and the English. He considered that the boundary between the two racial groups was rather stable, but stated '. . . the racial line is not now-a-days quite so hard as it was in times past'.

Within the present century it has been assumed that the ancient line of linguistic demarcation has become blurred to the extent that it can no longer be recognised. Certainly English-biased education has made more and more impact upon the Welshry, and from an examination of the Welsh language data in the Census Reports we can see how rapid the decline of Welsh has been. It is possible to compare the information for four census years—1931, 1951, 1961 and 1971. Some of this information is summarised on Fig 5. The percentages refer to individual parishes.

1931   The greater part of the Welshry contained over 80 per cent of the Welsh speakers. The Englishry contained less than 10 per cent of Welsh speakers, and across the centre of the county there was a narrow belt (one or two parishes deep) where 10–60 per cent of the people could speak Welsh.

1951   The Englishry was still solidly English-speaking, but in the Welshry the number of Welsh speakers was declining rapidly. Much of the St David's peninsula and the area between Trefgarn and Goodwick now contained less than 80 per cent of Welsh speakers, and the 'Landsker Zone' with lower percentages of Welsh speakers was becoming broader.

1961   The area with less than 10 per cent Welsh speakers was growing, and there was a marked reduction of Welsh speakers in the Landsker zone. Whereas in 1951 the upland area was solidly Welsh, now the Welsh-speaking 'core' had broken down into separate groups of parishes, showing that the decline of the language was accelerating.

1971   Broadly a similar pattern to 1961, but with the status of Welsh still declining in the western part of the Welshry and especially in the Landsker zone.

From evidence such as this it is not surprising that many historians have argued that there has been no sharp division between Welshry and Englishry for many years. The language maps simply seem to show a slow gradation in a broad belt across the centre of the county between the solidly English south and the Welsh-speaking core of the north. In recent years some

160

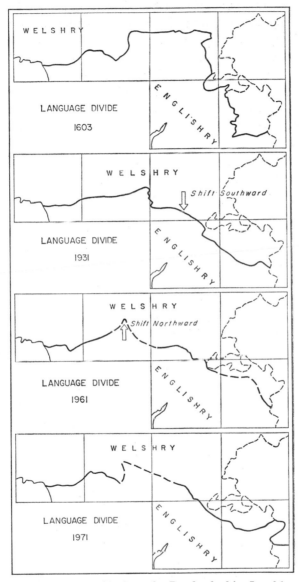

Fig 5 Maps showing how the Pembrokeshire Landsker has changed position over the years. Compare this with the Map on p 182

writers, intent upon proving that Welsh influence has always been strong in the Englishry just as English influence has affected the Welshry, have suggested that there is now no strong racial or linguistic line across the county. Major Francis Jones has even regretted the use of the term 'Landsker', implying that even if there is some sort of line between Welshry and Englishry it is too insignificant to deserve the blessing of a proper name.

But the Landsker is far from dead. In detailed field surveys undertaken across the Landsker zone in 1961 and 1971 attempts were made to establish the real status of the Welsh language in the centre of the county and also to discover whether there was any sharp divide between the Welshry and the Englishry. In 1971 a party of students undertook the survey and questioned 561 householders in the area. From their results there is little doubt concerning the continuing presence of the Landsker as a linguistic divide. Although most of the people questioned had not heard of the Landsker (indicating that the term itself has passed out of common usage), everyone was aware of the presence of the linguistic divide, and most of the interviewees had no difficulty in locating it with reasonable accuracy (Fig 5). Overall, its 1971 position is similar to that plotted for 1931 by D. T. Williams. Its sharpest section is in the west along the parish boundaries of the Trefgarn ridge; this matches the 1961 Census statistics, and has again been confirmed by those for 1971. The divide is also very sharp along the southern edges of New Moat and Bletherston parishes, coinciding partly with the course of the Afon Syfni; but here the census statistics fail completely to bring out the sharpness of the divide. In the centre of the county, around Spittal and Walton East parishes, and in the south-eastern lowland area between Pembrokeshire and Carmarthenshire, the divide is more difficult to find; here the mixed language loyalties of the present day provide an indication of the complicated settlement history of the Anglo-Norman period.

In spite of the slow decline of the Welsh language in the Landsker zone of Pembrokeshire, the linguistic divide is as easy to find as it ever has been during the past thousand years. It may be less easy to see than the distinctive landscape features of the Welshry and Englishry, but it is very much a reality in the minds of the local people. The Pembrokeshire Landsker, which has in turn been a fortified national frontier, a social and economic divide, and a linguistic divide, may be a historical relic, but it has remarkable persistence.

13 THE PEMBROKESHIRE COAST NATIONAL PARK

THE Pembrokeshire Coast National Park, created in 1952, is at once Pembrokeshire's crowning glory and its greatest headache. It covers 225 square miles, or just over one-third of the area of Pembrokeshire; it has about 180 miles of outer coastline followed in part by the coast path; it has at least twenty-four well-known sandy beaches and many that are less well-known; and it has at least ten main boating centres and fifteen centres for sea fishing. As shown in Chapter 2, among the immensely varied environments of the park are many stretches of cliffed coasts with intermittent sandy bays, the offshore islands with their huge seabird populations, the inner and outer reaches of the Milford Haven waterway, and the inland moors and wooded valleys of Mynydd Presely. As we have seen, the Pembrokeshire landscape provides the park's main asset, for it is something all can enjoy. But the complicated coastline of the county has created a major weakness from the point of view of park management. Because Pembrokeshire is a peninsula made up of peninsulas the national park is not a contiguous unit, but is made up of four detached portions (Map 4). This has led to very unusual problems of park administration and planning, even though the whole area of the park originally fell under the control of one planning authority.

We have already looked in some detail at the geology and landscapes of the park, and through the book we have seen something of the archaeological remains and other cultural features which lie within its boundary. We have not yet looked in any detail at the natural history, and the main part of this chapter is devoted to a brief survey of plant and animal life. The chapter ends with a description of the national park's tourist industry and a discussion of the land-use conflicts which are becoming more serious every year.

PLANT LIFE

In his book *The Pembrokeshire Coast Path* John Barrett, the pioneer clifftop walker, pointed out the huge variety of coastal habitats available for plant life. There are the cliff faces and clifftops, the storm-beach ridges at the heads of some sandy bays, the salt-marshes and valley floors, the sand dune areas as at Freshwater West and Whitesands, and the damp little valleys cut on clifftop sites by streams before they plunge into the sea. On many of the exposed clifftops plants have to adapt to gale-force winds and the burning of salt spray, but elsewhere there are stretches of coast-line where the effect of the wind is negligible and where plants can thrive in warm sunshine. The lee coasts on the eastern side of the Dale peninsula and between Saundersfoot and Monkstone Point are good examples. A similarly wide variation of habitats is found inland, from the exposed bleak hillsides of Mynydd Presely to the marshes and moorlands of the St David's district and the wooded steep slopes of the Gwaun valley and the beautiful Daugleddau. And everywhere the local factors of soil type, drainage conditions and aspect exert their own subtle influences over which plants will or will not thrive.

Because the climate of Pembrokeshire is mild and oceanic, plants can grow almost throughout the year. Spring comes very early, and some plants seem to make their own private decisions about which season is which. One or other of the two local species of gorse is in bloom at almost any time of the year, and even in the first week of January there are liable to be more than fifty flower species in full bloom. During February celandines and snow-drops are often in flower. In March these are joined by dandelions along the hedgerows and pink and yellow primroses around the fringes of the woodland. By the end of March the scurvy-grass is white on the clifftops, and there are bunches of violets for those who know where to look. Now the common gorse is reaching its full glory, and blackthorn is blossoming in the hedges. More and

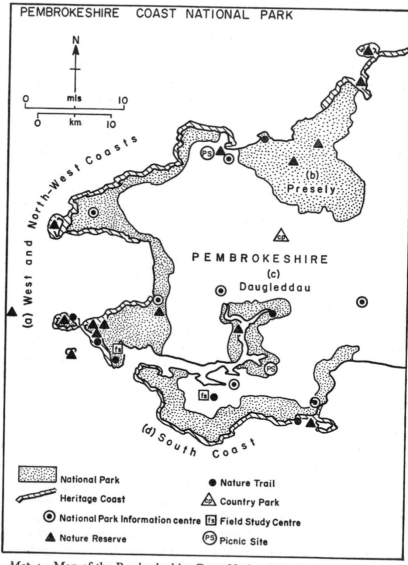

PEMBROKESHIRE COAST NATIONAL PARK

N

0   mls   10

0   km   10

(a) West and North-West Coasts

(b) Presely

PEMBROKESHIRE

(c) Daugleddau

(d) South Coast

National Park

Heritage Coast

National Park Information centre

Nature Reserve

Nature Trail

Country Park

Field Study Centre

Picnic Site

Map 4   Map of the Pembrokeshire Coast National Park, showing natural-history study facilities

more plants burst into bloom, including the sea campion, sea-pink, ox-eye daisy, and prostrate broom on the exposed cliffs. In the woodlands there are wood anemones, and on marsh valley floors wide patches of yellow marsh marigold catch the eye.

Daffodils are of course a great part of Welsh life, and there is local distress if they are not in bloom by 1 March, St David's Day. Spreads of daffodil are not so common as they were, but there are good springtime displays on the lawns of the old country estates, and occasionally they have spread into woodland from adjacent gardens. The truly wild daffodil is now very mixed up with the cultivated varieties, but Pembrokeshire has its own special species called the Tenby daffodil. This daffodil has the same bright yellow colouring over the whole flower, and it has a somewhat mysterious origin. Because of its unusual beauty and its early flowering qualities (it is usually out by mid- or late February) it became the object of a steady export trade to London. From the fields around Tenby, where it was previously abundant, half a million bulbs were dug up and exported between 1883 and 1885. The daffodil was almost exterminated, but now it has recovered again and it is quite common in old gardens and derelict cottage sites in several districts of Pembrokeshire.

Around Whitsuntide the spring blossoms are joined by blue-bells, thrift, red campion and foxgloves. The islands of Skomer, Skokholm and Ramsey are magnificent at this time; on the west coast of Skomer there is a sward of thrift several acres in extent, and further inland there are great sheets of bluebells inter-spersed with patches of the richly coloured red campion. Else-where, where there is more shelter and less competition, there are lesser celandines and primroses. As high summer approaches the colour subsides, and large parts of the island become blanketed with bracken.

The flowers of July and August are no less abundant. On the limestone cliffs of south Pembrokeshire one can see the reddish-purple flowers of greater knapweed, the golden samphire and three different species of sea lavender. On some of the salt-marshes there are purple and blue sea lavender, and sea aster and sea purslane. On the outer cliffs there are pearlworts, sea may-weeds, and many other delicate flowers, and banks of thyme and heather. And in many clifftop areas gentle green springy turf extends right up to the cliff edge. Inland, in the Presely Hills, the vegetation is quite different, with blossoming bog asphodel alongside sphagnum mosses, various rushes, cotton sedge, bilberry, bog myrtle, cranberry, and bog orchid. Further west the moorlands of Dowrog Common, Tretio Common and Trefeiddan Moor have other rather local plant species including a number of orchids and, in the pools of open water, plants such as bogbean, pillwort and water horsetail. These and many other local species are described in T. A. Warren-Davis's book *Plants of Pembrokeshire*.

There is now not a great deal of natural woodland left in the national park, and conifer plantations are being established in large areas of countryside particularly in Presely Hills. However, there are still several large areas of durmast oak woodland, as in the Gwaun valley and on the banks of the Daugleddau, and this is natural woodland creating an ideal habitat for many other plants, insects, birds and animals. Sycamore is also common, together with ash, elder, hawthorn, alder and birch. Higher up, out of the valleys, rowan and birch survive and succeed alongside the introduced conifers where many other deciduous tree species fail. Many of the damp woodlands have a prolific vegetation of mosses and ferns; and around the edges, where the tree canopy breaks up and allows light to penetrate, brambles build up impenetrable thickets.

The plants which live in the sea are somewhat less accessible than those which grow above sea-level, but they are no less interesting. Most of the outer coasts of Pembrokeshire are subject to a large tidal range and to attack by storm-waves through much of the year, so one would expect the growth of large seaweeds to be discouraged. But they are remarkably resilient, and where there is some shelter, several species thrive above and below the mean tide mark. One of them is *Porphyra umbilicalis*, which is still collected for making laver-bread, one of the great delicacies of Wales. Even on rocky headlands which are exposed to the full strength of storm-waves, larger seaweeds appear in the zone between mean tide-level and low-water mark. Particularly common are the wracks, the best-known of which is the knotted wrack with its thongs up to seven or eight feet long. Larger seaweeds from below low-water mark are seen best when they are uprooted and cast ashore during storms. Among these are saw wrack, thong weed and kelp; the latter, generally fastened tight to a rock surface by its powerful 'holdfast', can grow as much as twelve feet in a single season.

MAMMALS

Pembrokeshire is not particularly well endowed with the higher forms of life, and there are few mammal species. Without a doubt the Atlantic grey seal is the most interesting of the mammals of the national park. The seal herds are the largest in the southern part of the British Isles, and of the 2,000–3,000 grey seals around the Welsh coast most are concentrated around Pembrokeshire. The main breeding herds are on Ramsey Island (about 200 pups born annually), and probably there are 100 or so other pups born to smaller herds in caves and on isolated rocky beaches around the mainland coast. The seals enjoy basking in the sun, and even in bad weather they will often haul up on their own favourite beaches at the time of low water or to recover from a large meal. Generally they hunt at the time of high water. The herds around the Pembrokeshire coast are now used to man, and they show little fear; but they are still cautious and rather timid when humans are nearby, and because they are so ungainly on land they seldom stray far from the water's edge.

Most of the seal pups on the Pembrokeshire coast are born in late September or October (Plate 11a). They may weigh 30lb at birth. They are suckled for three to four weeks, putting on from 2lb to 4lb per day while the mother loses 100lb or more. The mother seldom feeds while suckling. When the pup weighs 90lb or so, the mother deserts it, leaving it to face the winter gales alone. The bulls mate with the females on their private beaches only ten to fourteen days after the birth of the pups. While many of the adults stay in 'home waters', the pups wander widely through the winter months, travelling as far afield as the Bay of Biscay, the English Channel, and the west coast of Ireland. But the centre of their tribal territory is the Celtic Sea and St George's Channel. The seals are fascinating creatures when studied

169

intensively, and a more detailed description of their habits is contained in R. M. Lockley's book *The Naturalist in Wales*.

Among the other large mammals of the county, deer were at one time numerous, as indeed were wolves and wild boars. All of these figure in Celtic mythology, but as a result of the medieval love of hunting nearly all the larger mammals were extinct in Pembrokeshire by 1600. After that date the only deer in the county were kept on private estates; there was a herd of fallow deer at Lawrenny, for instance, as late as the 1930s.

The next largest land mammals are the fox and the badger, both of which are very common. The county has the reputation of being great badger country, and a few years ago every small wood, copse and spinney had its own colony of badgers in residence. They are harmless, attractive creatures; long may they remain a part of Pembrokeshire wild life, for there are few enough mammal species left. Otters may still be common along many of the streams and rivers, but they are hunted by the local pack of otter-hounds and numbers have decreased. They are sighted occasionally in south Pembrokeshire (for example near Orielton), in the valley of the western Cleddau above Trefgarn and in the valley of the River Alun near St David's. Hares are becoming more common again in one or two areas after a period of comparative rarity, but the once vast rabbit population has still not recovered properly since myxomatosis, and the colonies are at present rather scattered and small. They are, however, abundant on Skomer, Skokholm and Ramsey. The elusive stoat is still quite common in Pembrokeshire, as is its cousin the weasel. The polecat is becoming much more common, and sightings of the animal have increased sharply in recent years. It has begun to breed in the county again, after a long break. The American mink has been breeding wild for twenty years or more, having escaped from some of the early mink farms. Moles and hedgehogs are common, as are a variety of rodents including the field vole, the water vole, the house mouse and the brown rat. The dormouse exists in small numbers, although Pembrokeshire seems to have no harvest mice. The black rat is found especially around the port of Milford Haven. Three of the British shrews are found locally. The red squirrel was once quite common in the woods around Benton, Lawrenny, Hook and Orielton, and also in the north of the county; but now it is so much reduced in numbers that it may even be extinct. In contrast the grey squirrel, a relatively recent arrival, is much more successful. Bats are quite common. Pipistrelle and long-eared bats exist in large numbers in many parts of Pembrokeshire, and some of the caves in the limestone cliffs of the Castlemartin peninsula house sizeable colonies of great and lesser horseshoe bats.

One animal which is a local curiosity is the Skomer vole, believed by some to be a unique subspecies. Certainly it is different from voles elsewhere in having a greater body-weight, a more tawny colouring and a less timid disposition than the mainland species. Perhaps it has evolved from ordinary mainland stock which was taken over to the island by the Iron Age settlers of 2,000 years ago.

BIRD LIFE

The abundant bird life of the Pembrokeshire Coast National Park is of course one of its great glories, and many naturalists consider that Pembrokeshire has a richer sea-bird life than any other county of England and Wales. The various species and their distributions have been well recorded in a number of recent publications, so there is little point in attempting a comprehensive survey here. Instead, the following paragraphs draw attention to some of the more interesting localities and some of the more unusual bird species of the county.

The vast seabird colonies of the Pembrokeshire islands can be counted as major tourist attractions, and perhaps it is no bad thing that the main nesting period does not coincide with the holiday months of July and August. The best-known of the islands is Skomer, now a national nature reserve managed by the West Wales Naturalists' Trust. David Saunders calls it 'without question one of the finest seabird islands in Europe'. There are large colonies of kittiwakes, razorbills and guillemots, and many puffin colonies. Manx shearwaters are numerous on the island, but because these birds are nocturnal they are seldom seen by day visitors. In the interior of the island there are large colonies of lesser black-backed gulls, and other nesting birds are oystercatchers, lapwings, curlews, short-eared owls and wheat-ears. There are shags and cormorants, too, and in common with the other coasts of western Britain, Skomer has seen an explosive increase in the number of nesting fulmars in recent years.

Ramsey and Skokholm are also superb bird islands. The latter is not so frequently visited, for it has no facilities for day visitors. However, Ramsey now has more day visitors than Skomer. Again the main nesting sea-birds are kittiwakes, fulmars, shags, guillemots and razorbills. Ramsey has no puffin colony today, although the bird certainly nested there 200 years ago. Probably rats caused the decline and fall of the colony, having been carried accidentally to the island on one of the farmer's boats. Ramsey is also well known as the island stronghold of the chough. Among the other islands Caldey does not have a rich variety of sea-bird colonies, but it does have a large colony of nesting herring gulls. The adjacent island of St Margaret's, which is a bird reserve, has one of the largest cormorant colonies in the British Isles—almost 350 nesting pairs. The most remote of the Pembrokeshire islands is Grassholm, an RSPB reserve with a justly famous gannet colony (Plate 11b). The island is only twenty-two acres in extent, and the gannetry occupies only one flank, but there are now about 16,000 pairs in residence. This makes Grassholm the fourth largest gannet colony in the North Atlantic, a surprising fact, for little over a century ago there were only about twenty pairs present. R. M. Lockley estimates that Grassholm supports about 60,000 gannets in the middle of summer, including the newly hatched chicks and other immature birds. The splendid white birds do their fishing over a wide area, and particularly within St Bride's Bay. There can be few more beautiful sights than gannets diving close inshore, wheeling and swooping on the bright, clean wind of a Pembrokeshire summer's day.

Among the most interesting of the seabirds mentioned above is the Manx shearwater, which certainly nests on Skomer and Skokholm, and in small numbers on Ramsey also. In its migration it covers vast distances, but in early summer it congregates on the Pembrokeshire islands. During the breeding season one partner sits quietly on its burrow during the day, but at dusk the areas around the colonies are transformed by tens of thousands of the

Plate 13 The beautiful old farmhouse at Garn. Note the long-house layout and the massive round chimney adjacent to the entrance

Plate 14 (above) The old post office at St David's, photographed in about 1870. This is a typical two-roomed cottage with a thatched roof and very small windows; (below) a long-house composed of distinct stepped segments on a steep slope in Trefin, north Pembrokeshire

birds screaming in from all directions in an endless multitude. And then at sunrise, all becomes quiet again. Skomer and Skokholm between them hold the world's largest concentration of shearwaters, probably totalling 135,000 pairs.

There are few large sea-bird colonies on the mainland of Pembrokeshire, although razorbills and guillemots nest on the outer cliffs of Dinas 'Island' and elsewhere. The same species, and more especially guillemots, nest close inshore on the famous limestone Stack Rocks, close to the Green Bridge of Wales on the south coast. In several other areas, too, fulmars, kittiwakes, and the various types of gull can be found nesting on the mainland cliffs.

The other birds of Pembrokeshire are of great interest, for they give some indication of the wide variety of habitats already mentioned. At present the list of breeding birds totals more than 102, and the majority of these are found on the mainland, each one in its own ecological niche. In addition, Pembrokeshire is superbly situated for receiving visitors, and there are some very exotic birds among the 304 species recorded. Among the birds which occur widely in the countryside we can include the heron, the buzzard, the mallard, the kestrel, the skylark, the raven, and the rock dove. Less common, but still definitely resident, are the peregrine falcon, the chough, the mute swan, the collared dove, the barn owl, the shelduck, the kingfisher and the dipper.

We may conclude this section with brief mention of one or two representative sites where different types of birds can be seen. The Gann Flat near Dale attracts many different waders and wildfowl. Typical are little grebe and goldeneye, Slavonian grebe and red-breasted merganser. Also during the autumn and winter there are wigeon, brent geese, greenshank, green sandpiper and little stint. In the Cleddau wildfowl refuge there are resident Canada geese, and also wintering parties of wigeon, teal, goldeneye and red-breasted merganser. In hard winters such as that of 1962–3 large numbers of white-fronted geese have visited the waterway. Around the shores in winter and spring there are lapwing, golden plover, curlew, redshank and dunlin. In the wooded Gwaun valley there are buzzards and ravens, together with dippers, redstarts, wood warblers, and grey wagtails. And higher still, on Mynydd Presely and the other uplands, one can see

L

redpoll, buzzard, raven, merlin, and ring ouzel. The lesser red-poll is found particularly in the new conifer plantations. During the summer there are meadow-pipits and nesting wheatears, and the air is filled with the songs of resident skylarks. During the winter snow buntings can be seen on Mynydd Presely.

TOURISM AND ITS MANAGEMENT

Pembrokeshire, with a current resident population (1971) of 97,295, attracts a large summer holiday population. The tourist industry provides employment for about 3,000 people and an annual income of some £10 million for the county. Many local people have come to depend on the tourist trade, although there are worries that its strong seasonal rhythm contributes to an unstable local economy. The major attractions are of course in the national park, and holiday accommodation is widely scattered throughout the coastal belt, but the greatest concentration of tourists' beds and holiday amenities lies in the south, around Tenby and Saundersfoot. At present the county provides about 5,000 beds in hotels, 5,000 in guest houses, 5,000 in private houses, 7,000 in furnished accommodation, 200 in hostels, and over 25,000 in static caravans, giving a total of some 47,000. In addition there may be a further 8,000 beds in touring caravans at any one moment, giving a peak holiday accommodation of perhaps 55,000. From these figures it is clear that caravan holidays have become increasingly popular. During August 1974 there were 9,208 caravans on sites in the county, and 5,471 of those were inside the national park. Caravan parks are a major amenity problem, and the Tenby–Saundersfoot area has already been designated a 'caravan saturation area'. Planning policy now dictates that no further caravan sites may be established within sight of the coast. Tents and tent sites are less of a problem, although there were over 3,600 tents in use by holidaymakers in August 1974.

Nowadays, almost all the holidaymakers who visit Pembrokeshire have their own cars, and this has encouraged many people to explore the county in depth. While the coastal resorts such as Broad Haven, Newgale, Tenby, Saundersfoot, and Whitesand

Bay keep holidaymakers busy during good weather, many of the attractions of the county's landscapes have proved to be popular with tourists. The city and cathedral of St David's have long been centres of holiday pilgrimage, as have the castles of Pembroke, Manorbier and Llawhaden. Haverfordwest has become the shopping centre for holidaymakers, especially since its castle now holds the County Museum and National Park Information Centre. Visitors are attracted in increasing numbers to the old village of Mathry, to Trefgarn Gorge and the Gwaun valley, to the county's remaining woollen mills, and in the south to the Bishop's Palace at Lamphey and to the secluded peace of Bosherston Pools. The supertankers in Milford Haven have proved an undoubted attraction, and the Llysyfran reservoir is already much visited. Wisely, the planning committee and other authorities have adapted to the mobility of the modern holidaymaker and to his increasing interest in the environment; information centres distribute fact sheets on a wide variety of topics, and many guides for the motorist have appeared in the last few years. One particularly successful venture is the Countryside Unit at Broad Haven, which disseminates information through its bookshop and exhibition centre. Under John Barrett the committee also pioneered the immensely popular organised coastal footpath walks devoted to simple field study.

Nevertheless, the majority of holidaymakers who visit the county come to enjoy the pleasures of the coast. The enjoyment of safe bathing and sandy beaches, spectacular cliff scenery and largely uncommercialised holiday settlements draws a large number of families, but many more are nowadays attracted by the prospect of good sailing at Solva, Little Haven, Dale, Saundersfoot, Lower Fishguard, Newport and elsewhere. Other popular sporting activities include sea angling, surfing (at Newgale and Whitesand Bay), water-skiing (as at Freshwater East, Burton and Dale), and golf, gliding and rowing. Already there is great pressure on holiday resources on the coast and it has been calculated that there may be a demand for 98,000 bed spaces at the holiday peak by 1985. The Tenby–Saundersfoot area has changed enormously in character over the last decade; it has been likened to a 'little Torbay' (Plate 15a), and there are fears that commercialisation is also going to spoil some of the other more attractive coastal areas. Symptomatic of these fears is the appearance of the informal Welsh Pembrokeshire Tourist Association, which seems not to be particularly racialist in intent, but simply wishes to preserve something of the unspoilt tranquillity of north Pembrokeshire.

Recognising the problems involved in planning for the tourist boom, the planning authority and other local committees have decided that future holiday development should be concentrated at fourteen centres. Using the criteria of coastal 'quality', the need to stick to national park objectives, the 'heritage coasts' defined by the Countryside Commission, and the location of National Trust properties and sites of special scientific importance, the planning authority has designated 'remote areas' which should be preserved as far as is practicable in their present natural state. In these areas additional holiday accommodation will, in theory, not be permitted, and certainly badly located developments will be cleared away.

Two major holiday developments have been encouraged by the county council. The first of these is at Broad Haven, where an already large holiday village is being expanded further, particularly through the provision of private houses and holiday chalets. The second is at Freshwater East, where an 'unsightly conglomerate of shacks and bungalows' has for many years been something of an eyesore. The bay is already an important south coast holiday centre, providing accommodation for 1,700 people, but the county council has put forward a comprehensive plan for its conversion to a holiday village with high-density holiday flats, houses, chalets and caravan sites with car parks and service centres. Most of the financial risk should be borne by a private company, eventually providing accommodation for about 4,000 holiday residents. Another private holiday development including a chalet settlement and yacht station at Lawrenny is already well advanced, and there have been other plans for development at Poppit Sands and elsewhere.

Thus, the Pembrokeshire tourist industry is changing character in a number of ways. The remoteness of the county will probably keep it beyond the range of most day-trippers from

England or even from urban South Wales, but more and more families will wish to stay in the county during the peak holiday months of July and August. The holiday trade has become more organised and is in places very commercialised, and careful planning is required to ensure that the national park remains an amenity. If the development of the remote areas can be carefully controlled, the charm of rural Pembrokeshire may be preserved; if not, the enormous benefit which the county gains from tourism may well turn sour.

14 BUILDINGS: MEDIEVAL CASTLES, PALACES AND CHURCHES

PEMBROKESHIRE is widely known as a county of castles, but it is not often realised how greatly its castles varied in design and function. Mostly, however, they were the products of the great colonising movement by the Normans in the early part of the Middle Ages, and many of the imposing buildings of today date from the fourteenth century or earlier. The same may be said of the magnificent bishop's palaces at St David's and Lamphey, which were two of the architectural splendours of Wales. And while the Englishry was being strengthened by massive stone castles and fortified residences and beautified by stone palaces, the increasing skill of the medieval stone-masons and architects was used, too, in ecclesiastical buildings. Fine stone churches were erected in many of the manorial settlements, and priories and abbeys also appeared on the landscape. In the sacred hollow selected by Dewi Sant for his monastery the early cathedral was raised, stage by stage, to its present magnificent proportions (Plate 5a). The legacy of this burst of military, ecclesiastical and domestic building is still with us. It fundamentally altered the cultural landscape of Pembrokeshire, and this chapter concentrates upon some of the medieval buildings which remain.

In Chapter 5 we have already seen how castles were essential for the establishment and then the defence of the Englishry. Some of the early earthworks and stockaded forts were built by the Welsh princes, but all the stone castles which were erected in twelfth- and thirteenth-century Pembrokeshire were the work of the Anglo-Norman lords. These castles were built and improved in several stages, and some did not reach their final form until the fifteenth century or even later. We have seen how several of the more important fortresses were used during the Civil War, and how Cromwell started the process of their demolition. Some castles were in a state of advanced decay even in George Owen's time, and the history of each castle can be related to such factors as its strategic importance, the wealth of the community which it protected, and the detailed history of warfare, politics and marriages among the medieval ruling families. The castles can be classified into four main types, as follows:

1 The great strategic fortresses (Pembroke and Haverford-west).
2 Other major castles (Newport, Cilgerran, Carew, Manorbier, and Tenby).
3 The Landsker castles (Roch, Wiston, Llawhaden, Narberth, Amroth and Laugharne).
4 The lesser strongholds such as Picton Castle and the smaller fortified structures at Dale, Angle, Benton, Upton, Bonville Court and Eastington.

In Map 5 the distribution of these castles is shown with respect to the medieval Landsker, the Englishry and the Welshry. Some forts and castles have entirely disappeared, while others can be traced only with difficulty. Some are not open to the public, for they are still used as private residences; and it should be remembered that the lesser strongholds mentioned here were but the most spectacular of a number of fortified residences which dotted the countryside. Some of these are mentioned later in the chapter.

THE STRATEGIC FORTRESSES

First and foremost among the medieval buildings of Pembroke-shire were the great strategic fortresses, upon whose successful defence the fortunes of the whole Englishry depended. Pembroke Castle (Plate 10a) was the most important of these, sited in the heart of the Englishry and capable of relief from the sea. It was the first and greatest of the 'round keep' castles of Wales, and has many of the classic early medieval features such as inner and outer wards, a strong outer curtain wall with defensive towers, a great gatehouse, and various inner ward buildings such as two

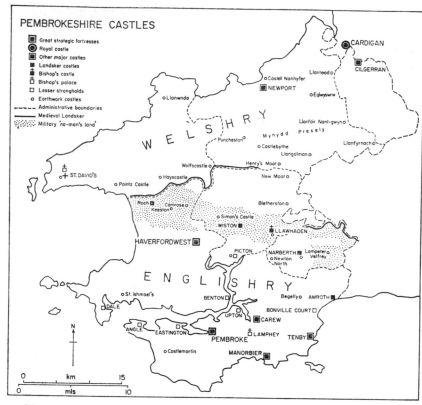

PEMBROKESHIRE CASTLES

- ▣ Great strategic fortresses
- ◉ Royal castle
- ▣ Other major castles
- ▪ Landsker castles
- ▪ Bishop's castle
- ⌂ Bishop's palace
- ☐ Lesser strongholds
- o Earthwork castles
- –––– Administrative boundaries
- ——— Medieval Landsker
- ░░░░ Military 'no-man's land'

Map 5 Map of early medieval Pembrokeshire, showing how the Landsker coincided with the boundary of the episcopal lordships. It also shows the main castle types of Pembrokeshire; note that the vast majority of castles are located in the present Englishry and in other parts of Daugleddau, settled during the early Middle Ages by the Normans and their followers

halls, a chancery and a chapel. After a long period of neglect the fabric of the castle was partially restored in the 1880s, and more extensive renovation has been undertaken since 1929. Now, quite naturally, the magnificent castle is a popular tourist attraction, partly on account of its architectural qualities and partly because of its Tudor associations; in 1457 Henry Tudor was born in the castle, and here he spent much of his boyhood.

The other great strategic fortress of the Englishry is at Haverfordwest, some way behind the Landsker but close enough to it to act as the main bastion in case of attack from the north and north-

182

east. Like Pembroke Castle, it was built as part of a planned Norman town, with its strong town walls, its riverside warehouses and quays, and its castellated and spacious parish churches. The castle was different from Pembroke Castle in design, being of the rectangular type. It was built on a fine strategic site, surmounting a steep, rocky bluff above the Western Cleddau river. It has a battlemented curtain wall up to twelve feet thick and a number of strong towers, and it was renowned as one of the strongest castles of Wales. But it was partly dismantled at the end of the Civil War and was sadly neglected thereafter. Today the remaining buildings are parts of the castle keep, surmounted on the northern side by the structure of the County Gaol which was constructed about 1820. Recently the buildings have been further extended, and the castle is now the home of the Castle Museum and Records Office.

OTHER MAJOR CASTLES

The other major castles of Pembrokeshire vary greatly in their style of building and in their state of preservation. At one extreme is Newport Castle, built as a stone fortress about the end of the thirteenth century and already in a state of disrepair by the mid-1500s. Little now remains of the original stone castle, but the gatehouse was converted into a residence in 1859 and is still in use today. At the other extreme are the spectacular fortresses of Carew, Manorbier and Cilgerran, all relatively well preserved and open to the public. And in between is Tenby Castle, built like Pembroke and Haverfordwest castles in conjunction with a walled town, but now preserved only in part. William de Valence planned to make Tenby impregnable, and the building of the massive town walls, in several stages, took fully 250 years to complete; but the castle has proved less resistant than the walls, and only a few fragments remain today, sharing a place on Castle Hill with Tenby Museum.

Cilgerran Castle occupies a commanding site above the River Teifi, and it is not surprising that it has long been a tourist attraction. The first castle may have been built here in 1093 by Roger, Earl of Montgomery, but the main buildings of stone and slate were constructed in the thirteenth century. The most splendid features of the castle today are the two great drum-towers which defend the landward side of the inner ward. Although Cilgerran maintained its status as an independent lordship throughout most of the medieval period it was too far from the main colony of Little England for safety, and it was assaulted by the Welsh princes time and again. In complete contrast, Manorbier, on the south coast, was so far removed from the ravages of the Welsh that, as far as we know, it was never beseiged. The fabric of the castle has survived well (Plate 12a). It was one of the seats of power of the de Barri family, and formed part of the lordship of Pembroke. The stone castle was built, stage by stage, through the twelfth, thirteenth and fourteenth centuries. It has an approximately rectangular inner ward with high curtain walls and corner towers. There is no keep, but a strong gatehouse was one of the later additions to the fabric. Today the picturesque castle is a great favourite with holidaymakers, and understandably so, for as it stands in ivy-covered splendour in its gentle valley one can picture the world of Giraldus Cambrensis eight centuries ago. Gerald was born here in 1146, and during the course of his travels and his involvement in the turbulent ecclesiastical politics of the Norman world he retained his love of Maenor Pirr, 'the pleasantest spot in Wales'. He described the graceful character of the twelfth-century castle and manor with the following words:

> The castle . . . is excellently defended by turrets and bulwarks; and is situated on the summit of a hill extending on the western side towards the sea port, having on the northern and southern sides a fine fish pond under its walls, as conspicuous for its grand appearance as for the depth of its waters, and a beautiful orchard on the same side, enclosed on one part by a vineyard and on the other by a wood, remarkable for the projection of its rocks and the height of its hazel trees. On the right hand of the promontory, between the castle and the church, near the site of a very large lake and mill, a rivulet of never failing water flows through a valley, rendered sandy by the violence of the winds.

Carew Castle was another subsidiary castle of the lordship of Pembroke. It stands on a low limestone outcrop surrounded by meadows and at the head of navigation of the Carew River. It was begun about 1200 to replace a simpler structure, and the west front, built around 1300, shows it to have been a typical medieval fortress. The most striking features are the massive round towers, castellated on top and supported below by spur buttresses which rise to first-floor level. Other features of the castle show it to have been altered greatly during the fifteenth and sixteenth centuries, and it eventually became a fine Tudor residence. Much of the rebuilding was done by Sir Rhys ap Thomas, who supported Henry Tudor on his march through Wales and who reputedly placed Richard's muddy crown on Henry's head after the triumph at Bosworth Field in 1485. After this Carew, somewhat surprisingly for a fortress so solidly established in the centre of the Englishry, became a great centre of Welsh culture, and in 1507 Sir Rhys gave the last of the great tournaments to be held in Britain. It has become something of a Welsh legend, and is described in detail by Edward Laws and Richard Fenton. The tournament lasted for five days, and was attended by the aristocracy from all over Wales, together with hundreds of retainers. The proceedings were started by mass in Lamphey Palace chapel, and continued with feasting in the great hall of the castle, accompanied by harp music and songs from the bards. There were contests in the tilting yard, wrestling, throwing the bar, tossing the pike and other athletic sports, and then deer-hunting in the park. There was more feasting and drinking, and theatricals in the evenings. And over it all presided the genial Sir Rhys, who had the good sense to take innumerable precautions in case the young knights in residence allowed family rivalries to break into real fighting and bloodshed. And at the end of it all, according to Edward Laws, '... although one thousand men had spent five days in company, not one quarrel, unkind word, or cross look had passed between them.'

Carew Castle passed to the famous (or infamous) Sir John Perrot in the middle of the sixteenth century, and he was responsible for the last major phase of reconstruction. He continued Sir Rhys's work of transforming the dark medieval fortress into a light airy palace, and he was responsible for the rebuilding of the north front with its series of beautiful mullioned windows overlooking the Carew River. But the castle was not to continue for long as a stately mansion-house. After the death of Sir John Perrot in the Tower of London the ownership of Carew changed several times, and the castle figured prominently in the Pembrokeshire campaigns of the Civil War. By 1686 it had long ceased to be used as a family home, and since then it has gradually declined to the status of a magnificent ruin.

LANDSKER CASTLES

The Landsker castles are something of a puzzle, because as a group they are very varied in style. Also, as we have seen in Chapter 5, the castles defended a military frontier only for a short period of time; even before 1150 the Anglo-Normans, helped by Flemish immigrants, were colonising the central parts of the county well to the north of the line of castles. Castles like Roch, Wiston and Narberth were seldom used as part of an overall Norman strategy to define and defend the frontier. The Normans themselves were never united enough to employ a common strategy against the Welsh. Probably the Landsker castles generally functioned, like the larger fortresses further south, as the defensive headquarters of individual baronies. Because they were so close to the periphery of the Englishry they were extremely vulnerable to raids by the Welsh, and it is understandable that they never prospered to any great extent. Wiston, Narberth and Laugharne castles in particular, exposed near the eastern flank of the Englishry, suffered greatly from Welsh attacks. Nevertheless, neither the English kings nor the lords of the Englishry had any doubts about the strategic importance of maintaining the defences of the eastern frontier. For example, after the destruction of Wiston and Narberth castles by the Welsh in 1220, Henry II instructed all knights and free tenants from the lordships to assist William, Earl Marshal, in their immediate reconstruction. This shows that there was some strategic design for the Englishry as a whole. But Narberth and Wiston continued to bear the brunt of Welsh attacks, and today very little remains of the original stone fortifications.

From the remains of the Landsker castles we can see how widely they varied in style. Laugharne Castle was probably begun in about 1100, but most of the imposing stone fabric visible today was the work of Sir John Perrot, who turned it into a fine mansion during the reign of Henry VIII. Narberth Castle was a simple rectangular castle with drum-towers at each corner. Probably it had no keep, but there was a fortified residential part. It was built about 1246, but it is not on the site of the original castle of Arberth which figures so prominently in Welsh history and legend. After a turbulent history of assault, destruction and rebuilding it came into the hands of the redoubtable Sir Rhys ap Thomas. He renovated it and made it habitable, but after his death in 1524 the castle continued its troubled existence. It was considerably battered during the Civil War, and after 1677 it ceased to be habitable. Now it is but a crumbling ruin, closed to the public and sadly in need of renovation before it is too late.

Wiston Castle was the centre of a lordship granted to one Wizo the Fleming. It was called Daugleddau, and it was the frontier territory settled by Flemings to provide a defence against the Welsh. The Flemings hated, and were hated by, the Welsh; and they were not too popular with the Normans either. They bore the brunt of many Welsh attacks, and the castle was never developed as a powerful stone fortress because it was too vulnerable and insecure and because the lordship was always short of funds. The early motte and bailey castle of Wizo himself was later modified by his sons, and a shell keep was built in stone on the 40ft-high mound. In 1220, as mentioned above, the castle and settlement at Wiston were savagely attacked by the Welsh, and in spite of Henry VIII's exhortations it seems that the keep was never properly reconstructed. Now, over 750 years later, only the base of the keep walls can be seen.

At the seaward ends of the Landsker lay the castles of Amroth and Roch. Little is known of the Norman Amroth Castle, but there are several earthworks in the vicinity, and there are records of a small stone castle at Earweare, close to the sea shore. There are no remains of this castle today (except perhaps for the restored gateway), for the modern Amroth Castle is a mansion-house dating from the early nineteenth century. Roch Castle is better preserved, standing on its imposing rock outcrop within sight of the sea and dominating the bleak countryside for miles around. The spectacular peel-tower was probably built during the thirteenth century by Adam de la Roche. Local tradition tells that he built the tower in order to defy a prophecy that he would die from the bite of a serpent; but adders thrived on the bracken-covered rocks around the castle, and one was carried into the castle by mistake inside a bundle of firewood. Of course it bit the luckless Adam, upon which he obediently died. The castle was never completed, although there are signs that curtain walls were originally planned to enclose an inner ward. In any case the tower was used and inhabited until about 1700. Among its more illustrious inhabitants were the Walters, the family of Lucy Walter who was mistress to Charles II. For about 200 years the castle was in ruins, but it was restored and extended in 1900–2 by the Viscount St David, and it has been further improved as a residence since then.

Llawhaden Castle, located between Wiston and Narberth on the eastern frontier, can certainly be classified as a Landsker castle; but it differs greatly from the others in that it was a bishop's fortified palace. As we have seen in Chapter 5, the episcopal lordship of Llawhaden retained much of its Welsh character even though governed by Norman bishops of St David's. The Normans were certainly aware of its defensive importance, and it was garrisoned strongly during periods of Welsh insurrection. But once the stone castle was built it seems to have been largely immune from the violence which attended the more lowly fortresses at Wiston and Narberth. This may have been due partly to the castle's great strength, and partly to the reluctance of the Welsh princes to commit violence against the bishop. And an early motte castle was built at Llawhaden in the early twelfth century, followed by a stone tower and curtain wall about a century later. The present impressive fortress took shape during a great rebuilding between 1250 and 1300, and other major additions to the fabric were made in the early fourteenth century. When it was complete the castle was a lavish fortified mansion, fit for the entertainment of bishops and their important guests, and providing accommodation for a large household staff and a large garrison. Until the 1530s it was maintained as a palace on the grand scale, but the infamous Bishop Barlow is said to have commenced the dismantling of the castle so that the sale of the lead roof could provide a dowry for one of his daughters. A sad end indeed for a military structure of such magnificence.

Most of the lesser strongholds of Pembrokeshire have faded out of history because their original motte and bailey structures were never replaced by more permanent stone buildings. Professor Grimes estimates that there were at least thirty such sites in Pembrokeshire, many of them associated with the church, mill and manor house of the typical manorial settlement. Some of the strongholds remained as lords' residences for several centuries; elsewhere (as at Picton) the manor house was moved away from the castle mound with the advent of more peaceful times, especially in the better protected parts of the Englishry. Some of the strongholds were built on prehistoric sites, as at Nevern and Walwyn's Castle. Elsewhere the conical flat-topped mounds and their earthworks were built by the Welsh and then taken over and adapted by the Normans with their superior castle-building techniques. Some of these old strongholds are still impressive, even though they support no ruined buildings today. For example, there are the castle mounds at The Rath (Rudbaxton), New Moat, Hayscastle, Camrose, Pointz Castle, Castlemartin and Puncheston.

Perhaps the best-known of the early strongholds which developed into fortified residences are the 'castles' around the Daugleddau waterway. The best preserved are at Benton, Upton and Picton. Benton was probably built as a subordinate fortress for the protection of the lordship of Rhos; like Roch Castle, it seems to have been a home of the de la Roche family. Little is known of its history, but it seems never to have been particularly large, comprising only a thirteenth-century peel tower and a small irregular courtyard protected by a thick curtain wall. The tower contained no fireplaces, so possibly the original residential part of the castle was at the opposite end of the court. From the end of the Civil War until 1930 the castle was in ruins, but after that it was rebuilt, almost single-handed, by Ernest Pegge. Now it is in good repair and is used again as a private residence. Upton Castle, on the other side of the river, is still a very imposing building. Its frontage comprises three drum-towers, and there was a gateway at one end. When it was built, probably in the thirteenth century, there was probably a walled enclosure at the rear but no trace of this now remains and the greater part of the building of today was constructed in the eighteenth century. Upton Castle can never have been a serious fortress in military terms, and it seems rather to have been a fine example of a medieval fortified house. For many generations it was occupied by the Malefant family and its descendants, and it is still used as a private residence.

Further up-river, on a commanding site above the confluence of the Western Cleddau and the Eastern Cleddau, is Picton Castle. As noted above, it does not occupy the original motte site, and the oldest part of the castle building of today was probably commenced in about 1302 by Sir John Wogan. The western half of the castle was added about 1800 by Lord Milford, but it retains the style of a Norman fortress with its battlements and projecting bastions. The castle has been continuously occupied since it was built, and since it seems to have been by-passed by the more violent of the conflicts between the Welsh and the Normans even its older section is still in a remarkably good state of repair.

Near the outer reaches of Milford Haven are two other fortified residences, at Angle and Dale. The Old Rectory at Angle is similar in some ways to the peel towers at Roch and Benton, although it occupies a much less imposing site. The original 'castle' at Angle seems to have been square, protected to the north and west by a moat and on the south side by an inlet of the Haven. Now only the single tower remains, roughly square in plan with a rounded projection housing a corner stair. It was probably three storeys high, and entered at first-floor level across a drawbridge. An interesting feature of the exterior wall is a row of stone corbels which must have supported a wooden walkway near the top of the tower. The house may have been a baron's residence, for there is a dovecote nearby as well as other medieval antiquities. But there is no accurate record of the history of any of these buildings. Across the Haven, Dale Castle was probably built originally by

Plate 15 (left) Tourist pressure at Saundersfoot. The old coal-exporting harbour (now a popular sailing centre) is at the top, right

(right) the new Haven Bridge shortly after the lifting of the centre span in December 1974

Plate 16 (above) The Llysyfran reservoir under construction; *(below)* an aerial photograph of the Esso refinery near Milford, showing the massive new oil tanks on the clifftops

Robert de Vale as his manor. The south wing may be on the site of the original fortified house, and it has a number of vaulted rooms and battlemented external walls. Most of the building is, however, of nineteenth-century date, and the castle is still used as a private residence.

Most of the other old fortified halls of Pembrokeshire have disappeared or are in ruins, but some of them have been preserved at least in part. One which has disappeared is the three-storeyed fortified house at Bonville Court near Saundersfoot. This probably consisted of two towers set corner to corner protecting other buildings behind, but no plans of the building survive, and it was probably abandoned in the 1700s before being destroyed in the Bonville's Court colliery workings in the present century. Another interesting building which was probably fortified is 'The Palace' at Cresswell, a rectangular structure with a turret at each corner. It may have been the home of Bishop Barlow in the sixteenth century, but the age of the building itself is in doubt. Other fine fortified houses (much modified by the hand of time) can still be seen at Eastington near Rhoscrowther, and at Monkton Priory Farm near Pembroke. Eastington, in its heyday, must have been particularly impressive, with its embattled parapet and turret and its fortified wall-walk. The Old Rectory at Carew has a corbelled tower of uncertain date, and a fine arched doorway. And on Caldey Island there is an old battlemented tower with walls four feet thick and a vaulted basement. This was probably a free-standing fortified residence in medieval times, but subsequently it has been incorporated into the monastic buildings. Undoubtedly there must have been many other fine fortified houses in the county, but their remains have been built into more recent structures and lost almost without trace.

THE BISHOP'S PALACES

During the Anglo-Norman period the diocese of St David's was the largest in Wales, and its lands provided the greatest revenues. Not surprisingly, the bishop's palaces of the time were built to reflect the wealth and power of the bishop, and in addition to the fortified palace at Llawhaden other fine residences were built at

Trefin, St David's and Lamphey. Of the former nothing survives, but much of the fabric of the St David's and Lamphey palaces remains, and from the ruins we can gain some idea of the building techniques and life-style of the age.

The Bishop's Palace at St David's is justly famous, and some authorities consider it superior architecturally to the adjacent cathedral. The palace was built as a successor to an early motte and bailey castle which served as the bishop's residence until the thirteenth century. The first major building on the site of the present palace took place between 1228 and 1293, but the palace attained its final splendour under Bishop Gower (1327–47). He was an inspired builder, and it was he who was responsible for the great hall with its vaulted basement and the magnificent arcaded parapets. This must have been a fine fortified building, stronger and much more imposing than the early smaller hall which is connected to it at right-angles. It had a fine entrance archway and a rose window, and the great east gable was flanked by turrets. Bishop Gower even added ornament to an already lavish design by using alternate areas of purple and yellow stone for parts of the parapet and the gable end. The Tower Gatehouse and the high defensive wall surrounding the whole of the cathedral close were also probably improved by Bishop Gower, although they must have existed in something like their present form during the late thirteenth century. With the coming of the Reformation the Bishop's Palace at St David's fell upon evil days, and again it was Bishop Barlow who hastened the decay of the buildings. It does not seem to have been occupied permanently since the end of the sixteenth century.

The bishop's residence at Lamphey was another fascinating building. It was constructed as part of a pleasant rural retreat for the bishop, nestled in a little valley and surrounded by fishponds, orchards, and vegetable gardens. There was also a windmill and a dovecote, and two watermills. The adjacent park held a herd of about sixty deer. Some of the buildings of the palace date from the early thirteenth century, and a fine, well-appointed camera, or private apartment, was added by Bishop Richard Carew between 1256 and 1280. He obviously employed imported stone-masons for the work, which is of superior quality to that undertaken by Bishop Bek around the end of the century. But again it was the redoubtable Bishop Gower who gave the palace its greatest splendour, adding a new hall and remodelling the court-yard, giving it a battlemented wall and a new gatehouse crowned with his characteristic arcaded parapet. There were various other phases of rebuilding, but after the Reformation the palace passed from the Church to the State, and in Elizabethan times it was a home of the Devereux family who were later the Earls of Essex. Now it is a ruin, looked after by the Department of the Environment.

CHURCHES GREAT AND SMALL

Earlier in this book we have seen how Little England acquired characteristic churches typified by high castellated towers during the early medieval period (Plate 6a). Like the castles, fortified residences and bishop's palaces, the churches were the products of an unsettled age, and it is worth mentioning a few typical examples here.

Some of the earliest churches, dating from the period of colonisation between 1100 and 1400, have been greatly modified since. In particular, there was a great phase of church rebuilding in the later part of the nineteenth century, and on many of the parish churches of today only the castellated towers remind us of their medieval origins. The churches are not particularly distinguished architecturally, and it has been said that Pembrokeshire churches are seldom real works of architecture at all. They have been referred to as 'wild and wondrous structures' full of character, and they are in turn charming, grotesque, and picturesque. The simplest churches were built on a straightforward rectangular plan with a tower at one end or near a side entrance. Later on a wide transept or aisle was added, and some churches also have lengthened naves or added vestries, all contributing to the usual 'patchwork' style.

Typical churches, dating from the thirteenth and fourteenth centuries, with high, tapering towers and castellated parapets, are at Steynton, Johnston, Ludchurch, St Thomas's (Haverford-west), Newport, Begelly and Gumfreston. Other churches, like St Martin's (Haverfordwest) and St Mary's (Tenby) have had spires added on top of their medieval towers, and there is an ancient leaning spire on the church of St Illtyd on Caldey Island. Other churches have squat towers dating from the medieval period, as at Rudbaxton, Nevern, Llawhaden and Uzmaston. Some churches have their own particular quirks of character. For example, the church at Llawhaden has an old northern tower and a later southern tower; the latter was built during fourteenth-century extensions to the nave and chancel. A sad remnant of a once-proud church occurs on the shore near Slebech. Here are the ruins of a church formerly associated with the local headquarters of the Knights of St John of Jerusalem, with walls and church tower surrounded by thick undergrowth. It is not certain when the church was built, but it may date from the fourteenth century.

The most imposing of the early medieval churches were built in the main towns, where there were rich patrons, large congregations and skilled stonemasons and carpenters. We have already referred to the fine churches of Haverfordwest, and it is worth noting here that St Mary's Church at the top of High Street is thought by some to be the finest parish church in Wales. It is austere and spacious, and has a fine thirteenth-century arcade of pointed arches made by skilled craftsmen. In its style and size it gives some indication of the importance of the medieval town. St Mary's Church (Pembroke) is another fine Norman church dating from the thirteenth century; and St Mary's (Tenby), with its fine tower and spire, is said to be the largest of the medieval parish churches in Wales.

Of all the ancient churches of Pembrokeshire, the crowning glory is of course St David's Cathedral (Plate 5a). It is at least the third to stand on this site, for the Viking raiders seemed to enjoy the occasional sally into Dewi Sant's 'Vale of the Roses'. The present structure was begun about 1180, but several centuries of work under a succession of bishops were needed before the building assumed anything like its present form. The plan of the cathedral is a simple one, and is not much different from that designed for Bishop Peter de Leia in 1180. Some of the internal ornament was the work of Bishop Gower, and the exterior has been much modified because of structural defects. The first tower collapsed in 1220, and an earthquake demolished part of the structure in 1248. The present tower is a low one, but it was even lower in the fifteenth century and lower still in the fourteenth century. It did not acquire its pinnacles until the cathedral was safe from raiders. The exterior is plain to the point of austerity. The west front was rebuilt in 1789 by John Nash, when it was about to collapse from the outward pressure of the Norman arches, and there was further rebuilding under the guidance of Sir Gilbert Scott in 1863. The result is somewhat drab, but at least these remedial works rescued the cathedral from ruin, for parts of it had been in a sad state of decay in the seventeenth and eighteenth centuries.

While the exterior may be uninspiring, the interior is exquisite. The slope of the floor gives the building a strange feel, but the eye is attracted by other things. There is the magnificence of the late Norman arcades, the superb nave ceiling of black Irish oak, dating from about 1500; the fourteenth-century stone screen built by Bishop Gower; the fine fifteenth-century choir stalls; and the delicate fan-vaulted ceiling of the Holy Trinity Chapel. Then there is the shrine of St David, the altars, and the tombs of assorted notables. And one can see delicate carving in stone and wood, reaching perfection in the rich pendants of the nave roof.

Like most cathedrals, St David's is not exactly consistent in style either without or within, and a troubled history has left its mark. But it is still very much the symbol of the power of the church in this remote saintly corner of the western world, even if it came to be the symbol of Norman ascendancy and Welsh decline. It is still a worthy place of pilgrimage.

THE MONASTIC HOUSES

The monastic communities of the Age of the Saints were succeeded by a number of Norman foundations, and the buildings from these later foundations still survive in a number of localities. Religious houses were St Dogmael's Abbey, Pill Priory near Milford, Haverfordwest Priory and Friary, Monkton Priory, and Caldey Priory. There were medieval hospices at Llawhaden and at Whitewell, St David's. Then there was the Commandery of the

Knights of St John at Slebech, mentioned earlier in this chapter. All of these establishments were of immense importance in the confused world of Anglo-Norman Pembrokeshire; as Major Francis Jones has said, 'together with the parish priests, the good monks were the main, indeed the only, civilising agents of that barbarous age . . .'

The best-known of the monastic ruins is at St Dogmael's, where the abbey was founded with rich endowments in 1115 on the site of an older Celtic monastery. Most of the building took place after 1200, but the greatest construction work was during the fourteenth century. Building was still going on right up to the Dissolution of the Monasteries in 1536; after that time the abbey fell into ruin, but the abbey church became the parish church and continued in use for a while. The north and west walls of the church stand almost to their full height, and the many other remnants of buildings around the cloister are today carefully preserved by the Department of the Environment.

St Mary's College, adjacent to St David's Cathedral, must have been a fine building, with its high walls and large windows; but John Nash was allowed to use it as a stone quarry during his restoration of the west front of the cathedral, and this did it no good at all.

No other monastic ruins in the county are so well preserved. Haverfordwest Priory stands in ivy-covered ruin on the banks of the River Cleddau just below the town, while Pill Priory near Milford is nowadays simply a twelfth-century chancel arch in the midst of much later dwellings. Parts of Monkton Priory are incorporated in Priory Farm, and the choir and sanctuary became the chancel of the parish church. This was restored in 1887, and its lofty spaciousness gives a clue to its origins. There are few traces of the hospices at Llawhaden and Whitewell, or of the once-famous Whitland Abbey. At Caldey the old Norman priory has been subject to alterations and repairs over the years, but many of its medieval rooms remain in use to this day. Here, at least, the monastic tradition of the Celtic saints and their Norman successors has been revived; the Cistercian community of Caldey is very much a part of Pembrokeshire life today.

15 BUILDINGS: HOMES FOR RICH AND POOR

MOST of the buildings in Pembrokeshire are the homes of its inhabitants—town and suburban houses for rich and poor, farmhouses, country cottages, and country mansions. The majority date from the past 100 years or so, but there are many interesting domestic buildings of much greater age in both Englishry and Welshry.

On the whole this was not a county of vast, rich estates, so there is little to compare with the magnificent country houses and parks so lovingly created in the counties of England between 1550 and 1800. The Pembrokeshire country houses were smaller and less imposing, but they have many interesting architectural features, and like the medieval churches and fortified residences they provide a link with the castle-building techniques of the Anglo-Norman community. The smaller farmhouses and country cottages have many features of interest, and in the towns there are fine buildings ranging from the well-known Tudor Merchant's House in Tenby to the town houses of the eighteenth-century gentry in Haverfordwest.

Near the old ports of the county there are commercial buildings such as the warehouses of Haverfordwest, St David's and Fishguard; and in Chapter 10 mention has already been made of the wide range of buildings connected with various industrial activities. There are also bridges, harbourworks and jetties, lighthouses and monuments, stations, embankments and viaducts dating from the railway era, and military buildings like the Milford Haven forts, many of them still in a good state of repair. In this short chapter there is space only to look at a few of these buildings, but the following paragraphs may give some idea of the architectural heritage of domestic buildings in Pembrokeshire.

COUNTRY COTTAGES

Most of the cottages scattered around the Pembrokeshire countryside used to be the dwellings of farm labourers and small craftsmen. Probably they were similar in style in both parts of the county, although there were of course local differences according to the raw materials available and the wealth and skill of the builder.

Many of the simplest and most primitive cottages have of course disappeared or have been altered and enlarged over the years. The most primitive cottages of all, which were still being built after 1840, were the 'one-night' shacks put up on waste or common ground by the landless peasants. The squatters would seek the help of neighbours, relatives and friends in the provision of raw materials and especially labour for the nocturnal building operation; but the *tŷ unnos* was not meant to last. It was built of turf and rough wooden beams, perhaps with a roof of grass or rushes, and it was usually built in May or June so that it could be replaced during the summer months by a second, more permanent, dwelling. Once this second dwelling was habitable, the original turf building became the cowshed or pigsty. Not surprisingly, most of the squatters' homes have vanished long since, for they did not have the quality of permanence about them. But several of the little hamlets which arose out of the squatters' settlements do remain, particularly in the north of the county on the fringes of Mynydd Presely.

Many of the Pembrokeshire country cottages of the 1700s and 1800s were built with mud walls and a rough-thatched roof. If help was forthcoming in the construction of the cottage, the total cost even at the end of the eighteenth century might be no more than £10. Most cottages were built to a simple rectangular plan (Plate 14a), with mud or clay walls five or six feet high and up to four feet thick. These were referred to as 'clom' walls, and they were strongest where clay could be employed in their construction strengthened with chopped straw, rushes or twigs. Generally there was a low, thatched roof. The quality of the thatching was generally poor, and the bundles of hay or straw were kept on with long poles or cord running along the length of the roof. There was a fireplace at one end, and a rough wattle and daub chimney, more often than not leaning out from the gable end of the cottage at a crazy angle. There was generally a low front door centrally placed in one of the longer walls, with a small window on each side. The windows were simply openings in the walls, for glass panes did not come into common use until much later. The floors were of damp, compacted earth. The simplest cottages had only one room, although articles of furniture were often used as partitions to create separate rooms. They had only a single storey and no lofts. Nowadays it is difficult to imagine the poverty and squalor of life in cottages such as these.

Not all of the cottages of this type were in the country districts, for they were common in the towns and villages also. Some of the most wretched cottages were built at the time of Pembrokeshire's 'industrial revolution', when many farm labourers were forced to leave the land and seek employment in the coal-mining districts. Many cottages for colliery workers were hastily erected around Begelly (where many of them seem to have been built by squatters) and at Kilgetty and Saundersfoot. In the middle of the nineteenth century the squalor of the buildings and of their inhabitants attracted much comment. Each cottage was made of a mixture of mud, road scrapings and stones, and its roof was thatched with straw. Sometimes a low wall of earth and wooden boards served to divide the cottage in two. A fire was kept burning continuously in the hearth, filling the interior with fumes and smoke but helping to keep the walls and floor dry. Not surprisingly, when the collieries and the Stepaside Iron Works closed, the cottages were abandoned and soon crumbled away. Within living memory there were over forty clom cottages in and around Stepaside. Now they are all gone.

In some parts of the county, especially where clom walls could be strengthened with shale fragments, cottages of this type are still in use, although not as dwellings. Generally they have been preserved because the old thatched roofs have long since been replaced by slate or corrugated iron. Thatch was never a very good roofing material in the wet and windy climate of Pembrokeshire, and hardly any thatched buildings remain. The best preserved is at Penrhos, near Maenclochog, where it is kept as a miniature museum.

The majority of eighteenth-century cottages still standing in the county have stone walls and slate roofs. Generally they conform to the traditional design; but the later cottages (dating particularly from the decades following the arrival of the railway in West Wales) are more elaborate. They have higher walls, larger windows with glass panes, back doors, internal walls, paved floors, and sometimes fireplaces and chimneys inside both gable ends. Some cottages were given interior ceilings and second floors or lofts, and porches and out-houses were often added. But still the design of these cottages was basically rectangular and symmetrical. The building materials varied according to the nature of the local bedrock; hence the cottages are made of limestone blocks in parts of south Pembrokeshire, slate slabs at Abereiddi and Trefin, Old Red Sandstone slabs on some of the shores of Milford Haven, and purple Cambrian sandstone near St David's. Mudstone or 'rab' fragments were often used around Haverfordwest, and where flagstones were available in the Ordovician and Silurian shales these were occasionally used for roofing purposes also. Very often the exteriors of cottages were colour-washed in pink, white, grey and various shades of yellow, and it was not at all uncommon for each of the four walls to be given a different colour. This custom probably arose from the need to seal the outer walls of clom buildings with a lime wash, and it was later extended to stone-built walls also.

Slate roofs have been used since the medieval period in some of the areas of Anglo-Norman settlement, but slate only became widely available for use on the cottages of poor people within the last 150 years or so. Naturally this coincided with the growth of slate-quarrying operations at Abereiddi, Rosebush, Sealyham and elsewhere. The original method of roofing with slate was to drill a hole through each slate, and then to fasten it to a thin, split batten by means of a wooden peg. All the battens were nailed on to the rafters, but no nails were used on the rows of slates themselves. The finished roof was rendered underneath with lime mortar, which had the effect of cementing slate, peg and batten together and keeping out the wind. As the decades passed and the wooden pegs began to rot, a thin coat of mortar would be applied to the outside of the roof in an effort to keep the slates in place. Over the years more and more mortar, or a sand and cement wash, would be applied, making the roof heavier and more liable to rot. Sometimes wires would be passed from one eave to the other, over the ridge, and again heavily grouted. Eventually the whole roof would slide off or collapse, or else be repaired with a patchwork of corrugated iron sheets.

FARMHOUSES

There are several different types of farmhouse in Pembrokeshire, showing the influence of both Welsh and Anglo-Norman building traditions. From the Middle Ages onwards, the homes of the husbandmen and yeomen were much more substantial structures than the cottages of the agricultural labourers, and they were generally built of stone. Many were completely rebuilt in the later sixteenth and seventeenth centuries, and many more were enlarged. At this time new farmhouses also appeared in many areas as agriculture became more prosperous, more efficient, and free of the conflict and destruction of the preceding centuries. But most of the new farmhouses were built to a fairly consistent local style.

Many of the Pembrokeshire farmhouses are based upon the medieval tradition of the open hall. The early medieval buildings were built with massive stone walls and they probably had no chimneys. But then gigantic fireplaces and chimneys were added, sometimes in awkward positions attached to the outside of an end wall or a side wall. Sometimes later renovations and alterations to farmhouses involved the demolition and rebuilding of nearly all the walls, so that the rebuilt structure was in effect added to the old fireplace and chimney! It follows that Pembrokeshire fireplace and chimney units were built to last, like that which stands in glorious isolation today in the middle of a cottage garden in Carew. From medieval times they were a part of the local building tradition, and Peter Smith considers that they are among the most remarkable architectural features of the region.

The chimneys come in three main types. The tall round chimneys of Pembrokeshire are well known, and they are locally referred to as 'Flemish chimneys'. However, there is no evidence that they had anything to do with the Flemings, for their distribution does not at all coincide with that part of the Englishry settled by the Flemish immigrants. They are, however, found on the halls and large farmhouses of the medieval gentry, and there are at least twenty-three of them. All occur in the Englishry, and the greatest concentration is found in a belt between Monkton, Pembroke and the Tenby area where limestone was commonly available as a building material. The slightly lower and less elegant conical chimneys are found mostly on the St David's peninsula, although there are at least two to the south of Milford Haven and another at Garn, near Fishguard (Plate 13). These generally belong to very old farmhouses which may have been the homes of the lesser gentry or the more prosperous yeomen. The most unusual are the square chimneys which are often built above fireplaces of extraordinary size, sometimes out of all proportion to the building which they serve. Occasionally there are exceptionally capacious ovens, too, fitted on to fireplace and chimney in unusual forms. These units are often situated to one side of the ridge. There are some splendid examples in the Englishry, as at Dover (Bosherston), Bangeston (Stackpole Elidor), Palmer's Lake (Penally) and Thornton (Bosherston).

There are various types of farmhouse plan, and these can be classified according to the number of rooms, their arrangement, and their relationship with the fireplace and chimney unit. The simplest subdivision seems to be between houses with gable-end chimneys (located either inside or outside the house wall) and houses with partly projecting fireplaces. The farmhouses at Rhosson, Clegyrfwya, Croftufty and Llaethdy, all near St David's are, or were, typical examples. Generally, there is a central passage running across the house from front door to back door. There are large rooms on either side of this passage, and sometimes smaller rooms as well under the main roof. There may be a loft to increase the living area beneath part of the roof, as in the magnificent fifteenth-century farmhouse at Garn. Small side-aisles or 'pent-houses' built on to the side wall are used as store-rooms, dairies or extra bedrooms, and they effectively increase the size of the living-room without increasing the span of the roof. In centuries past the main roofs of farmhouses such as these would have been thatched, with stone slabs or slates used on the roofs of the side-aisles.

An old type of farmhouse which is particularly common in the Welsh parts of Pembrokeshire is the so-called long-house. This is even more common in adjacent Cardiganshire and Carmarthen-shire, where several splendid examples have been studied. The typical long-house consisted, as its name implies, of a long, rec-tangular building, which was divided into three main segments. At the upper end was the dwelling-house, and at the lower end the cow-byre; between these was a connecting section used as a cattle-feeding walk. This central section usually had the main door and the main hearth. Some of the long-houses had lofts providing a second storey to the dwelling-house, and indeed hay-lofts were necessary for the cattle-shed also. Sometimes the lowest section of the building was a stable, entered through a separate door. Some of the long-houses had cruck-construction roofs, and they were originally thatched with straw or reeds. Turf was sometimes used to protect the ridge of the building, and often the dwelling-house was whitewashed. There were many local varia-tions on the long-house theme, and in the last century or so some of the more successful farmers have ejected the cattle from their homes in to separate cow-sheds, thus allowing the whole of the long-house to be used for domestic accommodation. There is a fine example of a long-house in the village of Trefin, where the building is in four connected segments running straight down a steep slope (Plate 14b).

Many of the old Pembrokeshire farms are hybrid buildings showing some characteristics of the long-house tradition and some of the Anglo-Norman tradition. The Welsh tradition is seen in the highly elongated rectangular form and the central passage running between opposite doors; and the style of the Anglo-Norman castle-builders is seen in the massive, thick stone walls, the arched doorways, the peculiar fireplaces, chimneys and ovens, and the stone staircases, recesses and benches.

COUNTRY MANSIONS

While the farmers were farming and the poor cottagers were trying to survive, the landed gentry of Pembrokeshire flourished. During the sixteenth century the manors of the Middle Ages were consolidated, and the landed gentry on their fine estates still wielded almost feudal power over their tenants. In addition to the old-established families there were many squires and lesser gentry. Some of these kept their place in the ranks of the gentry through their ancient pedigrees, but others rose through successful trading in the towns to join the ranks of the socially acceptable. From about 1570 onwards, there was a burst of house-building in Pembrokeshire as affluent families renewed or rebuilt their family seats to reflect their living style and (especially) their status. Many of the fine mansions of Pembrokeshire date from the period 1570–1800.

Among the great families were the Philippses of Picton Castle, the Owens of Orielton, the Barlows of Lawrenny, and the Campbells of Stackpole; and there were other well-known families at Slebech, Boulston, Llwyngwair, Sealyham and Manorowen, to mention but a few. Some of these families prospered, and as they did so their fine stately homes were rebuilt and enlarged. Other families (particularly the smaller gentry) built their homes and found their small fortunes dissipated. Between 1670 and 1750 many of the lesser Pembrokeshire gentry mortgaged or sold off their estates, and in 1810 Richard Fenton wrote that '. . . in several parts of this county mansions frequently occur in ruins, some abandoned for others more suited to the taste or views of the different owners, many by falling to heiresses, who have conferred their hands and properties on strangers, but the far greater number owing to the vicissitudes of human affairs and the precariousness of human possessions . . .'

Some fine mansions remain to remind us of past glories. The house at Orielton (Plate 12b) was originally a fortified medieval manor, but the powerful Owen family rebuilt it with a plain, classical east front in 1743. The south front was more elaborate, and there was a landscaped vista across lake and woodland. During the eighteenth century the estate and the house were great centres of the county's social life, and as the family prospered the house was extended even further in 1810. Now the complex of buildings houses the Orielton Field Centre, run by the Field Studies Council. At Picton Castle, as we saw in the last chapter, a large, new, castellated block was added in 1800, and the old west tower of the castle was demolished to make way for it. In 1768 Sir William Hamilton incurred great expense in making improvements to Colby Hall, and the cost of rebuilding Slebech Hall in 1776 was so crippling that the owner was forced to sell the estate soon afterwards. The great house at Landshipping was improved in 1789. Completely new mansions were built in this period at Ffynhone (1790, designed by John Nash) and at Boulston (about 1800). The former, although remodelled in 1904, is still the finest country house in the whole of the Welshry. Close to the idyllic harbour of Lower Fishguard, Richard Fenton built the fine house called Glynamel. There are other interesting stately homes still in a good state of preservation at St Brides (Kensington Hospital), Saundersfoot (Hean Castle), Lydstep, Llwyngwair near Nevern, Manorowen, and elsewhere.

Sadly, or perhaps inevitably, some of the great houses are now demolished or have been reduced to ruins. The stately mansion at Stackpole Court, home of Baron Cawdor, which was embellished within by works of art and beautified without by extensive renovations in 1715, has now been demolished. Close to Haverfordwest are the ruins of Haroldston mansion, the home of the picturesque Elizabethan Sir John Perrot. We can still gain some impression of its former grandeur even though it has been in ruins for over 200 years. In the south of the county there are the last remnants of Scotsborough in the little valley of the Ritec. Henllys, the home of our old friend George Owen, is lost without trace. The same can be said of the mansions of Rickeston and Llanrheithan in Dewisland, and many other fine houses. Unlike the castles and the churches, the mansions of Pembrokeshire were not built to last.

BUILDINGS: HOMES FOR RICH AND POOR

By way of conclusion to this chapter it is worth mentioning some of the fine domestic architecture of the main towns. Most of the interesting buildings date from the period when the Pembrokeshire gentry were at their most affluent and when the merchants of Haverfordwest, Pembroke and Tenby could still afford to live in reasonable style.

The most interesting of all the old buildings is the Tudor Merchant's House in Tenby (Fig 6). It dates from the fifteenth century, and it has a gabled front and a corbelled chimney. It is still carefully preserved, and is a popular tourist attraction. Next door is Plantagenet House, of similar age; this has a fine round chimney. There are few other traces of medieval buildings in the town, for the greatest part of its fabric dates from late Georgian to early Victorian times. Nevertheless, the regiments of hotels and boarding-houses along the cliff-tops above both North Beach and South Beach are quite magnificent monuments to the early efforts of Sir William Paxton, the creator of the modern holiday resort.

Haverfordwest has a number of fine town houses, some of them dating from the affluent years of the eighteenth century when many of the gentry built and maintained winter residences there. While the local gentry congregated in Tenby during the summer, Haverfordwest was the centre of the winter social scene. A number of the houses of High Street and Hill Street were the residences of the élite, and parties and balls were held virtually every night during 'the season'. The best-known of the town houses is Foley House in Goat Street, built by John Nash in 1794 for Mr Richard Foley. It has been preserved (somewhat garishly) and is now the headquarters of the Dyfed County Council Industrial Development Unit, the nerve centre for the Celtic Sea oil search.

Elsewhere in the town there are other interesting buildings, but local people apparently failed to notice them until many of them were recently scheduled for preservation. Hermon Hill House has a Regency bow front, and may also have been designed by Nash. And in Barn Street, Gloucester Terrace and elsewhere

Fig 6 A sketch of the Tudor Merchant's House in Tenby, one of the town's most popular tourist attractions

there are most attractive rows of town housing in a variety of different styles. The splendid wrought iron work of the terrace at the bottom of Barn Street is particularly fascinating.

Along the main street of Pembroke there is a wide variety of domestic architecture, from houses at the castle end with projecting Tudor corbels to the more familiar styles of the modern shop fronts. The irregular roof-line of the street has a medieval look about it, and this is of course enhanced when one is looking towards the castle. Here again is a reminder that in Pembrokeshire the medieval world is not very far away even when we are within sight and smell of the ultra-modern Pembroke powerstation.

16   THE REDISCOVERY OF MILFORD HAVEN

T HE most recent chapter in the life story of the Milford Haven waterway is part of the story of the British oil industry. During the early 1950s the oil companies were thinking in terms of vastly increased tonnages for their oil tankers, to enable them to keep pace with the enormous rise in the demand for petroleum products and to reduce their own transporting costs. Both the BP and Esso petroleum companies began planning for oil tankers of 100,000dwt or more, and the immense advantages of Milford Haven as a potential oil port became apparent. It had a wide and sheltered waterway, and could accommodate vessels of 55ft draught at all states of the tide. Tidal scour was efficient, and there was no silting problem and thus no need for continuous dredging. Land was cheap on both sides of the Haven, and was available for large-scale construction projects. Moreover, the government favoured the development of the Haven. Consequently the decision was taken in 1957 to embark upon the creation of a major oil port, and in 1958 government legislation was passed setting up the Milford Haven Conservancy Board. By 1959 the Esso and BP companies were hard at work with building projects on the shores of the Haven, and the modern oil port was born. Since then there have been other large schemes also, and these are shown in Map 6.

THE OIL INDUSTRY

The Esso oil refinery, near the village of Herbrandston, was the first refinery to be built on the shores of Milford Haven. It began working in the autumn of 1960 and is now the second largest re-

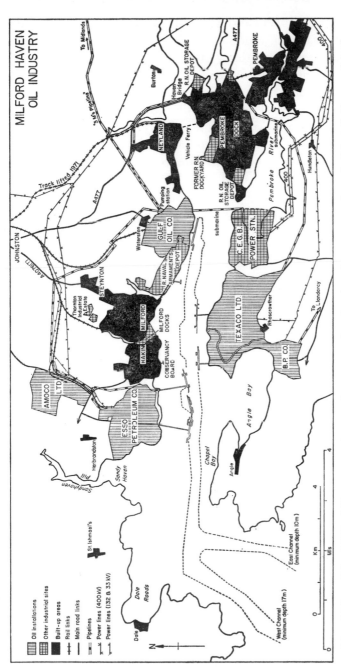

Map 6 Map of the Milford Haven waterway at the present day showing the concentration of oil installations and jetties

finery in the British Isles. At first it was able to refine only about 4½ million tons of crude oil each year; but now, after a large expansion project costing £26 million to complete, it can refine 15 million tons of oil per year. The refinery site covers 643 acres, with the refinery plant itself more or less surrounded by almost a hundred oil tanks (Plate 16b). The largest tanks, on the clifftops around the western edge of the refinery, store the crude oil. The smaller tanks hold various products such as petrol, diesel oil and jet fuels. Most of the crude oil is imported in the Esso supertankers which are a common sight in the waters of Milford Haven. The Esso jetty, stretching about 3,000ft out from the shore, has a long pier head with five berths for shipping. These are used by tankers of all sizes up to 285,000 tons, and nowadays more than 2,000 vessels use the jetty each year. Most of these are small tankers which carry about eighty per cent of the refined products to other British ports. About eighteen per cent of the products are pumped along a pipeline to Birmingham, Nottingham and Manchester. At present 375 staff are employed at the refinery.

The deep-water terminal at Popton Point, near Angle, was built by the BP company in the years 1958–60 and was officially opened in 1961. Its cost was approximately £7 million. There is no BP refinery on the site. Instead, the terminal was built to import crude oil for the existing BP refinery at Llandarcy, near Swansea, which had no facilities suitable for handling super-tankers. The terminal and the refinery are connected by a buried pipeline over sixty miles long. Its construction was an impressive civil engineering project. It involved the crossing of twelve major roads and thirty-seven rivers. The greatest obstacle of all was the River Tywi below Carmarthen, crossed at a point where it was about 1,500ft wide at high tide. When it was brought in to use the pipeline was the longest crude oil pipeline in the British Isles, able to carry 5 million tons of oil per year. Since 1960 the Llandarcy refinery has been expanded to refine over 8 million tons of crude oil per year, and the capacity of the pipeline has also been increased (by the building of a 'booster station' with three pumps at St Clears) to 9·2 million tons per year.

The jetty at Popton Point stretches 1,350ft from the shore, and the 'jetty head' is 2,370ft long, providing three berths for super-tankers. The first tanker to berth at the terminal was the 42,000 ton *British Statesman*, and in 1965 the first 100,000 ton ship to enter the Haven berthed at the BP terminal amid great publicity. This was the *British Admiral*. Nowadays even this vessel seems small in comparison with tankers of 250,000 tons which are frequent visitors to the Haven.

The BP company holds 383 acres of land on the south shore of Milford Haven, of which less than 300 is currently used. The offices and control centre for the terminal are inside the old Popton Fort where there are also storage tanks for bunker oil and water supplies. The main tank-farm is about a mile away at Kilpaison, on the shore of Angle Bay. The tanks hold a total of half a million tons of crude oil, and four of them (each holding 75,000 tons of oil) are among the largest in Europe. Recently two 50,000 ton tanks have been built on Popton Point to store fuel oil for the Pembroke power-station.

In 1962 Texaco chose Milford Haven as the site for its first UK refinery. It was opened in October 1964. It is the only refinery on the south shore of the Haven. The tank-farm and refinery are built in the middle of a 925 acre site, near the small village of Rhoscrowther. Since it was built the refinery has been enlarged so that it can now refine about 10 million tons of crude oil per year. Nevertheless, the refinery and tank-farm still only occupy 475 acres of the large site. The crude oil is imported in super-tankers and smaller vessels, although only two of the five berths on the jetty can accommodate tankers of more than 100,000 tons. This situation will soon be improved by a large jetty extension. The refinery produces petrol, jet fuels, kerosene, diesel oils, fuel oils and liquefied petroleum gases. About ninety per cent of these products are shipped out, for road access to the refinery is poor and there is no rail link. The refinery employs about 320 persons, and Texaco estimates that it contributes at least £1½ million annually to the local economy in the way of rates, salaries and local purchases.

In 1966 the Gulf Oil Refining Company started to build its refinery, petrochemical plant and deep-water marine terminal in the inner reaches of Milford Haven near the village of

Waterston. The installations, which cost £39 million, were formally opened by the Queen in August 1968. The refinery and its tank-farm are built on an exposed flat site close to the coast. The three berths of the jetty are quite close to the shore and they are not nearly so noticeable as the Esso, Amoco, Texaco and BP jetties further down the Haven.

Because the Gulf refinery is six miles from the mouth of Milford Haven it does not have access to the deepest channel. The largest vessels which can be handled at the jetty at present are 165,000 tonners. However, this presents no great difficulty to the company for it has an importing strategy which involves the use of a deep-water terminal in Bantry Bay, Ireland. 'Mammoth' tankers of 325,000 tons (such as the *Universe Ireland*) call at Bantry Bay approximately every ten days with cargoes of Kuwait crude oil. After brief storage in a tank-farm this is transhipped in smaller tankers which take it to the Gulf refineries at Waterston and Europoort (Holland). The refinery can process about 5 million tons of crude oil per year, and although there is a rail link most of the products are sent out by sea. Some of the products are used on the site in the Gulf petrochemical plant, which is the only one in the Milford Haven area. The petrochemical industry started here in 1969 with the production of benzene, a clear liquid which solidifies below 5·6°C and so has to be shipped in special tankers. Some benzene is made into cyclohexane, which is used in the manufacture of nylon. There are other products also, shipped partly to the Rotterdam chemical industry and partly to other European customers.

The £30 million Amoco refinery is the latest addition to the oil installations on Milford Haven. Building started in 1971 and it came 'on stream' in October 1973, with a refining capacity of 4 million tons per year. Unlike the other Milford Haven refineries the Amoco site lies well away from the coast, about two miles inland near Robeston Cross. It does, however, have its own jetty a short distance east of the Esso terminal. The jetty runs about 3,000ft from the shore near Gelliswick Bay out to the deep-water channel. The main berth can handle tankers of 275,000 tons, and the second and third berths are designed for loading smaller tankers with refined products. Underground

214

pipelines connect the jetty to the refinery. The refinery at present occupies only 314 acres of the 845 acres owned by Amoco. All of the processing operations, and the tank-farm, are contained within a more or less rectangular perimeter. Closest to the sea are the large crude-oil storage tanks. To the east of them, and around the 'process area' itself, are the smaller tanks which hold the refined products. The refinery and administrative buildings are in the north of the site, and on the eastern edge are the railway sidings. Like the branches serving the Esso and Gulf refineries, these have been specially built to link up with the main railway line between Milford and Johnston.

Pembroke power-station, which is located in Pennar Gut on the south shore of the Haven, is one of the largest in Europe. It was planned in 1964 and completed in 1973, having cost £105 million to build. It burns heavy fuel oil which is carried from the Gulf and Texaco refineries and the BP ocean terminal by buried pipelines. It is cooled by sea water pumped from the Haven at a rate of up to 55 million gallons per hour. In 1973 the power-station burned about 2 million tons of oil, and when fully used it may burn 4 million tons per year. This will allow the production of 2,000 megawatts, carried by the overhead power-lines of the national 'supergrid' towards South Wales, the Midlands and the Bristol region. These power-lines, which carry 400kV, are supported between the huge metal pylons which are now a spectacular part of the south Pembrokeshire landscape. The power-station provides employment for 495 people, and it contributes over £1¼ million to the local economy each year in rates and indirect contributions.

Of the vast network of pipelines which are essential to the workings of the Milford Haven oil refining complex, the most important is the pipeline linking Milford Haven with the Midlands and Manchester. It was built at a cost of £15 million in 1972-3 by a consortium of the Esso, Texaco and Gulf companies. Now it carries a variety of refined products (mainly petrol, kerosene and diesel fuel) in a pipeline which runs from Waterston to Seisdon in Staffordshire. From Seisdon there are smaller pipelines to terminals in Birmingham, Nottingham and Manchester. In its first operating year the pipeline carried over 2 million tons of products (mostly petrol), and this will be built up until over 9 million tons are carried each year.

While the developments of the oil-refining industry have been proceeding apace, the Haven has failed to attract any other type of major industry. Many industrial schemes have been proposed, amid great local interest, but none of them has come to anything. Even the petrochemical industry has failed to materialise, except on the Gulf refinery site, although it was widely thought at one time that companies like Fisons would be attracted to the Haven. Many other schemes for industrial developments have fallen through, and although some of them have encouraged great local hopes of increased industrial employment, others have raised great local opposition on environmental grounds. Above all, however, it is still true that the factor which militates most strongly against a more diverse industrial base around Milford Haven is remoteness from the major British markets.

The trappings of the oil industry in and around Milford Haven are considerable. The most important of the 'ancillaries' is the Conservancy Board, the body mainly responsible for controlling shipping operations in the waterway. It was set up as a unique civil port authority by Act of Parliament in 1958, since Milford Haven is the only new port in the UK to be established in the twentieth century. The Conservancy Board was charged with maintaining and improving the navigation of the whole tidal area of Milford Haven and the Daugleddau, regulating seaborne traffic, and providing lights, buoys and communications. Also, it was given the right to levy dues on all vessels entering the Haven, in order to finance its operations.

The Conservancy Board has its offices, signal station and small boat harbour at Hubberston Point, which gives easy access to all the refinery jetties and to the harbour entrance. The board has recently acquired increased powers, and the day-to-day running of its operations is in the hands of a general manager and secretary and a harbourmaster. The board employs sixteen pilots and operates five diesel-engined launches, three of which are always on duty. This pilotage, boarding and landing service has virtually eliminated delays to vessels requiring pilots, and in 1972 the launches logged a total of 12,164 hours actually under way.

The biggest project undertaken by the Conservancy Board to date was the £7½ million rock-dredging scheme of 1967–70, designed to improve the deep-water channel so that it could be safely used by 275,000 ton tankers at all states of the tide. New day and night transit lights were put up at West Blockhouse and Watwick Point, to supplement the existing navigational lights. The Watwick Point lighthouse is 48m high, making it the third tallest lighthouse in the world. In addition to operating the VHF radio port information service, the Conservancy Board signal station is the hub of telephone communications for Milford Haven. It controls the emergency services and co-ordinates the movements of the fleet of powerful tugs owned by Cory Ship Towage Ltd. It is also the operations centre for the sophisticated radar navigation system which has recently been brought into use for vessels entering and leaving the waterway.

The Milford Haven oil industry has grown at a spectacular rate. From the small beginnings of the oil trade the Haven had risen by 1968 to become Britain's leading oil port, handling 30 million tons of a UK total of 180 million tons. Now the Haven handles the second largest volume of cargo in Britain, and by 1976 it may well overtake London as Britain's busiest port. In 1973 over 28 million tons of shipping used the port. There were over 9,000 movements, and the cargo handled (mostly crude oil and petroleum products) was over 53 million tons. Now that the Amoco refinery is receiving cargoes of crude oil also, this record total is certain to be beaten easily in future years. Since 1965 the Haven has broken many shipping records both for the size of the vessels handled and the weight of single cargoes discharged. Vessels of over 300,000 tons are beginning to appear in the waterway, and cargoes of 225,000 tons are now commonplace.

The impact of the oil developments on Pembrokeshire has been enormous, and this can be measured in a variety of different ways. In terms of capital investment, something like £280 million has been spent on the oil installations, and capital expenditure is still going on in spite of the world oil crisis. Each phase of refinery construction has provided employment for over 2,000 workers, many of them locally recruited; and the completion of each refinery has been followed by severe unemployment. In 1974 the number of people directly employed in the oil installations was 1,849, and the industry is probably responsible for the creation of at least another 2,500 jobs in local firms. It is difficult to calculate the contribution of the industry to the local economy in cash terms; but including rates and local expenditure by the oil companies and the CEGB, one calculation puts the figure at about £6·7 million each year. As noted in Chapter 11, the need to provide services for the oil industry has resulted in better local roads, the reopening of Haverfordwest aerodrome to light aircraft, and the construction of the Haven Bridge. In addition, electricity supplies have been improved and the county has acquired a new reservoir at Llysyfran (Plate 16a) which not only improves water supply but also provides a welcome amenity for local people and tourists.

Most of the direct impact of industrialisation is of course felt around the waterway itself—in its farms and villages and in the three Milford Haven towns. Around the Haven, 3,262 acres of farm land has been lost to industry, and the appeal (and high wages) of refinery construction work has attracted many farm workers away from agriculture. Most of them will never return to the land.

But the farmers have obtained good prices for the land lost, and they have been forced to rationalise their farming activities to cater for their problems in finding farm labour. This may be no bad thing. The towns have experienced greatly increased trade, and many small firms have expanded to provide services for the oil industry. The oil companies have provided social and recreational facilities which have benefited all three of the town communities, and the arrival of many newcomers in the area has given a boost to social life and land values. Very few people have complained about the economic or social impact of the oil industry, although there has been much disquiet about the small number of permanent local jobs provided by the industry. Something like seventy per cent of jobs in the oil installations are held by local people, but the dreams of several thousand local jobs were never realistic. Since the oil companies came to Milford Haven technological developments in the industry have been so rapid that it has become one of the most capital-intensive of all. And the oil companies have come to Milford Haven to refine petroleum products as cheaply as possible—not to provide local jobs.

THE ENVIRONMENTAL IMPACT

It is inevitable that there should have been environmental problems in developing Britain's largest oil-refining complex in the county which contains Britain's most beautiful coastal national park. The oil installations are built around the middle reaches of Milford Haven, mainly between the coastal and inland sections of the park. But there has been much building inside the park also; the BP terminal and tank-farm are entirely within the park and the Esso, Amoco and Texaco refineries straddle the boundary. The Gulf refinery, further up the Haven, is built very prominently on a flat site, and although the power-station buildings are well shielded in the depression of Pennar Gut the 750ft chimney stack is now Pembrokeshire's most prominent landmark. In the south of the county there are now two rows of gigantic pylons transporting electricity solidly and inexorably towards the eastern horizon.

Nobody expected that the oil industry would be invisible, but it could have been made very much less visible than it is. During Milford Haven's first decade of development the oil companies, conscious of the fact that they were building on the fringes of a relatively new national park, attempted to minimise the visual impact of their installations. The Esso company embarked upon an elaborate landscaping scheme and an even more elaborate public relations exercise during the building of its refinery, and used earth embankments and sunken storage tanks on the slopes of a small valley in its attempt to blend massive structures into the landscape. The Texaco refinery was made considerably less obtrusive from Milford Haven because of a careful siting and landscaping scheme. The large BP tank-farm was built close to sea-level on the south shore of Angle Bay, and was well landscaped and coloured. And it was a happy idea on the part of BP to use the old Popton Fort as the administrative centre for the Angle Bay ocean terminal. On the other hand some aspects of the original construction works undertaken by the oil companies before 1970 were rather less pleasing to the eye. It was a planning aberration, for example, to allow the construction of five storage tanks for bunker oil and water on the rocky tip of Popton Point. It was a mistake to allow Texaco to build a group of storage tanks on another prominent clifftop site. And many local people now feel, in retrospect, that it was a planning disaster to have allowed the building of the Gulf refinery at all, on its prominent site adjacent to the village of Waterston where effective landscaping was impossible.

In the waterway itself the rocky headlands (such as Popton Point, Wear Point and Hubberston Point), which are the focal points of coastal landscapes, sprouted their inevitable jetties. The first three were built with long piers projecting to the edge of the central deep-water channel of the Haven. Having reached it, they spread their tentacles laterally towards east and west. In addition, navigational aids of various shapes and sizes appeared in and around the waterway, particularly during the major project undertaken by the Milford Haven Conservancy Board in 1967–70 to improve port facilities. These aids are prominent in the Haven entrance and on the cliffs to the west and north.

In recent years, sadly, visual pollution around the waterway has steadily increased. The new Amoco refinery, subject to stringent landscaping controls on the site itself, nevertheless makes a strong visual impact on many parts of the park which previously had no views of modern industrial buildings. The Esso company was given the blessing of the Alkali Inspector (who has the final word in such cases) to construct a 500ft smoke stack as part of its expansion programme. Recent extensions of refinery tank-farms have also made an impact. In order to store and supply fuel oil to the Pembroke power-station, the BP company constructed two 50,000 ton capacity tanks on a clifftop site immediately behind Popton Fort. These tanks are deeply sunk into bedrock in an attempt to reduce their effect upon the skyline. On the other hand, as part of its expansion programme Esso built equally large tanks on clifftop sites on the seaward margins of its original tank-farm. The visual impact of these is much more violent, for three of them occupy the hill summit adjacent to South Hook Battery, in an area which was strictly excluded from the first phase of refinery construction. Both the Esso and BP companies used strong civil engineering arguments to show that their new tanks could not have been sited elsewhere, and the planning authorities believed the civil engineers.

Marine pollution is, as yet, less of a problem in Milford Haven. The Conservancy Board prides itself that Milford Haven is the cleanest oil port in the world, but there are still occasional oil spills at the refinery jetties. These spills are always heavily fined by the Conservancy Board but this is no real deterrent since most spills are due to human error in piping crude oil or petroleum products between ship and shore. As the volume of shipping increases so does the risk of spillage and small spills are now frequently reported in the press. A big collision or berthing accident could cause fearsome pollution, and would provide a stern test for the emergency services. The Haven tugs are equipped for salvage operations, and they all carry fire-fighting apparatus including foam jets mounted sixty feet above the water-line. In case of oil spills the anti-pollution launch *Seaspray* is always on call with stocks of emulsifiers. In addition there is frequent patrolling in search of floating oil, and the oil companies have paid for research into the best ways of fighting oil spills.

Great concern has been expressed locally about noise and atmospheric pollution, particularly with respect to the Gulf refinery and the Pembroke power-station. The Gulf refinery plant is far too close to the village of Waterston, and the villagers have been involved in a long campaign against the company in their attempts to lessen the impact of noise, smell and dirt fall-out. The campaign has at times been bitter; the company has offered to buy the whole village and evacuate the population, and the villagers have resorted to various legal devices to obtain compensation from the company and even to close the refinery down. But Gulf is no more and no less guilty of pollution than the other companies operating around Milford Haven, and few people seem to have grasped the sheer scale of local atmospheric pollution. Working at full capacity, each refinery ejects between 50 and 100 tons of sulphur dioxide in its flue gases each day. At a conservative estimate this means that about 300 tons of sulphur dioxide is added by the refineries to the atmosphere above Milford Haven each day. Most of this falls to earth again a few miles downwind. The power-station is in a different league, for at full production it ejects 650 tons of sulphur dioxide daily. It burns heavy (ie cheap and filthy) fuel oil, and has no 'scrubbing' devices in its chimney flues to remove sulphur dioxide and other poisonous substances. Government regulations do not insist on their installation, and the simplest and cheapest method of disposal is to eject the waste gases at high velocity to an altitude of over 2,000ft in the hope that the wind will carry them away. The greatest fall-out of sulphur dioxide occurs about $6\frac{1}{4}$ miles away from the power-station, and above certain critical levels (already attained in some areas) plants are killed. All in all, the Milford Haven oil installations are capable of ejecting perhaps a thousand tons of poison into the Pembrokeshire atmosphere each day, and nobody seems to have noticed.

MILFORD HAVEN AND THE CELTIC SEA OIL SEARCH

Studies of the Celtic Sea and St George's Channel have shown geologists that there are probably large reserves there of crude oil and natural gas. These may not be as large as those of the North Sea, but in today's energy crisis both the government and the oil companies are desperate to discover and exploit all possible offshore oilfields. Drilling for oil and natural gas commenced in the Celtic Sea in 1973, and by mid-1974 crude oil and natural gas had already been discovered.

Milford Haven is extremely well placed for taking part in the Celtic Sea oil search. It has its own oil industry and there are sites which can be used as shore bases; the best of these are Pembroke Dockyard and Milford Docks. Pembrokeshire County Council encouraged the use of shore bases in the county, and now Dyfed County Council is maintaining this policy. Some local companies are involved in providing ship-building and repair and storage facilities. Celtic Sea Supply Base Ltd has been building up its work force and expanding the range of its industrial and service work; Govan Davies Estates and Marine and Port Services have developed their bases in the Pembroke Dockyard; and the Milford Docks Company is experiencing a new lease of life. And the vast number of services required for drilling operations in the difficult waters off the Pembrokeshire coast have encouraged many smaller firms to commit themselves to the Celtic Sea oil search as well. Near Haverfordwest the runways of Withybush aerodrome have been resurfaced, and are being used frequently by air taxi and helicopter services. Other helicopter bases are in use closer to Pembroke Dock.

By the beginning of 1975 the oil search had not really begun in earnest, partly because the oil exploration companies were fully occupied in the North Sea and partly because of a world shortage of deep-sea drilling equipment. This rather slow build-up has caused some local frustration, but it has at least allowed local commercial interests to prepare themselves carefully. And some progress is apparent. In the summer of 1973 Shell drilled the first unsuccessful 'wildcat' in the British section of the Celtic Sea, using the drilling rig *Transworld 61*. The rig was serviced from Pembroke Dockyard. In the winter of 1973–4 the drill-ship *Glomar Grand Isle* drilled a well for Arco; and this was followed by the drill-ship *Havdrill*, on charter to BP.

Local naturalists are worried that if oil is found off the Pembrokeshire coast the resulting pipelines will come ashore in the national park, requiring coastal terminals and pumping stations. Increased flying over the bird islands of Skokholm, Skomer and Grassholm by oil company helicopters could do great damage to local wildlife. Again, some people fear that now that oil has been found in the Celtic Sea the oil companies will soon want to establish offshore terminals in St Bride's Bay to handle ships of 500,000 tons and more. The effect of oil spills from such terminals could be disastrous for the local holiday trade, for the oil would come ashore on the sandy beaches of Broad Haven, Newgale and Whitesand Bay. Perhaps these fears are exaggerated, but at the time of writing there are signs that the new local government authorities are taking them seriously enough to evolve new strategies for controlling future development in Milford Haven. This is just as well, for the central government seems only to have been concerned with maximum development of the Haven 'in the national interest', regardless of the cost to the environment or the local community.

17 CONCLUSION: PEMBROKESHIRE, DYFED AND THE FUTURE

I N the foregoing chapters we have traced a number of threads which run through the landscape and the way of life of Pembrokeshire. Woven together these threads make up a rich tapestry—a tapestry which has more beauty and more variety than one has any right to expect in an area so small. And the tapestry is unique. It has a combination of colours and textures quite unlike those of adjacent parts of Wales. And yet these adjacent parts, the old counties of Cardiganshire and Carmarthenshire, have now joined Pembrokeshire to make up the new county of Dyfed. Times have changed; the seat of local government has been removed to Carmarthen, and the central government believes that Pembrokeshire is dead and buried. In this book we have seen that Pembrokeshire is very much alive and kicking even though it may have lost its name. Perhaps we may end on a note of nostalgia, looking at Pembrokeshire's immediate past and assessing its future role as part of Dyfed.

When local government reorganisation began, Pembrokeshire was slow to react. However, when it became clear that the county was to lose its identity and lose much of its control over its own destiny, a ground-swell of public disapproval started. During 1971 this swell gained momentum, with the enthusiastic support of the local press, and a 'Save Pembrokeshire' committee was formed to lead the fight for independence. Soon there was a thriving campaign in full swing, and the culmination of its activities was a delegation to the Welsh Office in London bearing a petition of 55,560 signatures. This represented the corporate voice of 79 per cent of the Pembrokeshire electorate, requesting the abandonment of the amalgamation scheme. However, unlike some other parts of England and Wales, Pembrokeshire was short of a strong establishment lobby, and the campaign failed. When the Local Government Act was passed it signalled the end of Pembrokeshire as a local government unit.

An interesting feature of the 'Save Pembrokeshire' campaign was that it revealed a strong unity of purpose in both Englishry and Welshry. The people of both halves of the county showed that, in spite of their traditional bickering in local council meetings and their petty animosities towards each other, they were united in their affection for the idea of Pembrokeshire. People from both north and south showed that they felt themselves to be, above all else, Pembrokeshire people. This was to be expected in the Englishry; but it was perhaps surprising that Welsh-speaking people showed themselves more inclined to face the future alongside Little Englanders than alongside their Welsh-speaking neighbours of Cardiganshire and Carmarthenshire.

Now Pembrokeshire belongs to Dyfed, and it is of course adapting itself to the new situation. To many the most interesting feature of the new county council is its aggressive pride in its own quality of Welshness. This is a consequence of the increasing self-respect of Welsh people throughout Wales, and of the upsurge in the popularity of the Welsh language over recent years. The campaigns of the Welsh Language Society and other groups have been remarkably successful, and hopefully they have come just in time to save the Welsh language and culture. The language has suddenly become respectable again, and it has become acceptable in many spheres where previously it was not tolerated. In Cardiff, Swansea and even Haverfordwest, Welsh lessons are in full swing.

The implications of the new situation are fascinating, especially when we look at them with respect to Little England. After centuries of numerical superiority over the Welsh-speaking people of Pembrokeshire, the people of Little England now find themselves very much in the minority in an aggressively Welsh new county. This will not do them any harm, and indeed they have always considered themselves Welsh, deep down, in any case. Eisteddfodau, welsh-cakes, Welsh costumes and cawl (leek broth) have always been as much a part of life in the Englishry as the Welshry;

o

and in 1972 Haverfordwest, below the Landsker, acted as host for the first time ever to that most Welsh of all Welsh institutions, the Welsh Royal National Eisteddford.

Sadly, the great occasion proved somewhat traumatic for many local people. The extremes of Welsh nationalism were demonstrated a little too openly for some tastes, and there seemed to be some disrespect for local traditions and for the English language, which happens to be the native language of the Englishry. Perhaps the Eisteddfod officials were a little insensitive towards local feelings, and perhaps local people were a little hypersensitive about quite small incidents which were not at all calculated to cause offence. But a great deal of offence was certainly caused by the lunatic fringe of the Welsh language movement, which defaced and smashed road signs all over Pembrokeshire. In all, damage costing £2,000 was caused, almost entirely to road signs which have English place-names such as Haverfordwest, Fishguard, Rudbaxton, and Milford Haven. This vandalism caused great local resentment, and although it was condemned instantly by the Eisteddfod organisers, it caused a quick backlash of vandalism against road signs bearing Welsh names.

Now everything is quiet again, and the Welsh language lobby has won a major victory in forcing the government to adopt bilingual road-signs for the whole of Wales. This involves the resurrection of Welsh place-names for south Pembrokeshire localities which have been English for about 900 years. Many of the medieval settlements of the Englishry will probably need to have Welsh place-names specially manufactured. South Pembrokeshire people are not quite sure how to react. They may see this as indicating a distinct lack of respect for the unique heritage of Little England, and as an attempt to destroy their own cultural identity. More likely, they will be amused by the farcical nature of the whole bilingual road-sign exercise. And after all, when the new road-signs are all erected, the lunatic fringe of the Englishry will have some convenient road signs right on their own doorstep to daub with red, white and blue paint.

While much has changed in Pembrokeshire, it has no need to fear for its identity or for its state of health. It has problems to face, certainly, particularly in its attempts to control the operations of Britain's greatest concentration of oil installations on the fringe of its smallest and most vulnerable national park. But the old county is economically healthy, and it is involved in national economic affairs to a greater extent now than ever before. The tourist industry is expanding, agriculture is relatively efficient, and manufacturing activities are gradually becoming more important. Pembrokeshire people are better off than they have ever been, and they know that their home area is a vital part of the new county of Dyfed. Most enticing of all is the prospect, or the hope, of industrial wealth and abundant side-benefits from the discovery and the piping ashore of offshore oil. As in the Age of the Saints, the people of Pembrokeshire are looking with faith in their hearts towards St George's Channel and the Celtic Sea.

BIBLIOGRAPHY

CHAPTER I

Barrett, J. H.   *The Pembrokeshire Coast Path* (1974)
Evans, R. O. and John, B. S.   *The Pembrokeshire Landscape* (Tenby, 1973)
Fenton, R.   *A Historical Tour through Pembrokeshire* (Brecon, 1903)
Fraser, M.   *Introducing West Wales* (1956)
Jennett, S.   *South-West Wales*, The Traveller's Guides (1967)
John, B. S.   *The Fishguard and Pembroke Area*, British Landscapes through Maps, No 16 (Sheffield, 1972)
Lockley, R. M.   *Pembrokeshire* (1957)
Mais, S. P. B.   *Little England Beyond Wales* (1949)
Miles, D. (ed).   *Pembrokeshire Coast National Park*, National Park Guide No 10, (HMSO 1973)
Price, J. A. (ed).   *Pembroke County Development Plan* (Haverfordwest, 1953)
Seymour, J.   *About Pembrokeshire* (Haverfordwest, 1971)
Stark, P.   *Walking the Pembrokeshire Coast Path* (Tenby, 1974)
Wight, M.   *Pembrokeshire and its National Park* (Tenby, 1971)

CHAPTER 2

Bassett, D. A. and Bassett, M. G.   *Geological Excursions in South Wales and the Forest of Dean* (Cardiff, 1971)
Brown, E. H.   *The Relief and Drainage of Wales* (Cardiff, 1960)
Evans, D. E.   *Pembrokeshire Coast Scenery* (Cardiff, 1973)
George, T. N.   *South Wales Regional Geology* (HMSO, 1970)
John, B. S.   *The Rocks: Geology of Pembrokeshire*, Pembrokeshire Handbooks (Llanychaer, 1973)
John, B. S.   *Scenery of Dyfed*, The Face of Wales Series, No 3 (Lanchester, 1976)
Lewis, C. A. (ed).   *The Glaciations of Wales and Adjoining Regions* (1970)
North, F. J.   *The Evolution of the Bristol Channel* (Cardiff, 1964)
Owen, T. R.   *Geology Explained in South Wales* (Newton Abbot, 1973)

CHAPTER 3

Atkinson, R. J. C. *Stonehenge* (1960)
Foster, I. L. and Daniel, G. *Prehistoric and Early Wales* (1965)
Grimes, W. F. *The Prehistory of Wales* (Cardiff, 1951)
Houlder, C. and Manning, W. H. *South Wales* (1967)
Lewis, T. P. *The Story of Wales*, Pembrokeshire Edition, Book I
(Llandybie, 1959)
Lewis, E. T. *Mynachlog-ddu: a guide to its antiquities* (Cardigan, 1972)
Moore, D. (ed). *The Land of Dyfed in Early Times* (Cardiff, 1964)

CHAPTER 4

Bowen, E. G. *Saints, Seaways and Settlements in the Celtic Lands*
(Cardiff, 1969)
Bowen, E. G. *Britain and the Western Seaways* (1972)
Bowen, O. *Tales from the Mabinogion* (1971)
Charles, B. G. *Old Norse Relations with Wales* (Cardiff, 1934)
Jones, G. and Jones, T. (eds). *The Mabinogion* (1973)
Leatham, D. *The Story of St. David of Wales* (1952)
Lewis, E. T. *Mynachlog-ddu: an historical survey of the past thousand
years* (Cardigan, 1969)

CHAPTER 5

Cambrensis, G. *The Itinerary through Wales* and *The Description of
Wales* (ed. W. Llewelyn Williams, 1908)
Fraser, D. *The Defenders* (Cardiff, 1967)
Laws, E. *The History of Little England Beyond Wales* (1888)
Lloyd, J. E. *A History of Wales from the earliest times to the Edwardian
Conquests* (1939)
Miles, J. *Princes and People* (Llandysul, 1969)
Phillips, H. *The History of Pembrokeshire* (1909)
Rees, W. *An Historical Atlas of Wales* (1972)

CHAPTER 6

Charles, B. G. *George Owen of Henllys* (Aberystwyth, 1973)
Howells, B. E. (ed). *Elizabethan Pembrokeshire: the evidence of George
Owen* (Haverfordwest, 1973)
Lloyd, H. A. *The Gentry of South-West Wales 1540–1640* (Cardiff,
1968)
Owen, G. D. *Elizabethan Wales* (Cardiff, 1964)
Thomas, H. *A History of Wales 1485–1660* (Cardiff, 1972)

BIBLIOGRAPHY

CHAPTER 7

Dodd, A. H.   *Life in Wales* (1972)
Jones, E. H. S.   *The Last Invasion of Britain* (Cardiff, 1950)
Kinross, J. S.   *Fishguard Fiasco* (Tenby, 1974)
Leach, A. L.   *The History of the Civil War in Pembrokeshire and its Borders* (1937)
Williams, D.   *The Rebecca Riots* (Cardiff, 1971)
Vaughan-Thomas, W. and Llewellyn, A.   *The Shell Guide to Wales* (1969)

CHAPTER 8

Howell, F.   *Stories at the Mill* (Haverfordwest, 1969)
Howells, R.   *The Sounds Between* (Llandysul, 1968)
——.   *Across the Sounds to the Pembrokeshire Islands* (Llandysul, 1972)
John, B. S.   *Ports and Harbours of Pembrokeshire*, Pembrokeshire Handbooks (Llanychaer, 1974)
Roberts, E. and Roberts, T.   *The Islands of Pembrokeshire*, Pembrokeshire Handbooks (Llanychaer, 1974)
Warburton, F. W.   *The History of Solva* (1944)

CHAPTER 9

Peters, E. E.   *The History of Pembroke Dock* (1905)
Rees, J. F.   *The Story of Milford* (Cardiff, 1954)
Richards, W. L.   *Pembrokeshire under Fire* (Haverfordwest, 1965)

CHAPTER 10

Hall, G. W.   *Metal Mines of Southern Wales* (Gloucester, 1971)
John, B. S.   *Old Industries of Pembrokeshire*, The Face of Wales Series, No 2 (Lanchester, 1974)
Rees, D. M.   *Industrial Archaeology of Wales* (Newton Abbot, 1975)
Stickings, T. G.   *The Story of Saundersfoot* (Tenby, 1970)

CHAPTER 11

Bowen, E. G. (ed).   *Wales* (1957)
Carter, H.   *The Towns of Wales: A Study in Urban Geography* (Cardiff, 1965)
Davies, M.   *Wales in Maps* (Cardiff, 1958)
Davies, M. F.   *Pembrokeshire* (1939)
Howells, R.   *Farming in Wales* (Llandysul, 1965)
Morris, J. P.   *The North Pembroke and Fishguard Railway* (Lingfield, 1969)

Price, J. A. (ed). *Haverfordwest 2000: draft development plan* (Pembrokeshire CC, 1973)
Price, M. R. C. *The Saundersfoot Railway* (Lingfield, 1964)
Scourfield, E. *The Welsh Farming Scene* (Cardiff, 1974)
Welsh Council. *A Strategy for Rural Wales* (HMSO, 1971)

CHAPTER 12

Gallie, M. *Little England's Other Half*, Pembrokeshire Handbooks (Llanychaer, 1974)
Harris, P. V. *Pembrokeshire Place-Names and Dialect* (Tenby, 1974)
James, D. G. *The Town and County of Haverfordwest and its Story* (Haverfordwest, 1957)
Lewis, E. T. *North of the Hills* (Haverfordwest, 1972)
Morgan, P. (ed). *Writers of the West* (Carmarthen, 1974)
Owen, T. M. *Welsh Folk Customs* (Cardiff, 1968)
Parry-Jones, D. *My Own Folk* (Llandysul, 1972)
Peate, I. C. *Tradition and Folk Life: a Welsh View* (1972)

CHAPTER 13

Davis, T. A. W. *Plants of Pembrokeshire* (Haverfordwest, 1970)
Howells, R. *Cliffs of Freedom* (Llandysul, 1961)
Hyde, H. A. *Welsh Timber Trees* (Cardiff, 1961)
Lacey, W. S. *Welsh Wildlife in Trust* (Bangor, 1970)
Lockley, R. M. *Grey Seal, Common Seal* (1966)
Lockley, R. M. *The Naturalist in Wales* (Newton Abbot, 1970)
Perry, A. R. *Welsh Wild Flowers* (1973)
Saunders, D. *A Guide to the Birds of Wales* (1974)

CHAPTER 14

Rees, V. *South-West Wales*, Shell Guide (1963)
Savory, H. N. *et al*. *Ancient Monuments of Wales* (HMSO, 1973)
Stickings, T. G. *Castles and Strongholds of Pembrokeshire* (Tenby, 1973)
Vaughan-Thomas, W. *The Splendour Falls* (Cardiff, 1973)
Wales Tourist Board. *Castles and Historic Places in Wales* (Cardiff, 1974)

CHAPTER 15

Barnes, T. and Yates, N. (eds). *Carmarthenshire Studies* (Carmarthenshire CC, 1974)
Peate, I. C. *The Welsh House* (Liverpool, 1946)

BIBLIOGRAPHY

Smith, P. *Houses of the Welsh Countryside*, Royal Commission on Ancient and Historical Monuments in Wales (HMSO, 1975)
Timmins, H. T. *Nooks and Corners of Pembrokeshire* (1895)

CHAPTER 16

John, B. S. *The Milford Haven Oil Industry*, The Face of Wales Series, No 1 (Lanchester, 1974)
Milford Haven Conservancy Board. *The Port of Milford Haven* (1973)

CHAPTER 17

Office of Population Censuses and Surveys. *Census 1971: Report on the Welsh Language in Wales* (HMSO, Cardiff, 1973)
Wales Year Book 1974/75. (Cardiff, 1974)

ACKNOWLEDGEMENTS

THE author gratefully acknowledges the following sources of the illustrations used in this book: Acrofilms Ltd, plates nos 1, 5a and 10a; Robert Evans, 2a, 5b, 11a, 11b and 12b; Cambridge University (J. K. St Joseph), 3a; Haverfordwest Central Library, 3b; Studio Jon, Fishguard, 4a, 6a, 6b, 12a, 13 and 15a; National Museum of Wales, 8b and 10b; National Library of Wales, 14a and Fig 3; Squibbs Studios, Tenby, 15b; Welsh National Water Development Authority, 16a; Esso Petroleum Ltd, 16b; *Illustrated London News*, Fig 4. Fig 1 is based on a diagram published by C. Houlder and W. H. Manning in their book *South Wales* (Heinemann Educational, 1966). We have been unable to trace the copyright holders of plates nos 9a and 9b. The remaining photographs and line drawings are by the author.

Abbeys, 197–8
Abereiddi, 87, 125
Age of the Saints, 47–54, 55
Agriculture, 83–91, 95, 144–9
Agriculture (Elizabethan), 71–5
Air raids, 113
Amoco Ltd, 210–23
Amroth Castle, 56, 187
Anglia Transwallia, 68
Anglo-Norman settlement, 58–64, 68, 152–6
Animals, 169–76
Animals, prehistoric, 87
Anthracite, 118–24
Architecture, 153, 180–209
Armorican mountain chain, 24
Arthurian legend, 49, 53
Atlantic convoys, 113

BP Co, 210–23
Badger, 170
Barges, 128–9
Barrett, J., 48, 165
Barrows, prehistoric, 41–3
Bats, 171
Beaches, 25
Beaches, coal-exporting, 120–1
Beaker people, 43–5
Benton Castle, 189–90
Birds, 171–6, 223
Bishop Barlow, 191
Bishop Gower, 194–7
Bishops, 57
Bishop's lordships, 155, 182
Bishop's Palace, 57, 69, 180–1, 193–5
Blackpool Mill, 88, 100, 130
Blood-groups, 155
Bluestones, 43–4
Boia, 50

Bonville Court, 191
Bonville's Court Colliery, 120, 123
Bosherston Pools, 177
Bowen, E. G., 53, 152
Bowen, James, 94
Brawdy, 135, 151
Brick-works, 131–2
Broad Haven, 123, 176, 178
Bronze Age, 43–5
Buildings, 140, 173, 174, 180–209
Bulb growing, 149
Burials, 40–2, 49, 55

CEGB, 215–22
Caldey, 37, 128, 196, 198
Caldey Abbey, 51, 197–8
Caledonian mountain chain, 24
Cambrensis, Geraldus, 38, 140, 184
Cambrian rocks, 22
Camden, W., 68
Camps, 45–6, 52
Cantref y Gwaelod, 39, 51
Cantrefi, 51
Caravans, 176
Carboniferous Limestone, 23
Cardigan, 11, 153
Cardigan Bay, 25, 38, 39
Carew, 64, 88
Carew Castle, 184–6
Car ferry, 111
Carmarthen, 153, 163
Carmarthen Bay, 14, 38
Carmarthen ironworks, 130
Carningli, 18, 20
Carns, 22, 29
Carreg Wastad, 92
Castell Malgwyn, 130
Castlemartin peninsula, 20, 36
Castlemartin tank range, 24, 150–1

Castle mounds, 189
Castles, 56, 81–2, 122, 140, 181–93
Cattle, 71, 73, 84–5, 146–8
Caves, 34–7
Cawdor, Lord, 92–4
Cawl, 225
Cells, monastic, 156
Celtic Sea, 115, 169, 222–3, 227
Celtic Sea oil search, 222–3, 227
Celtic settlers, 45
Celtic tribes, 47, 156
Cemais, 56–7, 65
Census data, 134
Chapels, 36, 86–90, 156
Charles, B. G., 67, 158
Chartists, 95
Cheese factory, 135
Chemical factory, 133
Chimneys, 173, 204–5
Church, 'Celtic' style, 70, 89, 156
Church, 'Norman' style, 59, 63, 153,
    195–7
Church of England, 89–91
Church types, 59, 63, 70, 89, 153–7,
    180, 195–7
Cilgerran Castle, 183–4
Circulating schools, 86
Civil War, 80–3, 103, 181, 187
Clay marl, 74, 145
Clegyrfwya (Clegyr Boia), 39–40
Cliffs, 28, 165
Climate, 144–5, 165
Clom, 200–1
Cnapan, 76–9
Coal industry, 117–24
Coal Measures, 23
Coastal scenery, 25–9
Coast path, 150, 164
Coedmore Forge, 129–30
Colby Moor Rout, 81
Collieries, 118–24
Conflict, 112
Coracle, 39
Corn, 72–3, 83–4
Corn mills, 88, 117
Cosheston, 17, 59, 100
Cottages, 134–5, 174, 200–3
Country estates, 199
Country houses, 134–5, 140, 199,
    206–7

Country life, 71–5
Countryside Commission, 178
Countryside Unit, 177
County Museum (Castle Museum),
    177, 183
Cromlechau, 40–3
Cromwell, Oliver, 82–3
Crop rotation, 84
Crops, 72–3, 147
Cruck roof, 205
Crymych, 85
Culm, 119
Cultural divide, 68–71, 152–63,
    186–9
Culture, Welsh, 47–53, 156–9, 185,
    225–7
Cymydau, 55

Dairying, 146–7
Dale Castle, 190–1
Dale Fort, 116
Dale peninsula, 13, 23
Dark Ages, 47–54
Daugleddau Estuary, 14, 20, 25,
    107, 119, 129, 165, 175
Davies, Howell, 89
Davies, Margaret, 55
Davies, M. F., 14, 153
Deep-water channel, 211–20
Defensible Barracks, 115–16
Defoe, D., 107
Deheubarth, 56
Demetae, 46
Description of Pembrokeshire, 65–79
Dewi Sant, 48–51, 180
Dewisland, 57, 72–3, 145
Dialect, 154
Dinas Island, 175
Dockyard, 15, 112–15
Drilling rig, 223
Drovers, 84–5
Druidston, 123
Duke of Wellington, 112
Dyfed, 13, 52–3, 224–7

'Earlies', 148–9
Earthworks, 45–6, 52
Eastern Cleddau, 107, 119
Efail-wen, 95
Eisteddfod, 226

Elizabethan Pembrokeshire, 67
Emery, F., 45
Employment, 110, 115, 132, 216–18
Enclosure movement, 95–6
Enclosures, 51–2, 84
English people, 68–71, 152–6
Englishry, 55–64, 68–71, 152–63, 180–98, 226
Environment, 19–30, 164–9, 219–23
Episcopal estates, 155, 182
Erratic boulders, 31, 44
Esso Petroleum Co, 192, 210–23

Farmhouses, 173, 203–6
Farming, 83–91, 95, 281
Fenton, Richard, 101, 206
Ferries, 119, 141–2
Fertiliser, 72, 74–5
Field patterns, 17, 51–2, 59, 152, 156
Field Studies Council, 207
Firebricks, 131
Fireplaces, 203–6
Firth Cleveland factory, 115
Fishguard, 22, 32, 92–4, 99, 103
Fishguard Fencibles, 92, 121
Fishguard Harbour, 125
Fishing, 76, 99, 109–10, 111
Fishlock, T., 154
Five Arches, 69
Flats, coastal, 29
Flemings, 58–9, 186, 204
Flemish chimney, 173, 204–5
Flimston clay-pits, 132
Flotsam and jetsam, 102
Flowers, 165–8
Foley House, 208
Fortifications, Milford Haven, 108, 115–16
Fortified residences, 181, 189–93
Fortresses, 56, 81–2, 181–93
Fox, 170
French invasion force, 91–4, 121
Frontier, 68–71, 186–9
Furze mills, 132

GWR, 126
Gallie, Menna, 158
Gannets, 172
Garden Pit disaster, 119
Gentry, 133, 140, 206, 208

Geological map, 21
Geology, 20–5
Glaciers, 31
Goodwick brick-works, 132
Grassholm, 139, 172
Graveyards, 90
Great Tanks Fire, 113–14
Green Bridge of Wales, 175
Greville, Charles, 108–10
Grey seal, 139, 169–70
Grimes, W. F., 52, 189
Guilds, 62
Gulf Oil Co., 210–23
Gwaun valley, 20, 165, 175, 177

Hafodydd, 51
Hakin, 111
Hamilton, Sir William, 110
Haroldston, 207
Harris, Howel, 86–9
Harris, V., 154
Hassall, C., 84
Haven Bridge, 137, 142–3, 191, 281
Haverfordwest, 36, 60–3, 89, 135–7, 151
Haverfordwest Castle, 83, 182–3
Head deposits, 32–3
Helicopter base, 223
Henry Tudor, 182–5
Heritage coast, 166, 178
Hill fort, 35, 45–6
Holiday developments, 178
Holiday industry, 121, 176–9, 191
Holiday sport, 177
Homes (buildings), 199–209
Homesteads, 51
Hook colliery district, 119–20
Hotels, 176
Howell, Florence, 100
Howells, B., 67
Howells, Roscoe, 101
Hubba, 54
Hywel Dda, 55

Ice Age, 18, 30–3, 37
Ice factories, 133
Ice sheets, 30
Immigrants, 58–63
Industrial Revolution, 117–33, 201
Industries, 117–33

Irish packet service, 111
Irish Sea glacier, 31, 44
Iron Age, 45–6
Ironworks, 88, 130–1
Islands, 167

James, G. D., 154
Jetties, 211–23
Jones, F., 57, 67, 103, 162, 198
Jones, Griffith, 86
Jones, John Paul, 103

Kellaway, G., 44
Kilgetty Colliery, 123–4
Knights, 56–64, 68, 152–6
Knights of St John, 196

Lamphey Bishop's Residence, 194–5
Landsker, 55, 68–71, 152–63, 181,
    186–9, 226
Landsker castles, 181, 186–9
Language, 153–63
Language divide, 160–3
Last Invasion of Britain, 91–4, 121
Laugharne Castle, 186–7
Laugharne, Rowland, 80–2
Lawrenny, 99, 178
Laws, E., 159, 185
Leach, A. L., 38
Letterston, 59, 141
Lighthouses, 104–6
Light industries, 110, 115, 133, 281
Lime, 74
Limekiln, 74, 87, 117, 128
Limestone quarries, 128–9
Little England beyond Wales, 14,
    55–64, 68–71, 152–63, 225
Little Haven, 123, 124
Llan, 48–9
Llanfyrnach mine, 129
Llangwm, 98, 138
Llanion Barracks, 113
Llawhaden castle, 57, 193
Llewellyn's churnworks, 133
Llysyfran Reservoir, 177, 192, 281
Loading-beaches, 123
Local government, 13, 136, 224–7
Lockley, R. M., 156, 158, 170, 172
Long-house, 174, 205–6
Lowland Hundred, 39, 51

Mabinogion, The, 52–3
Maenclochog, 125, 138
Mammals, 169–71
'Mammoth' tankers, 214, 223
Manorbier, 140, 151, 184
Manorbier Castle, 140, 184
Manors, 57, 153
Mansions, 140, 206–7
Markets, 75–6, 135, 149
Marloes, 102, 138
Martin, William, 56
Medieval hospices, 197–8
Medieval Pembrokeshire, 63–4, 140
Megalithic chamber, 41–2
Meltwater channels, 31–2
Menevia, 50
Merchants, 60, 99–103
Mesolithic people, 42–3
Mesolithic period, 37–9
Metal-working, 43, 45–6, 129–31
Methodist revival, 85–91
Middle Ages, 62–4
Milford (town), 15, 108–10
Milford Docks Co, 222
Milford Haven, 15, 25, 98–100, 107–
    16, 147, 164, 191, 210–27
Milford Haven Conservancy Board,
    210–23
Military establishments, 141, 150–1
Milk production, 147
Millstone Grit, 23
Ministry of Defence, 150–1
Missionaries, 48–51
Moel Drygarn, 46
Monastic houses, 197–8
Monuments, prehistoric, 34–46
Moorlands, 29, 168
Motte and bailey castles, 189
Mountain-building, 24
Mynydd Presely, 14, 22, 31, 35,
    53, 85, 125
Myths, 34–46

NCB, 120
Narberth, 57, 72, 98
Narberth Castle, 187
Nash, John, 197, 207–8
National Park Administration, 164
National Trust, 178
Natural history, 165–76

INDEX

Natural landscape, 19–33
Neolithic house, 39–40
Neolithic people, 39–43
Nevern, 47
Newgale, 176
Newport, 56, 63, 74
Newport Castle, 183
Newton Noyes, 151
New towns, 107–16
Neyland, 15, 110–11
Neyland foundry, 130
Nicholas, Jemima, 93–4
Nicknames, 155–9
Nolton-Newgale Coalfield, 123–4
Nonconformity, 86–91
Normans, 56–64, 68, 152–6, 180–98
North Pembroke and Fishguard Railway, 125

Ogam alphabet, 47
Oil industry, 15, 135, 141, 192, 210–23, 227
Oil spills, 221–3
Oil tanks, 113–14, 192, 212–20
Oil terminals, 210–23
Old Red Sandstone, 23
Open fields, 59, 83
Ordnance Survey maps, 11
Ordovician rocks, 22
Orielton, 140, 206–7
Otter, 170
Owen, George, 19, 23, 32, 38, 65–79, 104, 118, 135, 153, 159, 207
Owen, H., 65
Owen, Sir Hugh, 125

Palaeolithic period, 34–5
Palaeozoic rocks, 22
Parks, 140, 194–9
Parliamentary forces, 80–2
Paxton, Sir W., 208
Pembroke, 60–1, 122
Pembroke Castle, 56, 61, 82, 122, 181–2
Pembroke County Development Plan, 10
Pembroke Dock, 15, 112–15
Pembroke power-station, 15, 215–22
Pembrokeshire Coalfield, 15, 25, 117–24

Pembrokeshire Coast National Park, 14, 25, 164–79
Pembrokeshire Welsh dialect, 158
Pencaer, 20, 139
Peninsula fort, 45–6
Penrhos cottage, 202
Pentre Ifan, 42
Penygored tinplate works, 130
Peregrini, 48
Perrot, Sir John, 65, 185, 187, 207
Philipps, Sir John, 86
Picton Castle, 190, 207
Pig-iron exports, 131
Pigs, 149
Pilgrims, 49–51
Pilotage, 216
Pipeline (oil), 212–16
Piracy, 102–3
Place-names, English, 226
Place-names, Norse, 54
Place-names, Welsh, 51, 226
Planning, 136, 164, 176–9
Plant life, 165–9
Platform, erosional, 29–30
Poets, 158
Polecat, 170
Pollution, 221–3
Pollution (visual), 219–21
Popton Point, 116, 212–13
Population, 134, 176
Porth-clais, 53
Porthgain, 122, 127–8
Ports and harbours, 53, 98–100, 106
Potatoes, 148–9
Powell, R., 82
Poyer, John, 81–2
Precambrian rocks, 22
Precelly Hotel, 125
Prendergast mill, 132–3
Preseli district, 13, 134
Presely uplands, 14, 22, 31, 53, 85, 125, 147
Princes of Dyfed, 52, 55
Priories, 197–8
Produce, farm, 75–6
Pryderi, 53
Pwyll, 52–3
Pyr, 51

Quarrying, 124–9

Quaternary period, 30, 37
Quays, exporting, 119, 120

RAF, 114–15, 135, 151
RSPB, 172
Rab, 146, 202
Racial features, 155, 159
Railways, 106, 111, 120, 135, 138–41
Ramsey, 50, 54, 101, 169, 172
Raths, 45–6, 52
Rebecca riots, 94–7
Records Office, 183
Religious cells, 47–51, 156
Religious revivals, 85–91
Religious societies, 86–91
Residences, fortified, 57, 181, 189–95
Rhos, 63
Rhys ap Tewdwr, 56
Richards, W. L., 114
Roads, 84–5, 137–44
Road-signs, 226
Roberts, Bartholomew, 103
Roch Castle, 187–8
Rocks, 20–5, 124–9, 145–6
Rodents, 170
Roger of Montgomery, 56
Roman Period, 46
Roofing customs, 201–6
Rosebush, 121, 125–7
Roundheads, 80–2
Rowland, Daniel, 86
Royalists, 80–2
Royal yachts, 112
Rudwall custom, 72
Rugby, 156

SPCK, 86
Sailing ships, 99–100, 128
St Bride's Bay, 25, 123
St David, 48–51, 180
St David's Cathedral, 69, 196–7
St David's Head, 26, 46
St David's Peninsula, 28, 146, 160
St Dogmael's Abbey, 197, 198
St George's Channel, 48, 169
St Govan's, 36, 48
St Mary's Church (Haverfordwest), 63, 196

St Mary's College, 69, 198
St Justinian, 50–1
Saints, Celtic, 35, 47–51
Sands and gravels, 32
Sarnau, 39
Saundersfoot area, 120–3, 177
Saundersfoot Bay, 25–6
Saundersfoot Harbour, 120–3, 131, 191
'Save Pembrokeshire' campaign, 224–5
Sawmills, 132
Scott, Sir Gilbert, 197
Seabirds, 139, 171–5
Seafaring, 98–106
Sea-level changes, 30, 37–8
Seals, 169–70
Sea marl, 74
Sea-rovers, 53–4
Sea sand, 74–5
Sea trading (prehistoric), 15, 43, 135
Seaweed, 75, 168–9
Seithennin, 39
Settlements, Celtic, 51–3
Sheep, 73, 83–4
Shipbuilding, 99–100, 112–14
Shipping, 99, 111, 210–19
Shipwrecks, 100–5
Shipyards, 100, 111
Shopping, 111, 177
Silver-lead ore, 129
Skokholm, 101, 104, 170–5
Skomer, 20, 52, 54, 101, 171–2
Skomer vole, 171
Slate quarrying, 87, 124–7, 202
Smalls lighthouse, 104–6
Smelting, 88, 130–1
Smuggling, 102–3
Soils, 145–6
Solva, 87, 101, 103, 105
Sounds, 101
South Bishop Light, 104
South Pembrokeshire district, 13
South Wales Coalfield, 15, 117
Sport, 76–9
'Spud-bashing', 148
Squatters, 84, 200
Stack Rocks, 175
Stations (railway), 125–6

INDEX

Stepaside ironworks, 130–1, 201
Stone Age, 34–43
Stone axes, 43
Stonehenge, 43–4
Strategic fortresses, 181–3
Structures, geological, 20–5
Submerged forests, 18, 38
Sulphur dioxide, 222
Sunday School, 90
Sunderland flying-boats, 113
Supertankers, 210–23
Surnames, 155, 159
Surrender, French, 93

Tanneries, 117
Tartarus, 112
Tate, Colonel, 91–4
Tenant farmers, 83–4, 95
Tenby, 37, 60, 63, 69, 75, 81, 177
Tenby Castle, 183
Tenby daffodil, 167
Tenby Museum, 183
Tent sites, 176
Texaco Ltd, 210–23
Thatched roofs, 174, 201–2, 205
Thomas, H. H., 43
Thomas, Sir Rhys ap, 185
Thornton industrial estate, 110
Till, 32, 145
Tillage, 72–5
Toll-gates, 95–7
Tomb, 41–2
Tourism, 121, 176–9, 191
Tournament, medieval, 185
Towers, castellated, 59, 63, 70, 153, 195
Town houses, 208–9
Towns, Anglo-Norman, 60–3, 122, 183
Towns, modern, 106, 134–7
Town walls, 61, 63, 69, 183
Traction engine, 124
Trade, 60
Trading, coastal, 98–9, 106
Trawlers, 109
Trecwn, 141, 151
Trees, 18, 20, 29, 145, 168
Tref, 51
Trefgarn, 20, 170, 177
Trefin Bishop's Palace, 194

Tudor Merchant's House, 162, 199, 208
Tundra, 32
Turkey farming, 149
Turnpike trusts, 95–6
Twrch Trwyth, 53
Ty unnos, 200

Upton Castle, 190

Vale of the Roses, 196
Valleys, 29–30
Vaughan-Thomas, W., 91
Verteporix, 47
Vikings, 53–4
Village, manorial, 17, 59, 153
Village, names, 157

Warren-Davies, T. A., 168
Warrior, 115
Warships, 112
Water-board, 143, 192
Welsh language, 156–63, 225–7
Welsh language movement, 226
Welsh people, 47–54, 68–71, 156–9, 225–7
Welshry, 55, 68–71, 137, 152–63, 180–98
Wesley, John, 89
Western Cleddau, 20, 107, 170
West Wales Naturalists' Trust, 171
Whalecwm, 100, 133
Whitesand Bay, 35, 49, 177
Whiteside, H., 104–5
Whitland, 85, 147
Wildfowl, 175
Wild life, 139, 169–76, 223
Williams, D., 97
Williams, D. T., 163
Williams, Thomas, of Treleddyn, 91, 105
Williams, William, 86
Wiseman's Bridge, 123
Wiston Castle, 187
Wizo the Fleming, 58, 187
Woodlands, 29, 168
Woodside foundry, 130
Wool, 73
Woollen mills, 117, 132
Wrecking, 100–2

240